Practical social work

Published in conjunction with
the British Association of Social Workers

BASW
THE BRITISH ASSOCIATION OF SOCIAL WORKERS

Founding editor: Jo Campling

Social Work is a multi-skilled profession, centred on people. Social workers need skills in problem-solving, communication, critical reflection and working with others to be effective in practice.

The British Association of Social Workers (www.basw.co.uk) has always been conscious of its role in setting guidelines for practice and in seeking to raise professional standards. The concept of the Practical Social Work series was developed to fulfil a genuine professional need for a carefully planned, coherent, series of texts that would contribute to practitioners' skills, development and professionalism.

Newly relaunched to meet the ever-changing needs of the social work profession, the series has been reviewed and revised with the help of the BASW Editorial Advisory Board:

Peter Beresford
Jim Campbell
Monica Dowling
Brian Littlechild
Mark Lymbery
Fraser Mitchell
Steve Moore

Under their guidance each book marries practice issues with theory and research in a compact and applied format: perfect for students, practitioners and educators.

A comprehensive list of titles available in the series can be found online at: www.palgravehighered.com/socialwork/basw

---

Series standing order ISBN 0–333–80313–2

You can receive future titles in this series as they are published by placing a standing order. Please contact your bookseller or, in the case of difficulty, contact us at the address below with your name and address, the title of the series and the ISBN quoted above.

Customer Services Department, Macmillan Distribution Ltd, Houndmills, Basingstoke, Hampshire RG21 6XS, England

---

Practical Social Work Series

Founding Editor: Jo Campling

New and best-selling titles

Suzy Braye and Michael Preston-Shoot, *Practising Social Work Law* **(4th edition)**

Neil Thompson, *Anti-Discriminatory Practice* **(6th edition)**

Robert Adams, *Empowerment, Participation and Social Work* **(4th edition)**

Sarah Banks, *Ethics and Values in Social Work* **(4th edition)**

James G. Barber, *Social Work with Addictions* **(2nd edition)**

Christine Bigby and Patsie Frawley, *Social Work Practice and Intellectual Disability*

Jennifer Burton, *Practice Learning in Social Work*

Veronica Coulshed and Audrey Mullender with David N. Jones and Neil Thompson, *Management in Social work* **(3rd edition)**

Veronica Coulshed and Joan Orme, *Social Work Practice* **(5th edition)**

Lena Dominelli, *Anti-Racist Social Work* **(3rd edition)**

Celia Doyle, *Working with Abused Children* **(4th edition)**

Richard Ingram, Jane Fenton, Ann Hodson and Divya Jindal-Snape, *Reflective Social Work Practice*

Gordon Jack and Helen Donnell, *Social Work with Children*

Tony Jeffs and Mark K. Smith (editors), *Youth Work Practice*

Joyce Lishman, *Communication in Social Work* **(2nd edition)**

Paula Nicolson and Rowan Bayne, *Psychology for Social Work Theory and Practice* **(4th edition)**

Michael Oliver, Bob Sapey and Pam Thomas, *Social Work with Disabled People* **(4th edition)**

Joan Orme and David Shemmings, *Developing Research Based Social Work Practice*

Terence O'Sullivan, *Decision Making in Social Work* **(2nd edition)**

Mo Ray and Judith Phillips, *Social Work with Older People* **(5th edition)**

Michael Preston-Shoot, *Effective Groupwork* **(2nd edition)**

Jerry Tew, *Social Approaches to Mental Distress*

Alan Twelvetrees, *Community Work* **(4th edition)**

SUPPORTING FAMILIES

TERENCE O'SULLIVAN

First published 2016 by
PALGRAVE

Palgrave in the UK is an imprint of Macmillan Publishers Limited, registered in England, company number 785998, of 4 Crinan Street, London, N1 9XW.

Palgrave Macmillan in the US is a division of St Martin's Press LLC, 175 Fifth Avenue, New York, NY 10010.

Palgrave is a global imprint of the above companies and is represented throughout the world.

Palgrave® and Macmillan® are registered trademarks in the United States, the United Kingdom, Europe and other countries.

ISBN 978–1–137–30644–9 paperback

This book is printed on paper suitable for recycling and made from fully managed and sustained forest sources. Logging, pulping and manufacturing processes are expected to conform to the environmental regulations of the country of origin.

A catalogue record for this book is available from the British Library.

A catalog record for this book is available from the Library of Congress.

Printed and bound by CPI Group (UK) Ltd, Croydon, CR0 4YY

*To Toby and Eric
And
Those That May Follow*

CONTENTS

LIST OF FIGURES

PREFACE

This book will appeal to all those who are interested in supporting families and working with them to overcome the challenges they face. A wide variety of activities come under the rubric of 'family support', and *Supporting Families* focuses on home-based support where the worker builds relationships with families to promote family well-being. The following pages provide workers and students with ways of thinking about and working with families to overcome their difficulties. Families have an important place in people's lives and are human groups that potentially provide a caring, supportive and protective environment for their members. However, families can also become sites of anguish, harm, exploitation, violence and neglect.

From time to time all families face predicaments which they overcome using their own resources. However, families can find their resources insufficient or the difficulties they face so overwhelming that without outside help their situation deteriorates. Internal and external stressors act on families, causing tensions that result in them coming under strain. It is at these times that families need support from outside their networks, and if they don't get timely effective help they can enter a downward spiral, resulting in the family not carrying out its caring, supportive and protective roles.

The book will have wide appeal, covering as it does a range of skills and knowledge that workers need to support families and collaborate with interprofessional colleagues. It equips workers and students with the relevant knowledge and understandings they need to grasp some of the complexity of families. This includes good knowledge of what families are and how they are changing, and the importance of thinking about them as human groups that live in multilayered contexts and the ways these groups come under strain. As well as understanding the inner workings of families, workers need to think about the social and material contexts in which families live. To this end, *Supporting Families* uses an ecological framework to develop in-depth thinking about families, the problems they face and ways of overcoming those difficulties. The book includes models of supportive interventions focused on different levels of context that multi-professional networks or teams can combine together to help families resolve difficulties.

In addition to workers believing they are being supportive, family members need to experience them as supportive. As a consequence, the book stresses the importance of appropriate attitude and demeanour as well as specific skills and knowledge. Topics covered include effective communication, listening skills and learning from family narratives and interprofessional discussions. Highlighted is the ability to promote and engage in open dialogue that includes honestly discussing issues and concerns. Workers need an ability to construct and ask questions that promote reflection rather than defensiveness, and to be able to engage with different family members spanning different generations and family roles. The book covers the skills, knowledge and attitudes workers require to work collaboratively with different professionals, including having knowledge of and respect for different disciplines.

The book's conception of support is not restricted to emotional support or help in resolving immediate difficulties, but includes strengthening families and working towards change. To do this, workers require knowledge and a set of skills that enable them to build working alliances with family members. To build such alliances, it is necessary to understand the ambivalence families have about accepting help from outside their own networks. Families are often suspicious of workers, who need to manage the tensions between developing a degree of trust and emotional connection with family members, while at the same time remaining vigilant to the possibility that unbeknown to them something untoward is happening within the family. The approach requires workers to recognise and build upon family strengths and assets while listening to the family's narratives about the problems they face.

The book recognises that helping families is emotionally and intellectually demanding work, and to cope with these demands, workers need to have supportive supervision available to them. The quality of the supervision they receive will determine whether they can effectively support families and carry out their agency roles. The book explains what workers and their supervisors need to know about supportive supervision and what roles they have in achieving such supervision. It discusses how both individual or peer supervision needs to provide a safe space for deeper thinking and critical reflection about families and how to help them.

Chapter 1, 'Helping Families', sets out a family supportive practice that takes a whole family approach to prevention and early help and outlines the political, policy and legal contexts of this work.

Chapter 2, 'Understanding Families', explains a series of ideas, concepts, models and theories that help workers understand families as human groups in their social and material contexts.

Chapter 3, 'Families under Strain', explores the processes and ways families come under strain.

Chapter 4, 'Being Supportive', considers what being supportive involves and issues in working with different family members.

Chapter 5, 'Supportive Interventions', presents an ecological approach to helping families and different models of assisting them to meet the challenges they face.

Chapter 6, 'Working Collaboratively', focuses on how workers can effectively work together to support families, and stresses the need for a common family focus and the importance of respect for each other's expertise.

Chapter 7, 'Remaining Vigilant', explains how workers can remain vigilant towards their own thinking and emotions, and the possibility they are not seeing damaging processes within a family without this turning into surveillance.

Chapter 8, 'Supportive Supervision', stresses the importance of the supervisory relationship and how workers and their supervisors can effectively work together to support families.

The chapters use a number of features designed to help the reader get the most out of the book. At the beginning of each chapter is a *Chapter Overview* which highlights the topics covered. After a short introduction there is an illustrative family situation accompanied by a genogram which the chapter uses to give practical examples of the contents. In each chapter there are a number of *Research Focus* boxes that give the findings of international research into the topic in question. At the end of each chapter there is a bullet list of the chapters' key points and a number of *Reflective Exercises* and *Putting into Practice* activities. *Reflective Exercises* are primarily for individual study, and ask the reader to think about what they have read. Putting into Practice activities draw on the readers' experience and ask them, in a group or individually, to think about, apply, discuss or implement some of the ideas of the chapter. To deepen their understanding of particular topics, each chapter ends with *Further Resources* for the reader to follow up.

CHAPTER 1

HELPING FAMILIES

CHAPTER OVERVIEW

This chapter

- Presents 'family supportive practice' as a distinctive style of helping families, in which workers take a family approach to supporting families under strain.
- Explains how family supportive practice involves having a critical whole family perspective.
- Argues that family supportive practice can be a form of early help and prevention, but policymakers and practitioners need to be more precise about *what* they are trying to prevent and its *timing* in relation to 'problem' formation.
- Discusses how a continuing theme of social policy has been trying to achieve an appropriate balance between child protection and family support.
- Briefly describes how English law gives local authorities a general duty to support the upbringing of children in their families, but also gives them considerable discretion about how they do this and when they do it.

Introduction

This book sets out a family supportive approach to helping families, which aims to effectively support families when they are under strain. Even though lip service is often paid to 'work with families', this is often work with a child and/or a parent, but less commonly work focused on the whole family group or network. The chapters of this book will explore the knowledge, skills, attitudes and practices involved in family supportive practice, with the intention of setting out a framework for helping families. This first chapter sets out the notion of family supportive practice with its basic orientations as home-based, relationship building, ecological, preventative work carried out in particular policy, legal and political contexts.

The Poskitt family

The Poskitt family consists of Donna, 17 years old, and her son, Jason, who just had his second birthday. Donna and Jason live together, about a mile from Donna's family. She now rents a one-bedroom housing association flat, having initially lived with her mother and siblings. Her father holds the tenancy on trust for her until her eighteenth birthday. She finds living on her own difficult, particularly managing on a tight budget, but is happier than when she lived at home. Donna is the oldest child and has two sisters. Her parents separated some time ago, and her father now lives some distance away but keeps in contact with his daughter through social media. Her mother struggles to get by on a low income and in the past often called on Donna, as the oldest child, to look after her siblings and do chores in the house. Until she became pregnant, Donna took little interest in school, often being absent without good reason. Jason's father, Garry, who is a couple of months younger than Donna, is in contact with both his son and Donna, and still lives with his parents and is studying at Sixth Form College. He and Donna get on reasonably well, but she feels he could help more with Jason. Initially Donna experienced pressure from both her family and Garry's to have a termination, and family relationships became very fraught.

When Donna became pregnant, her attitude to school changed and she was lucky enough to attend a school that had positive attitudes and policies towards young, pregnant pupils. Just before Jason was born, Donna transferred to a local Young Parent Project that provided education and a crèche, and she is about to take her GCSEs. She plans to go to a local college and hopes to eventually go to university. Garry's family are still antagonistic towards Donna and show only limited interest in Jason. Donna feels his family resent her for distracting him from his studies. Up until Jason's second birthday Jason and Donna had the support of a family nurse, under the Family Nurse Partnership Programme. During the period when family tensions were at their height, the local Young Parent Project worked with the whole family and will stay in touch with Donna, Garry and Jason until Donna's eighteenth birthday.

Family supportive practice

Families are generally self-supporting systems, with members tending to support each other and work with each other to overcome any difficulties they face. For example, Bunting and McAuley's (2004) review of research into the informal support of young pregnant women and mothers found informal family support alongside that of partners and peers, on the whole, contributed to more positive outcomes. Broadly speaking, families have a supportive protective role in relation to its members; however, there are times when family groups and relationships are under particular strain and require support from outside. Before she became pregnant, apart from frequent usual ups and downs of their family life, Donna found her parents, siblings and grandparents generally supportive of her both practically and emotionally. When Donna's family learnt of her pregnancy, she experienced their reaction as anything but supportive, and the whole family came under strain and in need of support from outside. Home-based support and family-focused practice is one aspect of a broad range of activities and services under the umbrella 'family support'. A wide variety of both professional and non-professional workers, based in a diverse range of agencies and settings, are involved in helping families through home visiting.

Family supportive practice involves workers taking an inclusive approach to helping families that are under strain. Families come under strain when they cannot cope with external or internal stressors. Such strain results in tensions within family relationships that negatively impact on family well-being. When families come under strain, negative consequences can follow for individual family members, family groups, neighbourhoods, communities and society, whether the source of strain is from within or from outside the family group. Family supportive practice involves ecological thinking, and seeks to help families find their own solutions to resolve their difficulties so as to become self-supporting systems again. During her pregnancy, Donna became involved with a local parenting project. The project team took a family supportive approach which included seeing the family as a whole, including wider family relationships, family resources and family strains. As well as supporting Donna and Garry, the workers engaged with both their

Research Focus

Bunting, L. and McAuley, C. (2004) 'Research Review: Teenage Pregnancy and Motherhood: The Contribution of Support', *Child and Family Social Work*, 9(2), 207–215.

The authors provide a critical analysis of the research literature into the role of informal support in teenage pregnancy and motherhood. They found that support from family, partner and peers was different but complementary and generally had a positive influence on parenting, behaviour and practice. The paper also shows that informal support has complex dynamics which change over time and that when conflicts develop, particularly between mother and daughter, they generally have a negative impact.

4

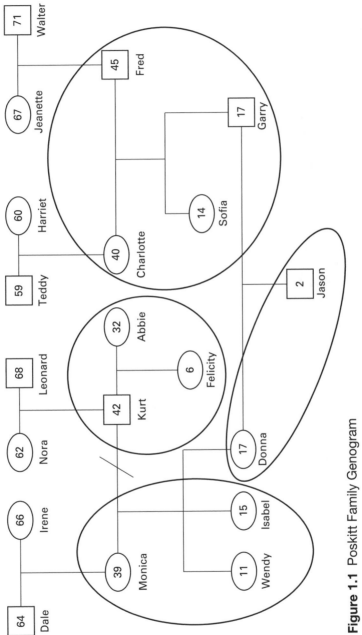

Figure 1.1 Poskitt Family Genogram

immediate and wider families. When Jason was born, the workers were at times working with four generations.

Family supportive practice is about understanding family practices, family relationships, resources and strains, even when the dominant configuration of a 'concern', 'problem' or 'difficulty' is in terms of an individual member. Morris et al. (2008: 60) identify three broad categories of family based service provision which are within the scope of family supportive practice. The first category is working with the family to support the service user, as when family members were engaged to support Donna when she was pregnant. The second is when workers recognise the needs of other family members arising out of their relationships with the primary service user, for example, when a family member misuses substances (Templeton, 2014). Finally, the third category involves whole family approaches which focus on the shared needs and strengths apparent in inter-family relationships and their collective assets, rather than addressing the needs of the service user or individual family member in isolation (Hughes, 2010). Hughes (2010: 546) identifies how in each of these categories, families can be framed in terms of potential resources to overcome difficulties, or as a source of problems. For instance, Orr, Barbour and Elliott (2014) point to the potential benefits of drug services adopting a family-focused approach in the treatment of adolescent and adult substance misuse, instead of the individual approach commonly adopted. They call for drug workers to more readily see 'families as part of the solution', rather than 'families as part of the problem'.

Whole family approach

The work of the Young Parent Project may not be typical and is perhaps comparatively rare (Morris, 2012: 19). 'Family support', 'family work' and 'social work with families' are not always what they seem. Morris et al. (2008) found when they reviewed the literature that there was repeated evidence of family based services or models, in reality being adult or children based, with little acknowledgement of the important difference between working with whole families as opposed to working with individual members of families in isolation. However, things might be changing with increased recognition and interest in whole family approaches in work with 'children and families'. For example, the 'Reclaiming Social Work' model, first piloted in the London Borough of Hackney, re-establishes a family focus within statutory social work (Goodman and Trowler, 2012: 11). Family group conferencing 'has generated considerable interest as a practical model that facilitates broader family engagement in care and protection' (Morris and Connolly, 2012), while family therapy continues as an established and effective approach to human difficulties (Stratton, 2011).

Whole family practice presents challenges, as it entails working with family networks and groups rather than individuals. It involves developing understandings of families, the strains they are under and how families can overcome those strains. Practitioners need to develop understandings of family life and practices, and the lived experience of individual family members through building relationships by means of listening to family narratives. Whole family practitioners do not restrict themselves to members of the household or those who are easier to engage. They carefully find out who family members construct as members of *their* family. Whole family practice requires skills in building trusting and honest relationships with the family group, as opposed to only selected individuals within the family (Morris, 2013: 206) and requires forms of practice that build on family strengths tailored to their specific circumstances.

Critical whole family approach

A whole family approach needs to take a critical form, in particular to counteract the twin dangers of losing sight of individual family members and ignoring the wider societal contexts. In taking a family approach, workers run the risk of losing sight of less powerful and/or less vocal family members while they focus on the family group, for example, child members of families slipping into background out of sight, while adult members get all the attention. In this chapter's case example there was a danger that the project workers concentrate their efforts on Donna and her family relationships and give less direct attention to her son, Jason. Taking a critical whole family approach recognises and is sensitive to the needs and uniqueness of each individual family member, no matter how young or old, and, when necessary, works with individuals, dyads and triads within the context of family relationships and practices, as well as working with the family group as a whole.

There is also a danger of not seeing how the wider social structures of society and social processes can underlie or exasperate family problems. Family orientated workers (and those who work with individuals) are in danger of seeing a family's problems as symptoms of 'individual' or 'family' malfunctioning, ignoring the impacts of the ways society is organised and structured. In an unequal society, many families experience multiple disadvantages which can play a major role in the development and continuation of family difficulties. Young pregnancy and motherhood is not only an individual and family issue but also a societal issue which some public discourses portray 'as a pernicious social problem where mother, children and society generally suffer' (Duncan, 2007: 307). For instance, part of Donna's daily reality is experiencing the impact of the stigmatisation of young motherhood.

Taking a critical whole family approach when helping families under strain involves having an ecological perspective that places family members, their relationships with each other, and their family life and practices in their environmental contexts. The next chapter fully explains what an ecological perspective involves, but basically it is seeing a family situation not only in terms of individuals but their relationships with each other and the impact that different layers of the wider contexts has on their family life, including their material environment, neighbourhood and society. Family supportive practice requires workers to have ecological understandings of not only families' living contexts, but the strains they are under and how the worker could help the family overcome them. This ecological approach underpins the whole of this book, particularly Chapter Two, Understanding Families; Chapter Three, Families under Strain; Chapter Five, Supportive Interventions; and Chapter Six, Working Collaboratively.

Prevention and early intervention

Family support and family supportive practice are often thought of as ways of preventing 'problems' and/or as a form of early intervention. However, there can be a certain ambiguity about the ways the terms 'prevention' and 'early intervention' are used. Biehal (2005: 22) points out that some policymakers and practitioners sometimes use the term 'early intervention' to mean intervention in the early life of a child, while others use it in relation to early stages in problem formation. Also 'prevention' and 'early intervention' are relative terms, with them depending on what policymakers and practitioners are trying to prevent. In fact, except in the most general of discussions, it is better to not use either term without making specifically clear what a policy, service or practice is trying to prevent and whether 'early' is in relation to early in the 'life of a child' or in the processes of problem formation. For instance, policies and projects in the area of young pregnancy need to be clear whether they are trying to prevent teenage pregnancy or promote good outcomes for young mothers and their children, or possibly both.

It is generally recognised that there are different levels of prevention which depend on the timing of help in relation to stages of problem formation, for example, Caplan (1964) distinguishes between primary, secondary and tertiary prevention that involve intervening

a) before the early stages of problem formation (primary prevention),

b) at the early stages of problem formation (secondary prevention) and

c) when the problem has had severe detrimental effects and attempts are made to limit or reverse the damage (tertiary prevention).

An example of primary prevention is universal children's centres, while 'crisis intervention teams' are examples of secondary prevention, and therapeutic services for maltreated children are examples of tertiary prevention.

Hardiker (2002) prefers the term 'intervention' to 'prevention' and developed an influential model consisting of five target levels: (i) 'general population' level, (ii) 'vulnerable groups' level, (iii) 'experiencing early stresses' level, (iv) 'experiencing severe stresses' level and (v) 'social breakdown has occurred' level. Family support through family supportive practice has potential roles on all these levels, but the primary focus tends to be families experiencing early stresses and severe stresses. Figure 1.2 shows the relationship between the Hardiker (2002) and Caplan (1964) models.

Examples of the different levels of prevention and intervention in relation to the chapter case scenario are:

● Sex and relationship education in all schools being part of the National Curriculum is *primary prevention* on the *general population* level in relation to preventing teenage pregnancy.

Intervention Levels 'Group Targeted' (Hardiker, 2002)	Levels of Prevention 'Timing of Intervention' (Caplan, 1964)
general population	primary prevention
vulnerable groups	
experiencing early stresses	secondary prevention
experiencing severe stresses	tertiary prevention
social breakdown has occurred	

Figure 1.2 Prevention and Intervention Levels Compared

- Identifying those young people most at risk of teenage pregnancy and providing targeted help is an example of *primary prevention* at the *vulnerable group* level.

- Projects and services to support young parents is *secondary prevention* at the 'early stresses' of pregnancy, birth and early parenthood, aimed at promoting good outcomes for both young parents and their children.

- Family caseworkers working with a young mother and her child when severe behavioural and emotional problems had become deeply entrenched is *tertiary intervention* at the *experiencing severe stresses* level, aimed at preventing breakdown of the family.

- Supportive work on reuniting a young parent and her child who was living in foster care is *tertiary prevention* aimed at preventing long-term separation of parent and child after *social breakdown has occurred.*

Related to different levels of prevention are services being organised into tiers corresponding to levels of need. Different jurisdictions have different arrangements for providing support for families that commonly takes the form of a continuum of provisions with services designed for particular levels of need. Within each area of England, agencies share assessment procedures, have a common language for different need levels and agreed multi-agency thresholds. Typically there are four levels for need in the continuum: *Level 1 Universal Services*, when children have their needs met by their family and the universal services available to all children, for example, schools, health visiting; *Level 2 Early Help*, when there are emerging concerns and a professional working in the same range of services as Level 1 provides additional support; *Level 3 Targeted Early Help*, when there are significant concerns, and specialist services are required, for example, the Youth Justice Service, CAMHS (Child and Adolescent Mental Health Services); *Level 4 Specialist Services*, when a child is at risk of significant harm or neglect, and statutory or specialist services from Children's Social Care are required. Agreed thresholds are required to mark the boundary between the four segments of the continuum. These thresholds are subject to change over time and depend on national and local government policies, priorities, funding and demand.

The school Donna attended until the later stages of her pregnancy is a universal service provided to all children of secondary school age. The family nurse working with Donna and Jason's family providing additional help is an example of Level 2 Early Help. The Young Parent Project becoming involved is an example of Level 3 Early Targeted Help. Children's Social

Care becoming involved if workers assessed Jason to be at risk of significant harm or neglect would be an example of a Level 4 Specialist
Service.

Social policy and family support

A government's social and economic policies have a profound impact on
families living within their jurisdictions. In this section we direct our attention to child welfare policies. Child welfare systems around the world differ in their orientation, some have a predominantly 'family support
orientation', while others have a predominantly 'child protection orientation'. Others try to achieve an appropriate balance between the two. It
should be stated that even though 'family support' and 'child protection'
can be presented as completely different activities requiring different
knowledge and skills, there are areas of overlap in the skills and knowledge required, especially if workers and families are to work together to
successfully implement child protection plans.

The focus here is the ever-changing policy context of child welfare in
England, from the setting up of Children's Departments, through the crea-
tion of generic family-orientated Social Services Departments, their grad-
ual dismantling and replacement with separate adult services allied to
health and children services allied to education. There have been shifts in
emphasis between child protection and family support, with achieving an
appropriate balance between the two being a continuing issue. In this
section we give highly selective highlights of post-war family welfare policy in England, outlining how social policy has changed since the Second
World War and will no doubt continue to change.

Post-war consensus 1945–1979

The post-war period was a time of reform, when, following the Curtis
Committee (1946) recognising the inadequacies of child care under the
poor law, the Children Act 1948 became law. This required local authorities to establish children's committees, appoint children's officers and set
up Children's Departments. James (1998: 173) argues that the Act motivated the first faltering attempts at preventative work with children and
their families. In 1971, Social Services Departments replaced separate
children, mental health and welfare services in England and Wales following the recommendations of the Seebohm Committee (1968). These

were to establish a 'community based and family orientated service', which provides one-door personal social services through the life course. The death of Maria Colwell in 1973 caused a public outcry and started a shift towards a 'child protection orientation' in child welfare services, with family support becoming comparatively sidelined.

The Tory years 1979–1997

The Children Act 1989 provided support for families whose children are in need, and protection for children who may be suffering from or likely to suffer from significant harm. The intention was to redress the failures and deficiencies of earlier practice by its emphasis on supporting families of 'children in need' and working in partnership with parents; however, child protection continued to marginalise family support. The publication of *Child Protection: Messages from Research* (Department of Health, 1995) initiated a refocusing debate about the balance between child protection and family support (Platt, 2001). A key finding of the research was that statutory child welfare services had too narrow a focus on forensic child protection investigations, to the neglect of family support. The key recommendation of the research was that policy and practice should refocus on supporting families in which there were 'children in need', rather than simply closing large numbers of non-substantiated cases despite the family needing support. How child welfare agencies respond to new referrals has remained an issue, particularly in relation to an appropriate balance between a forensic investigatory response and a supportive assessment response (Merkel-Holguin and Bross, 2015).

New Labour 1997–2010

The New Labour government had a broader view of family support, which Henricson (2012) refers to as a 'revolution in family policy'. Family support became a major contributor to New Labour's mission to combat 'social exclusion'. Parent–child relationships came centre stage, and family and parenting services mushroomed with Sure Start centres in every locality. The broad aims were to reduce child poverty, increase social mobility and improve child outcomes. In spite of a profusion of initiatives, New Labour did not achieve its self-imposed targets, and Henricson (2012: 12) raises the question of whether it was simply unrealistic to expect to change a highly unequal society like the UK solely through child and family initiatives targeting individual behaviour and family relationships.

In 2006, Family Intervention Projects were launched with the aim of reducing 'anti-social behaviour' and stopping the cycles of homelessness caused by it (White et al., 2008). These marked a shift in New Labour policy towards a national scheme of local projects targeted at specific groups that were engaging in various forms of anti-social behaviour or were considered to be 'at risk' groups. Typically, within the projects, highly skilled staff worked intensively with families in their own homes, taking a whole family approach, staying involved as long as necessary. Particularly relevant to the chapter case study was the Family Nurse Partnership scheme, also introduced in 2006, which provided a voluntary regular home visiting by specially trained family nurses to first-time young mothers 19 years or under, from early pregnancy until the child was two years old.

New Labour launched their 'think family' initiative in 2008 which advocated adult and children's services to join up around the needs of families, with there being no 'wrong door', and with all services looking at the whole family, building on family strengths and providing tailored support (Cabinet Office, 2008: 7). The Family Pathfinder programme was set up to test and develop the 'think family' model. Twenty-seven local authorities received additional funding to develop local family approaches to addressing the needs of families with multiple and complex problems. The evaluation of the programme concluded that there

Research Focus

Parr, S. (2009) 'Family intervention projects: A site of social work practice', *British Journal of Social Work*, 38(7), 1256–1273.

Sadie Parr draws on the findings of an evaluation of 'Signpost' Family Intervention Project and gives insight into the importance of the nature of the organisational context in which projects are set up. Signpost was one dominated by a social work ethos and gave professionals the opportunity to engage in creative practices then not possible in mainstream social work contexts. She argues that although Family Intervention Projects were framed within a 'problem family' discourse, with certain families being both the cause of anti-social behaviour and the site of its solution, it is the ethos and organisation of the specific local projects that shapes whether they can effectively help families. Where the dominant culture of projects is consistent with social work values, they give opportunities for skilled social workers and others to form supportive and productive relationships with families.

was a compelling case for local authorities and their partners to develop and implement intensive family support for such families (York Consulting, 2011).

Parton (2009: 68) points to the irony that just at the point when the community and family orientated Social Services Departments had been finally dismantled, the family re-emerged as a key object of social policy. In Chapter 6 you will see that children and adult services working together remains a challenge. An implication of achieving 'think family' is that those on 'the other side of the door' are able to look at the requirements across the whole family, rather than fragmenting needs or being focused on only one family member's experience (Clarke and Hughes, 2010: 528).

The 2007 world financial crisis and the following world recession rocked the last two years of the labour administration. Following the media and public outcry at the tragic death of 17-month-old Baby Peter in late 2008, there was again a shift in emphasis towards child protection, with the threshold of taking children into care lowered and social workers operating almost exclusively in the sharp end of child protection (Parton, 2011).

Research Focus

Rudoe, N. (2014) 'Becoming a young mother: Teenage pregnancy and parenting policy', *Critical Social Policy*, 34(3), 293–311.

Early pregnancy and motherhood are examples of areas of policy interest in recent decades. New Labour government's *Teenage Pregnancy Strategy* was part of a policy focus on improving 'parenting' in working class families. Naomi Rudoe researched the views of young women and staff at an alternative educational setting for pregnant young women and mothers. They were asked their views on the *Strategy*, in particular its aim of reducing teenage conceptions, increasing participation of young mothers in education, employment and training and the notion of the 'good mother'. She found the young women and staff held complex attitudes towards the strategy, parenting interventions and idea of the 'good mother'. Some of the young women thought it was a matter of choice whether to have a baby young, others were more cautious and thought it better to wait a while, but never a mistake. The staff were generally supportive of the ideas of parenting classes, but did not subscribe to a 'working class deficit' approach and stressed the need for parenting support for all social classes and ages of parent.

Austerity and retrenchment 2010–?

In the aftermath of the 2008 global financial crisis there was some continuity between the New Labour era and the 2010–2015 Conservative Liberal coalition government, but within a changed context of rigorously pursuing austerity policies, involving services and welfare cuts. Ball (2014) explains that in an austere climate of diminishing resources there was an escalation of families in acute need that precipitated a rise in demand for family support that services could not fulfil. Sure Start children centres continued in reduced and modified forms, Family Nurse Partnerships continued and 'Intensive Family Intervention Projects' morphed into the 'Troubled Families' initiative. Trying to change parental behaviour in targeted families continued, with a variation in tone and criteria as to which families need to change and why. The claim was that there was 'a group troubled families whose lives are so chaotic they cost the Government some £9 billion in the last year alone and can cause serious problems for their local communities through crime and anti-social behaviour' (Department of Work and Pensions, 2012: 1). Levitas (2012: 4) claims the figure of 120,000 is 'a factoid – something that takes the form of a fact, but is not', it being based on secondary analysis on 2004 survey data which found about 2% of the families surveyed had five or more of seven characteristics of social disadvantage.

Launched in 2011, the expectation was that the lives of 120,000 'troubled families' could be turned around by 2015. Local authorities were tasked with identifying 'troubled families' in their area using a set of criteria. These criteria had little resemblance to the multiple disadvantage criteria used in the original research that came up with the 120,000 figure. The national criteria that local authorities were to use to identify 'troubled families'

> Are involved in crime and anti-social behaviour
> Have children not in school
> Have an adult on 'out of work' benefits
> Cause high cost to the public purse

Hayden and Jenkins (2013: 4) found that in one particular city that was the focus of their research, only 90 families, of the 17,000 families in the local programme, met the first three criteria, and the authority had to rely on the fourth criteria that gave considerable local discretion as to who to include. The point is that the real picture is much more complex than the one the government portrayed in its policy statements about the existence of 120,000 'troubled families'. As Welshman (2012) makes clear, the discourse and rhetoric of the 'problem family' has proved resilient, spanning the period from the setting up of Pacifist Service Units (later renamed Family Service Units) during the Second World War in 1946, through to the 'Troubled Families' of the 2010–2015 Coalition.

In May 2015, the Conservative Party formed a majority government whose overriding priorities were shrinking the state and reducing the deficit and government debt. Austerity policies continued and the government cut public expenditure with increased vigour. The impacts fell particularly heavily on welfare benefits for families and local authority services, with knock-on effects to voluntary agency grants. Service thresholds become higher particularly for Children's Social Care, and staff and families come under ever-increasing pressure, with negative effects on morale.

Family support and law

There is a considerable and large branch of law known as 'family law' (Herring, 2011). This section will limit itself to one aspect of family law and will highlight important sections of the Children Act 1989 in respect of supporting families and safeguarding and promoting the welfare of children. Davis (2009) makes the claim that under the Children Act 1989, local authorities' first role is *not* child protection but supporting children and their families, with prevention being the first port of call. She goes on to state that child protection provisions are a safety net when family support has failed.

Section 17(1) Children Act 1989 states

> It shall be the general duty of every local authority [...]
>
> (a) to safeguard and promote the welfare of children within their area who are in need; and
> (b) so far as is consistent with that duty, promote the upbringing of such children by their families,
>
> by providing a range and level of services appropriate to those children's needs.

Section 17(1) raises at least four questions

What is the nature of this general duty?
When is 'a child in need'?
How are local authorities to safeguard and promote the welfare of 'children in need'?
When does promoting the upbringing of children by their families cease to promote and safeguard a child's welfare?

What is the nature of the general duty?

Brayne and Carr (2010: 259) explain how the duty under section 17 of the Children Act 1989 is a general duty and not a targeted, specific duty owed to any individual child, meaning that the duty to a specific child is very limited. Schedule 2 of the Act spells out the general preventative duties, inasmuch as they must take 'reasonable steps' to prevent children suffering ill-treatment or neglect, reduce the need for care proceedings and criminal proceedings against children, avoid the need to place children in secure accommodation and discourage children in their area from committing criminal offences (Davis, 2009: 109). Davis (2009: 109) goes on to say that Schedule 2 does not actually impose a duty to prevent children suffering ill-treatment or neglect, but a duty to 'take reasonable steps through the provision of services', with the word 'reasonable' allowing judgement, argument and justification.

When is a child in need?

As stated above, section 17(1) gives every local authority a duty to safeguard and promote the welfare of children within their area, but only those *who are in need*. The statutory meaning of 'in need' is given in section 17(10) which states that a child shall be taken to be in need if

> He is unlikely to achieve or maintain, or have the opportunity of achieving and maintaining a reasonable standard of health and development without the provision for him of services by a local authority under this part;
>
> His health or development is likely to be significantly impaired, or further impaired, without the provision for him of such services; or
>
> He is disabled.

Davis (2009: 111) states that 'the definition signals the section's preventative intention – it looks ahead to what is likely to happen if nothing is done. So children do not have to already be falling behind to qualify – it is enough to be clear they are likely to do so unless services are provided.' For instance, Donna's local authority assessed her as a 'child in need', enabling them to provide her with services.

How are local authorities to safeguard and promote the welfare of children in need?

Local authorities are to safeguard and promote the welfare of children in need by providing a range of services. Schedule 2, Paragraph 8, 'Provision for Children Living with their Families' states that

8. Every local authority shall make such provision as they consider appropriate for the following services to be available with respect to children in need within their area while they are living with their families –

(a) advice, guidance and counselling;

(b) occupational, social, cultural or recreational activities;

(c) home help (which may include laundry facilities);

(d) facilities for, or assistance with, travelling to and from home for the purpose of taking advantage of any other service provided under this Act or of any similar service;

(e) assistance to enable the child concerned and his family to have a holiday.

Although at first sight this seems an impressive list of provisions, the Act leaves local authorities with considerable discretion as to what they actually provide with the words 'as they consider appropriate'. Local authorities can fulfil their duty under the Act by providing grants to voluntary organisations, and a national charity runs the Young Parent Project with the aid of a local authority grant.

When does promoting the upbringing of children by their families cease to promote and safeguard a child's welfare?

In relation to the fourth question, Section 31(20) of the Children Act 1989 gives the grounds for a court to make a care or supervision order, which gives a signal as to when promoting the upbringing of a child by their family ceases to promote and safeguard the child's welfare.

Section 31(2) states that

(2) A court may only make a care order or supervision order if it is satisfied:

(a) that the child concerned is suffering, or likely to suffer, significant harm; and

(b) that the harm, or likelihood of harm, is attributable to:

(i) the care given to the child, or likely to be given to him if the order were not made, not being what it would be reasonable to expect a parent to give to him; or

(ii) the child's being beyond parental control.

Section 31(2) is known as the 'threshold criteria' and it is up to the courts to decide whether it applies, and for local authorities to decide whether to put a case before a court. Significant harm emerges as the important concept in determining whether a child remaining with their family ceases to promote and safeguard their welfare. Brayne and Carr (2010: 336) point out that given the limited statutory assistance from Parliament as to what they mean by 'significant harm', there has been wide variation and confusion in the interpretation of its meaning.

Like the Children Act 1989, the Human Rights Act 1998 reflects the tensions between family support and child protection. On one hand, Article 8 gives 'everyone the right to respect for his private and family life, his home and his correspondence'. Also, the European Court of Human Rights judged that the 'mutual enjoyment by a parent and child of each other's company constitutes a fundamental element of family life' (*W v. the United Kingdom ECHR*, para 59, cited in Munro and Ward, 2008: 227). However, there are exceptions to Article 8, including for the protection of health, and the European Court has given the expression 'private and family life' a broad interpretation, for example, the right to private life includes the right not to be subject to physical or sexual abuse (Williams, 2001: 839). Also, Article 3 states that 'no one shall be subjected to torture or to inhuman or degrading treatment or punishment'. So the right to a private and family life is not an absolute but a qualified human right.

Under the Children Act 2004, each local authority in England must make arrangements to promote cooperation between the authority and its relevant partners with the view of improving the well-being of children in the authority's area. In making arrangements the local authority must have regard to the importance of parents and other persons caring for children in improving the well-being of children.

Chapter Key Points

1. Generally families are self-supporting systems which sometimes require support from outside their family, community and friendship networks.

2. Within a critical whole family approach, family supportive practitioners do not lose sight of individual family members or wider societal contexts.

3. There are different levels of prevention in respect of targeted population and their timing in relation to stages of problem formation.

4. Over time and in different jurisdictions, government policies vary in the ways in which they frame when families need support, and what kinds of support they need.

▶

5. English authorities have a general legal duty to support the upbringing of children within their families as is consistent with their welfare, but legislation leaves them with considerable discretion as to how they do this, what services they provide and to whom.

6. There are inevitable tensions written into the Children Act 1989 between supporting the upbringing of children within their families and protecting children from harm.

7. Authorities and their partners have a legal duty to cooperate with each other in safeguarding children in their area.

Reflective Exercises

1. Think about the point-in-time of Donna finding herself pregnant at the age of 14, telling Garry she was pregnant, and them telling their families that Donna was expecting a child, and their reactions. Think about the relative merits and drawbacks of the local project workers focusing solely on Donna and her unborn child, compared with taking a whole family approach as briefly outlined in this chapter.

2. What do you think are the consequences for workers and families if authorities and agencies have to raise their thresholds for specialist services accepting referrals?

3. Child welfare systems around the world differ in their orientation, some having a 'family support orientation', while others have a 'child protection orientation'. Others try to achieve an appropriate balance between the two. What would you say the child welfare orientation is of the country you live in?

Putting into Practice

Think of a family you know that is under strain. It can be a fictional one if you wish. What do you think would be the best ways to support that family?

What do you think are the main challenges for practitioners in engaging and working with whole families?

Discuss whether it is practical for practitioners to take an ecological approach and have in mind the different layers of contexts and domains, ranging from individual family members right through to societal structures.

Further Resources

Clarke, H. and Hughes, N. (2010) 'Introduction: Family minded policy and whole family practice – developing a critical research framework', *Social Policy and Society*, 9(4), 527–531.

In this article Clarke and Hughes take a critical look at the idea of whole family practice.

Tunstill, J., Aldgate, J. and Thoburn, J. (2010) 'Promoting and safeguarding the welfare of children: A bridge too far?', *Journal of Children's Services*, 5(3), 14–24.

In this article Jane Tunstill and her colleagues contrast the optimistic intentions of Section 17 of the Children Act 1989 to produce a genuine continuum that will safeguard the welfare of children, and show how over the decades challenges have consistently skewed the balance between proactive family support and reactive crisis-driven responses in favour of the latter.

Thoburn, J., Copper, N., Brandon, M. and Connolly, S. (2013) 'The place of "think family" approaches in child and family social work: Messages from a process evaluation of an English pathfinder service', *Children and Youth Services Review*, 35(2), 228–236.

In this article Thoburn and colleagues describe the approaches and methods of a multidisciplinary team working with families with long-standing and complex problems. It identifies aspects of service that were associated with positive outcomes.

CHAPTER 2

UNDERSTANDING FAMILIES

CHAPTER OVERVIEW

This chapter

- Explores the contested term 'families', explains how they are changing and introduces the concept of 'family practices'.
- Explains the importance of family ecology in understanding and helping families.
- Analyses the social positioning of families in terms of 'social class', 'heteronormativity', 'ethnicity' and 'disability'.
- Considers the potential assets of family membership, in terms of 'social support', 'mattering' and 'social capital'.
- Examines family relationship dynamics, including power dynamics, gender dynamics and generational dynamics.
- Looks at the dynamics of time, including the ideas of 'social convoy' and 'family life cycles'.

Introduction

Workers need to develop good understandings of the families they work with if they are to effectively support them. Families are complex human groups embedded in social and material contexts; therefore, practitioners need relevant conceptual frameworks that enable them to make sense of what they hear and see. The quality of practitioners' understandings will depend, among other things, on the extent to which they can build relationships with family members that enable open dialogue, which is the subject matter of Chapter 3. In addition, workers need to be able to intellectually cope with the complexity of families as human groups. Drawing mainly on family studies, family dynamics and ecological theory, this chapter aims to explain frameworks, concepts and theories that can potentially help practitioners develop understandings of family situations that do justice to the complexities involved and assist in working with families to overcome their difficulties. Equipped with such frameworks, practitioners will be in a better position to develop in-depth understandings of families.

The chapter is wide in scope, ranging from the internal relationship dynamics of families to the social positioning of families in society. The chapter endeavours to present an understanding of families as human groups moving through time and living in an unequal society. To show that all families have family dynamics, family practices and a family ecology, I have chosen the chapter family scenario as a contrast to those in the other chapters, inasmuch as the McGovern family members have a relatively comfortable life.

The McGovern family

The term 'the McGovern family' refers to the family in the four-generation genogram (Figure 2.1). The McGovern family as portrayed consists of seven households and up to seven families, depending on how we define the term 'family'. They reflect at least some of the ways family forms have changed and become more diverse. Mary and Connor McGovern are a heterosexual married couple, who form a household together and represent a traditional, intact heterosexual family. They have four adult children, Liam, Fiona, Andrew and Sinead, all of whom have left home and formed households of their own. Connor's mother, Hannah, is still alive and lives alone in her own home, as does Mary's mother, Oonagh. Liam and his partner, Kate, are a cohabiting couple and have two children, Ellie, a child of their partnership, and Tyler, from one of Kate's previous relationships. Fiona shares a flat with housemates and has a non-resident partner, David. Andrew and Rachel separated some time ago and Andrew brings up their daughter, Cheryl, on his own. Sinead is married to Zoe and they have two children, Zoe's daughter Saad from a previous heterosexual relationship and their own child, Wendy, by known donor Richard.

The McGovern family, as depicted, shows that once we move outside the 'household' and view families as multigenerational and multi-household networks, their membership can get large and complex. As complex as the Figure 2.1 genogram may be, it does not show the full picture, as the adult children's partners' families of origin have not been included and many aunts, uncles, 'in-laws' and cousins are also missing. Like other families, the McGovern family relationships are characterised by various degrees of emotional and geographical closeness and distance. The McGovern family have generally not faced severe problems but rather the everyday ups and downs and issues of family life and relationships. The one exception is the fraught relationship between Liam and his stepson, Tyler, resulting on one occasion in Tyler running away from home.

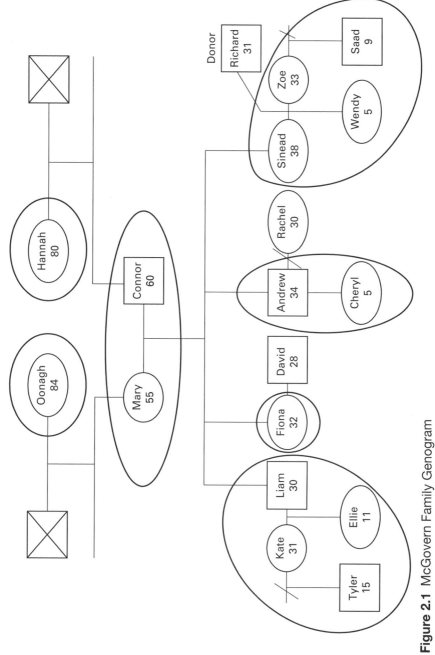

Figure 2.1 McGovern Family Genogram

The chapter consists of six sections: the first on what families are; the second on family ecology; the third on the social positioning of families along the dimensions of social class, heteronormativity, ethnicity and disability; the fourth on families providing the potential assets of social support, mattering, and social capital to its members; the fifth on family relationships and dynamics; and, finally, the sixth on the dynamics of time. Together, these sections give a picture of families as human groups with a diverse membership of individual human beings embedded in multilayered contexts and social meanings moving through time.

Families

The McGovern family, like others, use the term family in a number of ways, such as when family members refer to the whole family having attended a wedding, when they refer to their paternal great-grandmother Hannah's ring as being a family heirloom that passed down the generations and when Andrew and Rachel talked about starting a family. Within professional and theoretical discourses the concept of family is both complex and controversial, and we need to give some attention as to what we mean by the term families, as there can be some anxiety about how families are changing and what 'proper families' are.

What are families?

Some readers might regard the question 'What are families?' as redundant, as everybody knows what a family is. However, there is no straightforward answer to this question, and endeavouring to answer it reveals some important issues of relevance and interest to practitioners attempting to support families. Even through some sociologists question the continuing relevance of the concept of family (Wilkinson and Bell, 2012) it remains an important idea for practitioners, policymakers and people in general. As Silva and Smart (1999) point out, despite the growing consensus that diverse patterns of 'family life' exist, people still define particular aspects of the lives as 'family life' and feel committed to their 'family'.

Practitioners need to have a fluid and open perspective as to what families are, devoid of qualifying criteria in terms of gender, biological link, legal status, sexuality, number of parents, number of generations, co-residence or the presence of children. Family orientated practitioners are interested in the constellation of people that have significant connections to each other. Family members may view some members of these constellations as 'like family', for instance a non-related 'aunty', while others will be friends or neighbours. Also, the relationship a particular member has with other members will vary in terms of emotional closeness, levels of intimacy, as well as whether they live within the same household, nearby or some distance away. Each constellation member will have their own personal life and have connections outside the constellation as well as within.

Families are changing

Over the years, 'family forms' have been changing and have become much more diverse and fluid. Weeks, Heaphy and Donovan (2001) use the term 'families of choice' to reflect the range and mix of blood, partner, legal, affinity and friendship ties and commitments that now form families. Among the demographic changes are increased partner separation, rise in lone parent households, re-partnering and family reconstitution. There has also been an acceptance of same-sex-parented households and families. There have been changes in the roles men and women play, for example, increase in women's employment outside the home, coupled with a delay in childbirth and men no longer being the sole 'breadwinner' and an increase in cohabiting couples. The McGovern family reflects some of this diversity. There are two single-person households in the great-grandparent generation; there is a couple household in the grandparent generation; in the adult children generation there is a reconstituted family, a housemate's household, a lone-parent household, a cohabiting couple and a same-sex-parented family.

Practitioners set out to support people in their living contexts and recognise that many people have an open, flexible and fluid perspective on what constitutes 'family'; however, they also need to be aware that competing ideologies and discourses about what 'proper families' should be still exist in society. There have been debates about the meaning of these changes within sociology, politics and the general public. Jamieson et al. (2006) discuss the disagreement in sociology about just how fundamental are the shifts that have taken place in actual practices. They offer two different ways of interpreting the same trends.

> One ... in terms of the elasticity and constant stretching of the boundary of what constitutes 'family' as the constellations that people designate as 'familial' has become increasingly diverse. Another ... is to say that the idea

and ideal of family is losing ground to different understandings of how life should be lived.

(Jamieson et al., 2006: 1)

In the former interpretation, the changes are a welcome extension of family boundaries, practices and obligations. However, in the latter, changes in family and household composition is evidence of decline or decentring of family relationships that accompany an increase in the importance of individual choice in one's personal life. Within politics there are those that mourn the changes as moral decline and an end or weakening of 'the family', while others point to the diversity of family forms as something to be welcomed and celebrated. Those who narrowly define 'proper families' as a co-residing, heterosexual married couple with their biological children tend to deplore the changing family forms, but others welcomed the changes as heralding the end of rigid, narrow definitions as to what a family is.

What is important from a practice point of view is whether the changes positively or negatively impact on people's ability to support and care for each other and bring up children. In debates about the decline of 'the family' it is often forgotten that within the diverse family forms, the basic core of sharing resources, caring, responsibility and obligations remain. As Silva and Smart (1999) state, the emergence of new family forms does not mean the values of caring and obligation are abandoned, but that they remain central issues which continue to bind people to together. Furthermore, Golombok (2000: 99) argues that family structure makes little difference to children's psychological development instead, what really matters is the 'quality of family life'. It is the quality of human relationships, and having the material resources to sustain some quality of life that are important.

From 'the family' to 'family practices'

There was a time when sociologists studied 'the family' as a social institution, as part of a normative societal framework of how life should be lived. With the exception of some politicians and religious leaders, those inside and outside sociology have largely discredited and abandoned the idea of 'the family'. Sociologists think the term the family evokes an 'ideological stereotype of a heterosexual, two-parent nuclear family with a breadwinning husband and father, and a home-making wife and mother' (Edwards and Gillies, 2012: 64). They fear the concept is in danger of setting a fixed and static normative standard as something for people to live up to and be judged by.

Family sociologists have endeavoured to resolve these issues surrounding the subject matter of their discipline in a number of ways. One relatively straightforward way is instead of 'the family', it is now common to refer to 'families', which is thought to better reflect the different and changing ways of being a family. Now the word family is used much less on its own but rather as an adjective as in 'family relationships', 'family activities', 'family outing', 'family conflict' or 'family violence'. Another way sociologists have tried to get away from fixed notions of what families are is to focus on 'family practices', and the different ways of 'doing family' and 'displaying family'.

The term family practices is a relatively new term that focuses on what family members actually do in their family roles both within the family home and outside (Saltiel, 2013). Morgan (1996) was one of the first to use the term, among other things, to resolve some of the issues around the rigid notion of 'the family'. The term allows differences in the ways 'family' is done and different ways of doing 'family'. Families are what families 'do', rather than relying on institutional or membership definitions of family. Family practices are those practices that families construct as being in some way about 'family'. As Morgan states,

> Family practices are not just any old practices; they are also practices which matter to the persons concerned and which are seen in some way as being 'special' or 'different'. To 'mean' something to somebody is not simply to be able to identify, but to invest that object of identification with a degree of emotional significance. It should be stressed that this emotional/ evaluative aspect need not be positive; in family matters, as many have noted, we are dealing with love and hate, attraction and repulsion, approval and disapproval.
>
> (Morgan, 1999: 190)

The concept of family practices is particularly useful to workers, as it respects the different ways families have of 'doing family', that is, the different ways members interact with each other and go about their family lives. There can be considerable individual, cultural and social class differences in family practices, for example, whether children have a set bedtime or whether as a family they sit around a table together at meal times. When Sinead and Zoe formed a family together they brought with them different sets of family practices, differences that were resolved over a period a time.

Family ecology

Each family has its own ecology that consists of intra-familial and extra-familial environments in which family members live their lives.

Understanding family ecology involves simultaneously paying attention to many different levels of context. At their most simple, these levels of context are as follows: the personal level; the interpersonal level; the community and neighbourhood level; and the societal level. Practitioners taking an ecological approach will have the following in mind: the individual family members; their intra-familial environment, including family dynamics; their material resources, including housing conditions; and their extra-familial environment, including the wider family, the neighbourhood, local facilities and local community, as well as wider cultural, societal and governmental contexts of their lives, including, in an increasingly globalised world, the global economic system. They would recognise that family members have lives outside the immediate family context, with family members participating in local agencies, facilities, workplaces, schools and other institutions. Figure 2.2 shows the internal relationships dynamics of Tyler's immediate family, their relations with the wider families, their participation in schools, leisure places, local facilities, services, organisations and peer groups, and their interaction with friends and neighbours and the cultural, economic, structural and political contexts of their lives.

Multiple levels of influence

An ecological perspective is required if family practices and processes are to be fully understood. Parenting and child development are two important and related processes that occur within families. Bronfenbrenner's

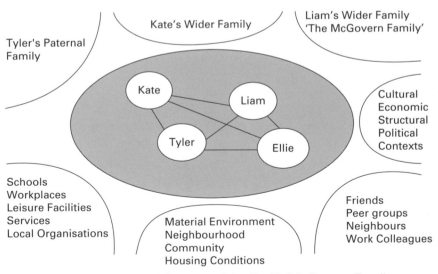

Figure 2.2 The Ecological Context of the Smith/McGovern Family

(1979) 'Ecology of Human Development Model' and Belsky's (1984) 'Determinants of Parenting Process Model' are two ecological models that complement each other and have been influential in the fields of child development and parenting. As ecological models, they concern multiple levels of influences on human behaviour and development. A common feature of both models is that they focus on an individual in their multiple-levelled environment, in the case of Bronfenbrenner, a child, and in the case of Belsky, a parent. Bronfenbrenner's model shows the various influences on child development, while Belsky's model shows the multiple influences on a parent's parenting practices. There will always be limitations on any model that endeavours to depict the processes of multiple influences on human behaviour and development, but they do enable greater depth of thinking about the processes involved.

Ecology of child development

Bronfenbrenner's (1979) ecological framework has had considerable influence on ecological thinking in the helping professions. Bronfenbrenner (1986) is interested in the ecology of families as a context of human development. He makes a distinction between the internal environment of families as a context of human development and the external environment of families that affect the capacity of families to foster the healthy development of their children. Within the framework, the ecological contexts of child development are five nested systems: microsystems; mesosystems; exosystems; macrosystems; and a chronosystem. Tyler participates in a number of microsystems, including the microsystem of family home, microsystem of his father's home, microsystem of his school, grandparent's microsystem and microsystem of his peer group. Mesosystems are the ways microsystems relate to each other and can impact on Tyler's development, for instance, events at home can affect Tyler's progress at school, events in school can affect his behaviour at home and arguments with his stepfather can affect his mood when he goes to school.

Exosystems are the extrafamilial environments parents participant in, especially places that children rarely enter, examples being a parent's workplace and their friends. Tyler's mother's and stepfather's workplaces are exosystems that affect the family environment, including their parenting. The chronosystem is how ageing, life transitions, life events and historical changes affect family processes, for example, Tyler's chronosystem includes the separation of his parents. The macrosystem (Bronfenbrenner, 1979) includes the wider societal influences on family processes and

Tyler's development. An economy in recession would be part of the macrosystem and would affect household income and so impact on the family environment in which Tyler lives and develops.

Ecology of parenting

Belsky's (1984) process model of parenting identifies the multiple determinants of parenting as consisting of three domains of influence. The three domains are:

- the parent's developmental history and their psychological resources;
- the characteristics of the child; and
- the contextual sources of stress and support, including co-parenting relations, social networks and work.

The model recognises both direct and indirect influences of the personal, interpersonal and social levels, as well as the potential of one domain to buffer the effects of another. The domain of a parent's developmental history and psychological resources directly influences their interactions with their child and indirectly influences the broader context in which parent–child relations exist. As when a parent's personality influences their choice and relationship with their partner, the willingness of their social network to offer help and their job satisfaction, a parent's developmental history and psychological resources affect their capacity for 'doing' good parenting. All four of Mary and Connor's children have had an upbringing that provided them with the capacity to be good parents, although factors outside 'their person' can infringe on this ability.

The model gives children an active role in parent–child relations and picks out a child's temperament as influential. As Belsky (1997: 12) states, 'because the parent-child relationship involves two parties, it is not surprising that attributes of each participating member affect the nature of the interactions that transpire'. It is not about a child's temperament per se but the goodness of fit between the parent's and child's characteristics (Belsky, 1984: 86).

The model sees the co-parent relationships, social networks and work as potential sources of support or stress. The amount and quality of supports available and intensity of environmental stressors will have an important impact on a parent's parenting (Ghate and Hazel, 2002). A parent can view their relationships with their partner as a source of support or stress. Likewise, a lone parent could perceive the lack of a partner as a source of support or stress. Andrew might find parenting without Rachel less stressful, as what he perceived as her aggravation was out of the picture. Support from a social network can cause more stress than it alleviates, and work can give a sense of satisfaction or frustration. The point is that one cannot assume that certain domains are sources of support or assume others are a source of stress. The model recognises parenting as a buffered system in which support in one domain can act as a buffer against stress in another, as when a supportive social network offsets a stressful co-parenting relationship.

Assessment frameworks

An ecological perspective can form the basis of assessment frameworks like the *Framework for the Assessment of Children in Need and their Families* (Department of Health, 2000) introduced in England in 2001. The framework includes a triangle with the sides representing three interrelated domains: child's developmental needs, parenting capacity, and family and environmental factors, each of which has a number of dimensions. The framework is reminiscent of Belsky's (1984) three domains in his process model of parenting: parent's developmental history and psychological resources; characteristics of the child; and contextual sources of stress and support. Local authorities commonly use the framework as the basis for their assessments of children in need in their area. The framework provides a common language for professionals to communicate with each other and consistency across the country. It has the potential to help workers to create ecological understandings of family relationships, the welfare of family members and their experiences of family life. However, whether workers can achieve this potential depends on the organisational context in which they work and how they use it in practice.

There are three main criticisms of the use of the framework. First, in a book entitled *The Missing Side of the Triangle*, Jack and Gill (2003) claim that there is comparative neglect of the family and environmental factors domain. Second, workers allowing the framework to have a stultifying effect on assessment practice means that questions are asked in a predetermined format, resulting in an intrusive style of questioning (Welbourne, 2012: 83). Third, workers might fail to analyse and integrate the discrete pieces of information that the framework encourages them to collect. The information collected using the framework needs to be integrated and analysed so as to be able to see 'the wood for the trees', for example, recognising that there is an interplay between parenting capacity, the challenges parents face, and the resultant impact on the welfare of children. If workers working with Tyler and his family are to use such a framework to produce quality assessments, they will need time to build relationships with family members, effective supportive supervision and the skill to not allow the instrument to stifle their practice.

Social positioning

Families occupy different social and economic positions in society. Common features of societies are gross inequalities of wealth and income, with families occupying different social spaces and corresponding levels of status and esteem. Important social dimensions of difference are social class, sexuality, ethnic difference and disability, all of which position families in society. The wider McGovern family are predominantly a heteronormative, middle class, White Irish family living in England, which gives them a relatively privileged position in British society. However, not all the 'family households' in the wider McGovern family occupy this privileged position. In terms of heteronormativity and ethnicity, Sinead and Zoe are a same-sex couple and Zoe is a British Asian, Andrew is bringing his daughter up alone, and Tyler is of mixed heritage.

Social class

A family's standard and conditions of living, the resources that have available to them, and their members' life chances relate to their location in society. There is a degree of upward and downward mobility but a tendency for the children to grow up to occupy a similar social, cultural and economic social location in society as their parents. Like their parents, Mary and Connor's four children all have good middle class jobs. Families play a major role in the reproduction of advantage and disadvantage (Crompton, 2006: 671) through the different volumes and types of capital possessed by its members. This enables advantaged families to maintain their privileged position and acts as barriers to disadvantaged families from being upwardly socially mobile. For example, a parent with social capital in the form of a network of contacts in prestigious positions can use these to get their children high-status work experience.

Although it is common to see class as no longer relevant (Beck and Beck-Gernsheim, 2002), some see class as a continuing, if changing, way societies are socially arranged (Crompton, 2006). There are a number of different ways of looking at social class. The Marxist perspective on class is that the most important division in society is that between the proletariat and the capitalists, that is, between those who sell their labour, workers, and those who own the means of production, 'capitalists'. In contrast to this, Bourdieu's (1986) influential perspective on class constructed class as the volume and type of capitals a person or family has accumulated. The BBC's Great British Survey Experiment (Savage et al., 2013) used Bourdieu's different forms of capital to develop a new model of social class. The model has seven classes ranging from an 'elite' to a 'precariat'. The authors claim the seven-class model recognises the continued polarisation of British society and class fragmentation of its middle layers. Many of the families practitioners come in contact with will be members of the precariat, a word formed by merging 'precarious' and 'proletariat'. The precariat was the most deprived class, with the lowest levels of economic, social and cultural capital. The term precariat reflects the often precarious and unstable position of disadvantaged families. Mary and Connor are members of the 'established middle class', while their children are members of the 'new affluent workers class'.

Savage, Warde and Devine (2005) see 'capital' as being distinctive through its potential to accumulate and its capacity to convert into other resources. Bourdieu (1986) describes four types of capital: social, economic, cultural and symbolic. *Social capital* is the size of a person's social network connections and the volume of capital (economic, cultural and/ or social capital) possessed by network members (Bourdieu, 1986: 249, cited in Barker, 2012: 731). *Economic capital* 'refers to material and financial assets, including ownership of stocks and shares' (Garrett, 2007: 359). *Cultural capital* consists of scarce symbolic assets, like education (particularly in the form of educational credentials), tastes, demeanour, styles of speech, mannerisms, pronunciation and dress. Garrett (2007: 359), drawing from Gunn (2005: 60), states that the body is an instrument of cultural capital, and for the middle class the long process of education inscribed a particular bodily manner or disposition. *Symbolic capital* is when others recognise economic capital, social capital and/or cultural capital as legitimate and give prestige, reputation and fame (Garrett, 2007: 359).

The relevance of social class for workers is that it shapes the lives of the families they work with, determines their position in society and reflects the volume of social assets they have to draw on in difficult times, the barriers they face in improving their position and the chances their children have of being upwardly socially mobile. As such, they need to take social class into account when working with families to improve their lives.

Heteronormativity

Heteronormative nuclear families, that is, 'opposite-sex two-parent families', still occupy a privileged position in society compared with 'same-sex two-parent families' and one-parent families (Wilkinson and Bell, 2012: 426). 'Privileged' in the sense of 'socially conferred benefits and advantages that result from mere membership' of a social group, in this instance heterosexuals (Montgomery and Steward, 2012: 162). Heteronormativity is the term used for the existence of this internalised set of social norms concerning the 'normal' and 'natural' sexuality being heterosexuality. As a result, some do not give all families equal esteem, constructing them as 'pretend families'. For instance, lesbian, gay, bi-sexual and transgender (LGBT) applicants for adoption may be scrutinised more closely than heterosexual couples and held to a higher standard (Hicks, 2000: 159). In a heteronormative healthcare system, professionals may assume 'parents' to be a man and a woman, with all communication and routines based on heterosexual couples (Röndahl, Bruhner and Lindle, 2009: 2339).

Heteronormative attitudes can include unfounded concerns about children growing up in lesbian- and gay-headed families, including developing psychological problems as a result of bullying by peers, having atypical gender development or adopting a lesbian or gay identity (something considered to be negative within heteronormativity). Zoe and Sinead generally feel accepted in the neighbourhood they live in, but their life is not free from disapproving looks and comments about their family set-up.

Research Focus

Golombok, S. and Badger, S. (2010) 'Children raised in mother-headed families from infancy: a follow-up of children of lesbian and single heterosexual mothers at early adulthood', *Human Reproduction*, 25(1), 150–157.

This was the third phase of a longitudinal study of the quality of parent–child relations and the psychological adjustment of children in female-headed families with no father present from infancy. This is in a context of diversification of family forms and concerns of some that the absence of a resident father would have a negative impact on a child's psychological well-being. Golombok and Badger compared 47 female-headed family households who had raised their child from birth with the absence of a resident father (27 families headed by single,

▶

heterosexual mothers and 20 families headed by lesbian mothers) with 39 two-parent heterosexual families. In this third stage of the research, the child had entered adulthood. The researchers found that the female-headed families were similar to the traditional families on a range of measures of quality of parenting and young-adult psychological adjustment. Where they did find differences between family types, they pointed to more positive family relationships and greater psychological well-being among young adults raised in female-headed families. The research shows the children raised in female-headed households from infancy continue to function well as they enter adulthood. The implication is that absence of a resident father from birth does not result in negative consequences on the psychological well-being of the child. Their research lends weight to the view that it is quality of family relationships that are important, not family composition.

Ethnicity

As well as families being located in society in terms of social class and sexuality, they occupy a position in an ethnic structure with considerable inequality existing between ethnic groups. However, the patterns of inequality are far from straightforward, with the ethnic composition of Britain being complex in a number of ways. First, there are many distinctly different ethnic groups in Britain, and even though the terms Black British, British Asian and White British are commonly used, each of these broad terms masks considerable complexity. For example, British Asian ethnicities would include a number of distinct ethno-religious groups, for instance, Salway, Chowbey and Clarke's (2009) research into the experience of Asian fathers in Britain included Bangladeshi Muslim, Pakistani Muslim, Gujarati Hindu and Punjabi Sikh fathers.

The UK benefits from its multi-ethnic makeup and the waves of immigration that have taken place over the decades and centuries. At any one time families can consist of first, second, third and fourth generations. Oonagh and Hannah are both first-generation immigrants from Ireland, their children Mary and Connor are second generation, Liam, Fiona, Andrew and Sinead third generation, Ellie, Cheryl and Wendy fourth generation. Some members of the McGovern family still define their ethnic identity as White Irish. Generally, members of White families have an advantaged position in European, North American and Australasian societies, although low-income White families face multiple disadvantages. So it is not just a case of advantaged ethnic majority and disadvantaged ethnic minorities. There is also appreciable economic and social inequality between different ethnic minority groups. In her study of parenting in Britain, Barn (2006) found that there were differences between ethnic minority groups in income, employment and housing. Equally, even though there are distinct ethnic groups in Britain, there is as much difference within ethnic groups as between them. Among some of the reasons for this heterogeneity is that social class and household type, i.e. two-parent compared with one-parent households, cut across ethnic boundaries. As a consequence, we can make no assumptions about a family's social location in society based on their ethnicity alone.

No matter what the socio-economic position of an ethnic minority family is, they can face racism and discrimination on a regular basis. Brimicombe et al. (2001) found that the ethnic composition of an area appears to have a significant effect on the rate of racially motivated incidents, with them being significantly higher where there is a large White majority. Racial abuse and harassment is a common form of racism, and Chahal and Julienne (1999) found that for those families who find themselves the targets for racial harassment and abuse, it had a profound effect on their daily and family lives. It could reduce their quality of life, impact on family relations and restrict their movements. For example, there was a reluctance to leave the home, not letting the children play outside, not going out at night, and daily tasks like hanging washing and putting rubbish out becoming negotiated risk-taking events. The everyday experience of racial abuse impacts on family member health and well-being, including experiencing anxiety, stress, depression and sleepless nights.

Disability

At the moment, members of the McGovern family are nondisabled, something that could change at any time. Families with one or more disabled members, whether children or adults, occupy a socially oppressed position in society. Within the social model of disability, disability is a form of social oppression; as Oliver (2013: 1026) states, 'we were not disabled by our impairments but by the disabling barriers we face in society'. Thomas (2004: 580) defines 'disability' as 'a form of oppression involving the social imposition of restrictions of activities on people with impairments and the socially engendered undermining of their psycho-emotional well-being'. She argues that this social relational model of disability does not preclude that impairments and chronic illnesses can directly cause some restrictions of activity, but these do not constitute 'disability' but are impairment effects (Thomas, 2004: 581).

Dowling and Dolan (2001: 21) argue that it is not the caring for a child with disabilities that reduces 'quality of family life' but the impact of societal disabling structures, attitudes and barriers. They explain how 'families with children with disabilities experience a range of inequalities that families with children without disabilities do not suffer' and that it is the whole family that suffer (Dowling and Dolan, 2001: 21). They give the example of families missing experiences such as going to the cinema, restaurants and the park to avoid public intolerance, staring and shunning.

Family assets

Practitioners need to be interested in the networks and relationships of people, as they potentially provide important psychological, emotional and social resources to their members, including social support, social capital and feelings that they matter. Members of the McGovern family are generally supportive of each other, have a reservoir of social capital that they can call upon when necessary and feel they matter to other members. The amount and quality of these resources can vary, and, where practicable, workers can work with family members to enhance the level of social support, social capital and a sense of mattering that are available to a particular member or all family members.

Research Focus

Muir, K. and Strnadová, I. (2014) 'Whose responsibility? Resilience in families of children with developmental disabilities', *Disability and Society*, 29(6), 922–937.

The starting point of this article is that families with children with disabilities are at higher risk of stress, financial disadvantage and breakdown. Muir and Strnadová argue that policy and practice have shifted towards family resilience, that is, their ability to cope with adverse circumstances. They ask to what extent 'family resilience' places another burden on families and the extent that family resilience depends on the availability of resources external to the family. They argue that many of the conceptual components of resilience that are the responsibility of family members still depend on external resources and supports being available for family members to interact with. There is danger that society places the responsibility for coping with such adverse circumstances solely on the individual family, with emphasis given to the 'family resilience' (Muir and Strnadová, 2014) while not tackling negative attitudes and failing to provide appropriate support for families.

Families and social support

Social support includes the support people receive from existing relationships, and potential sources are family members, friends, work colleagues and neighbours. Social support theory identifies the types and qualities of relationships that provide support. Dolan, Pinkerton and Carnavan (2006: 14) describe four types of support: 'concrete support', consisting of practical acts of assistance; 'emotional support', consisting of acts of empathy, listening and generally being there; 'advice support', including reassurance; and 'esteem support', in relation to how one person rates and informs another of their personal worth. However, whether one member finds another member supportive will depend on the qualities of the support offered. Dolan, Pinkerton and Canavan (2006) identify dimensions along which the quality of support can vary, including closeness of the person, whether the support can be reciprocated and its durability, including its accessibility and non-intrusiveness.

Tyler found the breakup of his parents very difficult and had difficulty in accepting his mum's new partner, Liam McGovern, as well as his dad starting a new family with someone else. During this period, he felt that both his parents had lost interest in him and he became very depressed. We could hypothesise that during this period the protective factor of social support diminished. Social support is an important protective factor and can have important beneficial effects on physical and mental well-being (Ochieng, 2011: 429). Stockdale et al. (2007) found that having someone to provide emotional support protected individuals from the negative consequences of stressful situations. In a prospective study, Khatib, Bhui and Stansfeld (2013) found that perceived low levels of family support predicted higher levels of depressive symptoms in a multi-ethnic sample of 11- to 14-year-old adolescents from a socially deprived area of London. They found that support from friends did not mitigate against the effects of lower levels of family support, possibly because family members provide more stable sources of support than peers.

Families and mattering

Mattering is an important aspect of the protective power of social connection, and mattering to family is particularly important during adolescence (Elliott, 2009) and old age (Dixon, 2007). Elliott, Kao and Grant (2004: 339) define 'mattering as the perception that to some degree and in any variety of ways, we are a significant part of the world'. Interpersonal

teenage sons abuse their mothers, particularly in sole-parent households. Typically, such mothers find it hard to enlist protective or cooperative forms of power from agencies to help them deal with the abuse. The authors hypothesise that agencies tend to frame the son's violence as being the result of poor parenting or delinquency, and fail to recognise the family dynamics involved in sons usurping the traditional form of patriarchal family relations by using violence to become the 'man of the house'.

Gender dynamics

Gender, the cultural expectations of what it is to be a man, a woman, a girl or a boy, has a marked impact on family dynamics and practices. It continues as an enduring feature of family life, and to understand families we need to understand gender relations and practices within families. West and Zimmerman (1987: 130) refer to 'doing gender', which they conceive as an ongoing situated activity in everyday interaction that meets or in some cases does not meet the cultural expectations associated with one's gender, that is, the cultural ideals of masculinity and femininity. While there have been changes, traditional ideals of masculinity and femininity still remain influential, for instance, men associated with being strong, protective providers and women associated with being caring, nurturing, homemakers.

Family practices are also gendered practices, that is, who does what in the home and family are gendered and often unequal. However, there is general agreement that there are emerging new forms of family life and changing family practices, many of which are associated with the shifts in relations between men and woman (Jackson, 2008: 125). This is particularly so in relation to the decline in the male breadwinner/female homemaker model, and changing aspirations of women which have included expecting more from partnering relationships, sharing domestic tasks and childcare, and working outside the home. However, feminist critiques of inequalities between woman and men in domestic partnerships (marriage and cohabitation) remain relevant, with women continuing to be largely responsible for the daily maintenance of social and bodily needs of their male partners and children (Jackson, 2008: 132, 137).

Adams and Coltrane (2005: 242) maintain that men whose upbringing has been based on the traditional ideals of masculinity predicated on the belief that men inhabit the public sphere (activities outside the home) and women the private sphere (activities within the home) may not be able to live up to the ideals of a democratic, sharing and caring family life.

They report that one of the most consistent problems identified by women with respect to their male partners is their lack of communication and emotional expression. Likewise, the children of men who adopt an emotionally remote and inexpressive style of masculinity experience remoteness in their relationship with their fathers. Adams and Coltrane (2005: 244) believe that feminism has given men the tools to resolve this disjuncture but it will require abandoning the assumption that masculinity is the antithesis of femininity and that to be a man, one does not have to prove one is not a woman.

Generational dynamics

Alongside gender relations, intra- and intergenerational dynamics make up a large part of the internal dynamics of families. Family relationships between generations and within a generation can involve conflict or solidarity as well as ambivalence (Bengtson et al., 2002). The wider McGovern family is a four-generation family, consisting of a great-grandparent generation, grandparent generation, parent generation and grandchild generation. Within each generation family members can occupy a number of gendered role positions, including but not restricted to parents (mother, father), child (son and daughter), grandparents (grandfathers, grandmothers), siblings (brother, sister) or grandchildren (grandson, granddaughter). Andrew is a father, a son and a grandson. These family roles form the basis for a number of intra- and intergenerational relations, some of which will be same-gender relationships and others opposite-gender relationships.

Psychodynamic theory postulates the interplay between the gender and generation positions influences dyadic relationships within families, although there has been limited conclusive research in this area (Russell and Saebel, 1997). The idea is that the gender of the parent and the gender of the child both contribute to the parent–child relationship (Russell and Saebel, 1997: 114). Theorists argue there are distinct relationship differences within father/daughter, father/son, mother/son and mother/daughter dyads. However, when considering the quality of family relationships, it is important to consider from whose perspective. Herlofson (2013) found the perceptions of relationship quality in family dyads could differ between 'her' and 'his' views and between 'views up' and 'views down' the generations.

An important set of generational dynamics occurs between siblings, with sibling relationships being the longest-lasting relationships in people's lives, longer than with parents, with children or with partners and like other relationships characterised by various degrees of closeness and distance changing over time (Edwards and Weller, 2014: 188). Birth order, gender mix and age spacing impacts on sibling dynamics, as do life stages. For example, sibling rivalry and conflict is usual in childhood but declines in adulthood (Van Volkom, Machiz and Reich, 2011). Sibling relationships have been found to be influential in childhood and adolescence, for example, Edwards and Weller (2014) show how childhood sibling relationships have a role in the construction, negotiation and contestation of masculinity and femininity. Siblings can be very supportive of each other and involve 'caretaker'/'looked after' relationships. Kosonen (1996) researched the views of 69 Scottish primary school children of their sisters and brothers and found that siblings were significant sources of support, and they primarily viewed 'sibling care-giving' as positive, but when it did have negative consequences, it included annoying domination and sometimes abuse.

The dynamics of time

The passage of time is an important context of family life and family development, with changes in family relationships and dynamics over time. Family members live their lives through time, with members being at different points in their lives. When working with families it is important that workers are explicitly aware that they see only a snapshot of a family at that particular point in time. To help place families in the context of time and understand some of the family dynamics associated with the passage of time, this section will briefly introduce two models of families and social networks moving through time together, 'social convoys' and 'family life cycles'.

Social convoys

Kahn and Antonucci (1980: 269) define a social convoy as a 'dynamic network of social support', consisting of people with whom an individual travels through time, the membership of which changes with exits and entrances. Fiona's social convey gained a new member on the birth of her niece Ellie. The term convoy, rather than 'network', captures both a protective supportive function and the movement through time (Levitt,

2005: 38). Convoy membership changes are most likely to occur during a member undergoing major life transitions, for example, birth of children, forming partnerships, ending partnerships, leaving school, changing jobs, moving house, leaving home, migration, retiring or death (Santos and Levitt, 2007: 827).

Levitt (2005: 38) defines social convoy as a person's perceptions of who is 'close and important in their life'. It is important to make no prior assumptions regarding convoy membership, as it is not uncommon for a person's social convoy to exclude a family member and include people not conventionally defined as family members in the centre of the convoy. Practitioners and researchers can use the idea of social convoy as a therapeutic or research tool that consists of a focal person in the middle represented by 'ME', surrounded by three concentric circles. In the first concentric circle, the focal person puts those 'so close, their life cannot be imagined without them'. In the middle concentric circle, they put those less close but still important, and in the outer circle the focal person puts those not as close as the others, but still important.

Family life cycles

The concept of social convoys contrasts with that of family life cycles; the former relates to changes in the membership of an individual's social network, and the latter to changes in family relationships that occur with the passage of time. Typically, theorists frame 'family life cycles' as stages of family development, apropos the presence and ages of children in the family home. The continuing validly and utility of the concept has been seriously questioned (Hoyle, 2013), with the major criticisms being that it cannot capture the life course experiences of families that do not involve children, that families do not follow the same cycle, and the growth of diversity in family forms means that any particular definition of 'the family life cycle' can only reflect one of many possible versions of family development over time. Equally, increasing separation, followed by re-partnering, means families do not experience an orderly addition of children but rather the sudden entry of step-children which is 'out of sync' with a chronological addition of children. Diversity of family forms, family practices and family life cycles mean that it may not be practical to develop a model that reflects the various development paths families can take. However, it is important to recognise that transitions can be emotional and stressful processes that require renegotiation and development of intergenerational relations.

Carter and McGoldrick (1989) developed a model that tries to reflect some of the variations in family life cycles and which focuses on intergenerational relations, family transitions and their associated developmental issues. They acknowledge 'family life cycles' vary with social class and ethnic group, while separation, entering new relationships and forming new families are becoming usual. Their 'intact-family life cycle' model is as follows: becoming a single adult; forming a couple; being a family with young children; a family with adolescents; launching children and moving on; and living in later life. There are common developmental variations within this cycle, for instance, the decision to separate, followed by either sole parenthood with resident children or sole parenthood with non-resident children, followed by parents entering into new relationships and forming a new reconstituted family. Other variations of family life cycles would include non-partnered people not ever becoming a member of a couple, and non-partnered people having children without a partner.

One potential value of the construct, family life cycles, is that it associates particular emotional transitions with particular stages of family development. Carter and McGoldrick (1989) identify the following family life cycle stages:

1. Leaving home, single adulthood: accepting emotional and financial responsibility for self. The chances are that in a couple of years Tyler will be undergoing this emotional transition.

2. Joining of families though partnership: commitment to new system. All of Mary and Connor's children went through this family transition some time ago.

3. Families with young children: accepting members into the system. Andrew and Rachel are currently in this family cycle phase.

4. Families with adolescents: increasing flexibility of family boundaries to include children's independence and great-grandparent frailties. Kate and Liam are in this family cycle phase at present.

5. Launching children and moving on: accepting multiple exits and entries into the family system. Mary and Connor have gone through this emotional transition.

6. Families in later life: accepting shifting generational roles. Oonagh and Hannah, and their children Mary and Connor, are experiencing this family life cycle phase at present.

As you can see, when you take a whole family approach, different parts of a multigenerational family are simultaneously going through different phases of the family life cycle. It is not so much about the details of these emotional processes but the idea that as a family develops through time, they can face emotional challenges related to changing family relationships and roles.

Chapter Key Points

1. Practitioners need to have fluid and open perspectives as to what constitutes a family, devoid of rigid qualifying criteria.

2. The concept of 'family practices' is useful to practitioners in that it enables them to refer to and respect the different ways families 'do family'.

3. Workers need to give due attention to a family's ecology, which will involve them in simultaneously paying attention to many different levels of context ranging from the individual to society.

4. Social structures position all families in society in relation to social class, heteronormativity, ethnicity and disability.

5. Social support, mattering and social capital are family assets potentially available to its members.

6. The relations of gender, generation and age shape family and power dynamics.

7. The ideas of 'social conveys' and 'family life cycles' can be useful but require care in how they are applied.

Reflective Exercises

1. Think about what you mean by the term 'family'. Make some notes.

2. Think about the volume of social capital you have available to you and compare this with someone you know. The volume of social capital a person has depends on the size of their network of connections and the volume of economic, cultural and social capital possessed by its members.

▶

3. Do you agree or disagree that heteronormative nuclear families, that is, 'opposite-sex two-parent families', still occupy a privileged position in society compared with 'same-sex two-parent families'? Give reasons for your answer.

4. Think about the relationship dynamics within your own family (however you want to define it). In terms of emotional closeness and distance, think about your intergenerational relationships (for example, you and your parents) and intra-generational relationships (for example, you and your brother(s) and/or sister(s)). Does gender, similarity and difference have an impact?

Putting into Practice

Draw your 'social convoy' at this point in your life. Write 'ME' in the centre of a piece of paper and surround yourself with three concentric circles. In the first concentric circle put those so close you cannot imagine life without them. In the middle concentric circle, put those less close but still important, and in the outer circle put those not as close as the others, but still important. If you are drawing the social convoy in a group, compare your convoy with someone else's.

Identify what 'family life cycle' phase you would place yourself in at this point in your life. Are there particular challenges you can identify as being associated with this phase?

Thinking about working with a family, which, if any, of the ideas in this chapter would you pick out that might help you understand that family better?

Further Resources

Adams, M. and Coltrane, S. (2005) 'Boys and men in families: The domestic production of gender, power, and privilege', in M. S. Kimmell, J. Hearn and R. W. Connell (eds) *Handbook of Studies on Man and Masculinities*, Thousand Oaks, CA: Sage, 230–248.
Adams and Coltrane's chapter focuses on and is critical of the false opposition between 'femininity' and 'masculinity' and how families reproduce the non-participation of men in family life.

Crompton, R. (2006) 'Class and family' *The Sociological Review*, 54(4), 658–677.
Rosemary Crompton's article critically explores the role of families in reproducing familial class position generation after generation.

Jack, G. (2000) 'Ecological influences on parenting and child development', *British Journal of Social Work*, 30(6), 703–720.
This article sets out the complex set of interacting factors that influence parenting and child development.

CHAPTER 3

FAMILIES UNDER STRAIN

CHAPTER OVERVIEW

This chapter

- Presents an *Assets and Stressors Model* of families using their assets to deal with family stressors.
- Explains how particular interplays between family stressors and family assets can result in family well-being, family resilience or family strain.
- Considers the rival explanations and narratives as to what causes families to be under strain and how families can overcome them.
- Looks at Domain Theory as a way of exploring the multifactorial nature of family difficulties, challenges and problems.
- Examines a number of challenges families can face, namely poverty, work–family conflict, life events, disability, mental distress, substance misuse and family violence.

Introduction

This chapter is concerned with the processes involved in families coming under strain and needing support. As explained in Chapter 1, 'strain' appears to be an apt metaphor for the consequences of the various pressures that families can experience that may cause suffering and harm. Many other terms have been and are being used for families that need help and support, including 'dysfunctional families', 'problem families', 'chaotic families' and 'troubled families'. Over time, such terms tend to be abandoned as stigmatising, but it could be that whatever term is used will eventually carry a stigma, as, unfortunately, the families themselves are often stigmatised. The merit of the term 'families under strain' is that it is part of a framework for understanding families in difficulties.

In various ways, families experience problems, difficulties, challenges and issues which they eventually resolve within their own extended networks. At times, a family, for a number of reasons, may not resolve their difficulties and need support from outside. Either the difficulties they face are too great for their collected resources or their collective resources are too small to resolve even moderate difficulties. Workers need to be able to develop understandings of the factors associated with a particular family coming under strain, the nature of the difficulties they face and the resources they have to overcome those difficulties.

The Drury family

The Drury family consists of two children, Conrad (3 years old) and Kayla (5 years old), their mother Diane (25 years old) and their father Steve (24 years old). From the very start, Diane's parents were against her marrying Steve, thinking he was unsuitable for their daughter. Steve getting into a fight with Diane's brother nine months ago strengthened their view of Steve's unsuitability. The assault resulted in Steve's conviction for grievous bodily harm and him receiving a three-year prison sentence. The Drury family is a low-income household with Diane working part-time at a local hotel, and before his imprisonment, Steve worked at a recycling centre. Steve and Diane rent a house in a disadvantaged urban area with few amenities and are in rent arrears and currently threatened with homelessness. Diane has been trying to lessen the emotional impact on Conrad and Kayla of their father's absence by being open about where he is and taking them to visit him, but such visits are taking their toll. The family have always found it difficult to manage living on a low income without support from outside the immediate family. Since Steve's imprisonment, Diane has been completely ostracised by her family and become increasingly isolated. Inevitably, the change in family circumstances is putting the family under strain, with Diane finding it increasingly difficult to cope and finding some solace in alcohol. This has resulted in changes in her parenting practices, with the children's school noticing a deterioration in her and her children's appearance and demeanour.

Family assets and stressors model

Figure 3.2 is a schematic depiction of an 'assets and stressors model', loosely and selectively based on Sullivan (2015); De Haan, Hawley and Deal (2002); and Lavee, McCubbin and Olsen (1987). The model depicts an interplay between family stressors and family assets, resulting in one of three processes: either family problem-solving, family coping or family non-coping. Family stressors are challenges and issues that families face and are forces that can result in families coming under strain. Family assets are the resources and strengths that families have available to deal with those stressors. They can emanate from both within and outside the

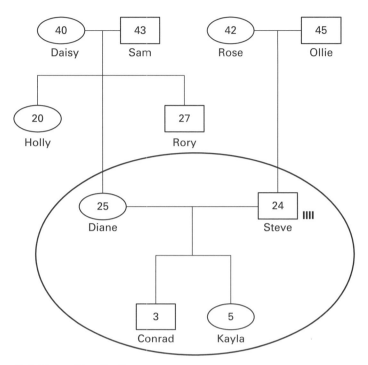

Figure 3.1 Drury Family Genogram

family. For example, they can emerge from individual family members, family relationships, neighbourhood and community settings, and services, or the culture and society the family live in.

'Family problem-solving' is the process of families engaging in actions to meet and resolve family challenges and, if successful, results in 'family well-being'. 'Family coping' is a process of families engaging in actions to withstand the stressors and, if successful, results in 'family resilience'. The concept of coping is used here for a less than satisfactory state of struggling to withstand the pressures of dealing with the stressors. 'Family non-coping' is the process of coping mechanisms failing, which eventually results in 'family strain'. As seen in Figure 3.2, the processes of family problem-solving, family coping, and family non-coping do not invariably result in family well-being, family resilience and family strain, respectively. For instance, the model shows family problem-solving will not always be successful in achieving family well-being but may establish family coping. Likewise, a family initially coping with stressors may not continue to do so, or a family that initially does not cope eventually copes and ultimately meets the challenges it faces.

Family well-being, family resilience and family strain

Within the model family well-being, family resilience and family strain are possible outcomes of an interplay between family assets and family stressors. Theorists define family well-being in several ways (Zimmerman, 2013: 10) and we will conceptualise it as when family relationships and practices create a positive supportive climate that promotes family members' emotional, intellectual and physical health and development. In physics, 'strain' is the distortion that occurs when a structure cannot withstand the tensions created by the load placed upon it. Likewise, 'family strain' is the 'distortion' that can occur in family relationships and family practices when the family cannot cope with the tensions created by family stressors.

The concepts of family well-being and family strain are not so widely employed as 'resilience'. Resilience is a concept that relates to when individuals or families exposed to stressors continue to cope, while others exposed to similar stressors do not (Luthar, Cicchetti, and Becker, 2000; Luthar, Sawyer and Brown, 2006; Rutter, 1987; Rutter, 2006; Ungar, 2011). Hill et al. (2007) point out that 'there is no consensus on the definition of resilience but rather it has a cluster of meanings associated with doing better than expected in difficult circumstances'. Researchers and theoreticians use the concept of resilience in various ways, and it can refer 'to the process of, capacity for, or outcome of successful adaptation despite challenging or threatening circumstances' (Masten, Best and Garmezy, 1990). Here, we are using the concept of resilience as the outcome of successful coping. Resilience is usually an individual-level concept but can also be conceptualised at the family level or the community level. 'Family resilience', which has been developed from the concept of individual resilience, is a family continuing to manage (but not thrive) despite family stressors (De Haan et al., 2002; Hawley, 2000; McConnell, Savage and Breitkreuz, 2014; Patterson, 2002; Walsh, 2003).

Applying the family assets and stressors model entails a case analysis that results in a case formulation which will be a particular reading or framing of the family situation. Among the family stressors impacting on the Drury family at present are low family income, poor relationships between Diane and her family and, more recently, parental imprisonment. Among the family assets are Diane and Steve's strong relationship and Diane's wisdom in being open with the children about where their father is and taking them to visit him. At present the interplay between family stressors and family assets is resulting in the family just coping despite the stressors, with Diane continuing to take her son and daughter to school, go to work and carry out household tasks. However, there is a danger that

construct different causal narratives of the development of problems within families. These explanations can be either deliberately or unthinkingly targeted on a particular layer or domain of reality, for instance, focused on individuals, families, communities or wider society. Workers and theories can frame 'problems' and their 'solutions' as individual problems, family problems or societal problems, for example, poor mental health has been seen in all these ways. Although workers interact with and work with family groups, there should be no assumption that just because they are working with the family group, family strains have their root causes within the way family members interact with each other or their particular 'family practices'. Workers need in-depth understandings that recognize that human difficulties have multifactorial origins, with different factors on different levels concurrently interacting with each other.

The development and continuation of problems or difficulties involves complex processes occurring over time, and it is useful for practitioners to have some understanding of how the mechanisms/processes underlying the development of difficulties operate. For a number of reasons, it is not possible to have an objective view of any family situation, including the Drury family, and human beings engage in 'meaning making' activities to interpret and frame the information that their senses perceive. This means workers need to be explicitly aware of the constructed nature of their understandings and assessments and to be as systematic and free from biases as possible. In the Drury family situation, we can identify a number of factors potentially involved in Diane being on the verge of not coping and in bringing about changes in the children's appearance and demeanour at school. These factors include Steve committing an offence and his subsequent imprisonment, the deepening of the rifts within the wider family, the pressures of bringing up two young children alone on a low income and the relatively young age of the parents.

It is easy to have simplistic notions of what is causing family difficulties, such as simple linear 'cause and effect' models of causality. For instance, A causes B, as in, the cause of the current difficulties experienced by the Drury family is Steve being an unreliable person and an irresponsible father who let himself get into a position of seriously injuring another man. This may or may not be true, but it simplifies a complex multifactorial situation. In reality, there are complex mechanisms involving the interplay of factors located in different levels of reality, and as human beings we try and make sense of situations the best we can. Reductionist explanations reduce human behaviour to a single level, for example, individual behaviour or character or the way society is organised, whereas ecological explanations construct problem development as involving the interplay of multiple factors on multiple levels of reality. For instance, relatively young parents bringing up children on a low income, with wider family conflict, parental imprisonment and lack of family support services for those left behind.

A theory of how social reality is structured might help practitioners do justice to the complexity, by showing the interplay between different factors on different levels that result in a family's state of being. One such theory is Layder's (2006: 272) 'domain theory' that portrays social reality as consisting of multiple interrelated domains. Houston's (2010a) adaptation of Layder's work consists of five domains: 'the domain of the person', 'the domain of situated activity', 'the domain of social settings', 'the domain of culture' and 'the domain of polity/economy'. The theory depicts people having agency, that is, the human capacity to influence what happens. This capacity operates within enabling and constraining structures; therefore, how people act in any particular situation depends on a complex interplay between sets of influences (Houston, 2010a: 75). Figure 3.3 is a schematic representation of this multilayered social reality using the example of Kayla.

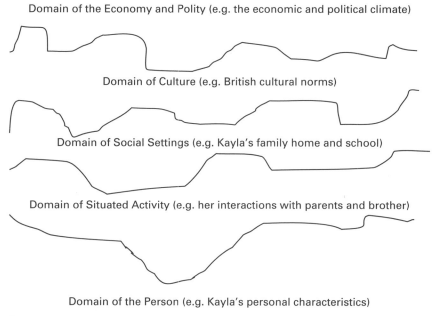

Domain of the Economy and Polity (e.g. the economic and political climate)

Domain of Culture (e.g. British cultural norms)

Domain of Social Settings (e.g. Kayla's family home and school)

Domain of Situated Activity (e.g. her interactions with parents and brother)

Domain of the Person (e.g. Kayla's personal characteristics)

Figure 3.3 Schematic Representation of Multilayered Social Reality

In the Drury family, each individual has their own unique 'domain of the person', which includes their accumulated life experiences (their psychobiography), their body and its biology, their personal identity, personality, emotions and human agency. The domain of situated activity includes the interactions between people, that is, what happens when members of the Drury family interact with each other and with people outside the family. The domain of social settings forms the immediate environment of these interactions, so would include the family group, the prison and prison visits, Diane's workplace and the school the children attend. Layder (2006: 280) explains that

> [Social] settings vary in their organisational form. In some, relationships are formal and tightly structured such a schools, universities, hospitals, industrial/commercial firms, government bureaucracies and so on. Others are based on informal, loosely patterned relationships such as friendships, partnerships, family networks. Although their form is variable, social settings are clearly distinguishable from other domains in that they are local aggregations of *reproduced* social relations, positions and practices.

Members of the Drury family also live their lives in a cultural context, that is, the 'domain of culture', which includes historically accumulated cultural knowledge, norms, social expectations and taken-for-granted ways of doing things. It also includes fashions, images and different forms of art, including music, objects and documents of various kinds. Within 'the domain of polity and the economy', the economy includes the circulation, distribution, accumulation of money, goods, services and material resources, while 'polity' is a whole system of politics and government, including political organisations and the instruments and activities of government and the state.

The important point about the different domains of social reality is that the domains are not independent of each other; rather, there is a constant interplay between them. The significance for families coming under strain is that the processes producing that strain result from an interplay between a number of factors located in different domains and not as simple as A causes B. By way of illustration, Diane being on the verge of not coping is located in the domain of the person, but it has strong interrelationships with the other layers of reality: the domain of situated activity, including interactions with her children; the domain of social settings, including the family group, the prison visits, her workplace; the domain of culture, including the pressures she feels as a woman to maintain her appearance even though she does not feel like it; and the domain of economy/polity, including her economic position in society as a low-wage earner, govern-ment austerity policies and the laws and policies that sent her husband to prison without any support services for the family he left behind.

Family challenges

What I loosely refer to as 'family challenges' are aspects of family life that, to varying degrees, can be framed as family stressors, family strains and/or aspects of family dysfunction, depending on how people formulate the family situation. Families can face a wide range of challenges, including family violence, mental health problems, disability, substance misuse and addiction, poverty, severe debt, overcrowding, relationship and behav-ioural problems, homelessness and threatened homelessness, and neglect. Such challenges can reverberate through the family and have a negative impact on family life, and family members' individual well-being. It is not uncommon for family challenges to occur together and be interrelated to each other, and when this happens the chances of serious harm to family members occurring are greatly increased (Welbourne, 2012: 171). Wood-cock and Sheppard (2002) found that families with a combination of parental depression and alcohol misuse had significantly higher levels of relationship problems, particularly parenting problems, than those in which the parent was depressed but did not misuse alcohol.

Poverty

This section focuses on low family income as a family stressor that puts considerable strain on family life and family relationships. Many families cope well despite living on a low income (Ghate and Hazel, 2002: 191), but living on a low income puts many other families under strain. Poverty is a relative phenomenon, as what people regard as the necessary require-ments for living change over time and between different parts of the world. Townsend (1997: 31, cited in Callan et al., 1996: 6) defines the condition of poverty as when 'resources are so seriously below those com-manded by the average individual or family that they are, in effect, excluded from ordinary living patterns, customs and activities'. It is com-mon in Europe to define low-income households as those that have an income of less than 60% of the national medium household income. Liv-ing on a low income can mean doing without everyday necessities, such as food, clothing, fuel for lighting, heating and cooking, and managing a low budget takes a great deal of energy, time, skill and ingenuity. However, poverty not only has material consequences for family members, but also social and psychological ones, including doing without social necessities like holidays and birthday presents.

Jo (2013) draws attention to the significance the emotional side of poverty, which he refers to as the psychosocial dimensions of poverty and is interested in the actual feelings of being poor and experiencing hardship. He picks out the emotion of shame for specific attention. Shame involves failure to live up to the standards that others expect of us, that is, others whose approval is important to us (Lazarus, 1991: 241). Jo (2013) says that the 'others' that judge can be real or be the inner voice of the mind reflecting the judgements of the dominant discourses in society. Shame and other emotions like humiliation can have negative effects on psychological health of family members, which in turn impacts on family relationships and family functioning. In her review of research into the lives of disadvantaged children in the UK, Ridge (2011: 76) found children were negotiating complex family terrains where family needs were in tension with the children's own social and material needs. There was an overwhelming need to keep up with peers and not stand out as different. She refers to research by Elliott and Leonard (2004) who found children from low-income families struggling to get the right trainers to disguise the reality of their economic situation at home so as not to become the victim of teasing or bullying.

Research Focus

Ridge, T. (2011) 'The everyday costs of poverty in childhood: a review of qualitative research exploring the lives and experiences of low-come children in the UK', *Children and Society*, 25(1), 73–84.

This review of 10 years of qualitative research into the lives and experiences of children who reside in the UK and who live in low-income families shows that poverty penetrates deep into the heart of childhood, penetrating every aspect of their lives, from material disadvantage to limiting social relationships and social participation, to the hidden aspects of their lives, including feeling shame and suffering from marginalisation. Tess argues that policymakers often overlook and easily disregard social repercussions of poverty, especially when policy concerns focus on perhaps more tangible concerns such as child welfare, school attendance and performance.

Work–family conflict

Work–family conflict exists when parents find that the demands of work interfere with their home and family life. A parent's actual experience of work can have strong influence on the level of work–family conflict that exists. Darcy and McCarthy (2007) researched the antecedents of work–family conflict by asking about levels of job involvement, job stress and colleague support. They found the significant antecedents differed depending on family cycle stage. For families with a preschool child, work–family conflict was less if there was work colleague support, for families with a youngest child 6–12 years old, work–family conflict was more when job involvement was high, and in families where the youngest child was 12 years old or more, work–family conflict was more when job involvement and job stress were high.

Having a family member or members in employment is often a family asset, particularly when they receive a living wage and are reasonably happy in their work. However, in many families, trying to achieve a balance between work and family life is in itself demanding and stressful. This stress still predominantly falls on mothers, as 'men and women experience the demands of work and family differently as it is generally women that assume greater responsibility for domestic and caring work whilst participating in paid work' (Wattis, Standing and Yerkes, 2013: 3). Like many mothers, Diane employs coping strategies when negotiating the boundaries between paid work and family, chief among these are working part-time, which unfortunately has the consequence of lower income. Despite working part-time, she still feels the amount of time work takes and the amount of job stress it generates makes it difficult for her to fulfil family responsibilities and have some time for herself.

Life events

Life events are occurrences in a person's life that require or entail change, such as the imprisonment of a family member, death of a family member, loss of job, eviction, breakup of an intimate relationship, family member being involved in a serious accident or the family moving house. Falloon et al. (1993) distinguish between ambient stressors that are the day-to-day hassles of family life and life events that are discrete stressors independent of day-to-day difficulties. Family members can experience life events at any time, and they can either be direct or indirect stressors acting upon the whole family. Life events involve transition, and the impact of an event will depend on how the family or family member perceives what has happened. Even positive life events such as getting a new job can generate stress, albeit more likely a lower level than a life event perceived as negative.

Steve's imprisonment is a negative life event for him and his partner, Diane, and their two children, Conrad and Kayla. For Diane, she needs to navigate the transition from co-parenting with Steve to being the head of a one-parent household. Conrad and Kayla need to adapt to the absence of their father and to their mother parenting alone, while Steve needs to adapt to a new relationship with Diane, Conrad and Kayla, from co-residing father to non-residing father. Steve's imprisonment produces material pressure in the form of a reduction in family income and relationship pressures in the shape of arguments over him leaving Diane to run the household single-handed and parent alone.

Disability

It would be a mistake to equate having a disabled family member with a family being under strain, but families with one or more disabled members are as varied as other families and as such can come under strain. Impairment and disability can be factors in that strain, but, like other family stressors it is often when they co-occur with other factors, for example, low income, that the combined effect can be considerable. Research into the impact on family life of having a child with a disability in the family has usually been from particular family member perspectives rather than families as a whole, for example, from mothers' perspectives (Green, 2007), less so fathers, siblings (Burke, 2010) and grandparents (Miller, Buys and Woodbridge, 2012) but more rarely the disabled child. Green (2007) found the lives of mothers of children with disabilities are much more emotionally complex than is generally assumed. The mothers felt caring for a child with disabilities had positive impacts on them, including increased confidence, skill and assertiveness. Emotional distress was much more likely to result from financial stress and time constraints than from being a mother of a child with disabilities. The emotional distress they did experience was associated with negative social attitudes, the perceived stigma of disability and the lack of services.

Parents with learning disabilities can face multiple challenges, including struggling with literacy, abstract concepts such as time, and everyday practical tasks (Tarleton and Porter, 2012: 234). However, there is no basis for the stereotypes and assumptions that parents with learning disabilities cannot parent and cannot learn the skills they require (McConnell and Llewellyn, 2002: 306). Strain in families with one or two parents with learning disabilities tend to result from their support needs not being met, the prejudices they are subjected to and the fear their child will be removed. Parents with learning difficulties face a struggle to hold on to their children, as it is estimated that authorities place two in every five of such children outside the family home (Booth, Booth and McConnell, 2005: 353). Booth, Booth and McConnell (2005: 353) argue that it is an open question whether this is evidence of widespread parenting failure or, alternatively, differential treatment of parents with learning difficulties, with them being subjected to higher standards than non-disabled parents. Like non-disabled parents, parents who have learning difficulties can neglect their children, but professionals and courts should base their judgements on careful assessment and evidence, not on stereotypes or assumptions.

Mental distress

Having one or more family members experiencing mental health issues can be a family stressor impacting on other family members and family functioning. Both child mental health and adult mental health problems can have significant influence on family life and can be one reason why some families need support. Families vary in their capacity to cope with the challenges of mental health issues. Diane has previously suffered from low mood and is feeling increasingly down about her situation. Depression is the most common mental health problem, and maternal depression can severely interfere with parenting and have considerable impact on a child's welfare and development. 'It is estimated that children of depressed parents are between two and five times more likely to develop behaviour problems than children whose parents are not depressed' (Smith, 2004: 5). However, parental mental health problems do not automatically equate with poor behavioural or emotional outcomes for children, with less than half of children whose parents experience mental health issues developing such outcomes.

Children can suffer when parenting becomes a struggle because of mental health issues. Diane's change of mood is beginning to disrupt her parenting and is likely to have unintended negative impacts on Conrad and Kayla. With Diane being preoccupied and withdrawn, she is less emotionally available to them and less able to give them the attention they need, and this may negatively affect her judgement of their behaviour. However, 'the parenting capacity of adults with mental health problems is a continuum, ranging from unimpaired to severe' (Rouf, Larkin and Lowe, 2011). When parenting capacity is affected, 'parenting can include insensitivity, increased criticism of children and high levels of expressed anger', the effects of which will differ depending on the child's age (Cleaver, Unell and Aldgate, 2010, cited in Rouf, Larkin and Lowe, 2011).

Substance misuse

Substance misuse is a term that can be used for alcohol and drug use that leads to social, physical and psychological harm (Knoll, 2004: 129). This could be harm to one's self and/or harm to others in the form of neglect or violence. The stress caused by their intoxicated behaviour can result in other family member developing problems (Copello, Velleman and Templeton, 2005: 370). Diane's drinking has not reached a hazardous level, which Manning et al. (2009: 4) define as 'a pattern of alcohol consumption that increases the risk of harmful consequences for the user and others'. Substance misuse can create negative and harmful dynamics within families and can impair parenting, but harm is not inevitable and rarely occurs as a consequence of substance *use* alone (Manning et al., 2009: 11). Knoll's (2004: 134) review of research into the experience of children and young people who live in a family where a parent misuses substances found that 'parental substance use had very little adverse impact, providing the family was functioning and supportive. Substance use per se did not mean that everything automatically fell apart.' It is parental *misuse* of substances and its associated dynamics that had a detrimental impact on children in particular.

Knoll (2004) found a number of common features that resulted in the tensions and stresses of living in a family which is organised around the substance-using parent. The needs of the children were in danger of being unseen both by family members and outsiders. Because of children's innate sense of loyalty, their awareness of people's opinions of drinkers and 'druggies' and fears about professional intervention, they were often trapped in a position where they could not ask for help or acknowledge the fears to outsiders (Knoll, 2004: 136). One difference between the family dynamics of the legal use of alcohol and the criminality surrounding illegal drug use is the association of the latter with criminal activity, and the greater stigma gave an added imperative to keep the family secret (Barnard and Barlow, 2003: 46).

Family violence

Interpersonal family violence is a source of severe strain and harm, and it negatively affects family functioning, individual family members and their relationships with each other. Violence within families can take many forms, including parental child abuse, intimate partner violence, older adult abuse, sibling violence and parent abuse. Different forms of family violence can co-occur within the same family and can relate to each other. The perpetrators of family violence have often been the victims of violence or exposed to violence within their family of origin (Holt, Buckley and Whelan, 2008). Victims of family violence can also be the perpetrator of violence on another member of the family, as when an adolescent son abused by his father is violent towards his mother.

Family violence can be a distortion of gender and generation relations within families, and it can be both intra- and intergenerational. Intra-generational violence can take the form of sibling violence or intimate partner violence, while intergenerational violence can take the form of child abuse, parent abuse by children or elder abuse by adult children. Whether within the same generation or between different generations, family violence is commonly recognised as gendered, with males being the perpetrators and females the victim, as in brother-on-sister violence, son-on-mother violence and male-partner-on-female-partner violence. However, there is increasing recognition that males can be victims of female violence (Drijber, Reijinders and Ceelen, 2013).

Violence in the home has a damaging effect on families that is not limited to the direct impact on the victim. For example, exposing children to intimate partner violence can be a damaging form of emotional abuse (Holt et al., 2008; Meltzer et al., 2009). Exposure to domestic violence is not limited to directly witnessing the violence, and it includes hearing but not actually seeing the violence taking place and indirect exposure by witnessing the outcomes of the violence, including injuries to their parent, broken objects and their parent's emotional state (Meltzer et al., 2009: 491). Meltzer et al.'s (2009: 500) analysis of data collected in a national survey of the mental health of children and young people in the UK 'suggests that one child in 25 or one in every class is exposed to witnessing severe domestic violence at home'. The study found that in the UK 'children that witness domestic violence do indeed have a greater likelihood than other children of developing conduct disorders but not emotional disorders'.

As discussed in the previous chapter, parent abuse by children represents an inversion of conventional family power relations that breaches the traditional parent–child relationship (Tew and Nixon, 2010: 585). Parent abuse is when a child is violent towards a parent and can have a background of the child's exposure to intimate partner violence within the family. Parent abuse commonly takes the form of adolescent sons against their mothers, particularly lone mothers (Tew and Nixon, 2010: 585), with their physical size and strength being a factor (Jackson, 2003: 325). Jackson (2003: 326) found that a son's drug use could indirectly contribute to him being violent towards his mother, for example, when she attempts to refuse him money and tries to restrict his movements outside the home to limit his access to drugs.

Chapter Key Points

1. All families have assets with which they endeavour to cope with family stressors.

2. The interplay between family assets and family stressors results in family well-being, family resilience or family strain.

3. Families, popular discourses, and professionals can construct different causal narratives of the development of problems within families.

4. Domain Theory provides a framework for understanding the multifactorial nature of families being under strain.

5. Families face challenges, including low income, work–family conflict, life events, disability, mental distress, substance misuse and family violence.

Reflective Exercises

1. Think of a family challenge that a family you know faced. In what ways, if any, did it cause tensions within the family that resulted in the family being under strain?

2. Do you agree that it is not possible to be truly objective about a family's situation? Think about the reasons for your answer.

3. What do you think the popular discourses about the causes of poverty are? Construct an alternative narrative about why some families live in poverty.

Putting into Practice

Apply the Family Assets and Stressors Model to a family you worked with or know. Identify the stressors the family faced and the assets they had to engage with those stressors. What would you say were the family's responses to the challenges? Were they family problem-solving, family coping or family non-coping, and was the eventual outcome family well-being, family resilience or family strain?

Have you or someone you know worked with a family when the explanation as to why the family were under strain differed between the professionals and family members? How would you sum up the difference between the two sets of explanations?

Identify the multiple stressors impacting on a family you worked with. Work out how the different stressors could have interacted with each other and what the cumulative effects were.

Further Resources

Chapter 6 'Social Work and Poverty: A Complex Relationship', in P. Welbourne (2012) *Social Work with Children and Families: Developing Advance Practice*, Abingdon: Routledge, 89–115.

This chapter covers many of the issues surrounding families living in poverty, including children's views of poverty, and poverty as a challenge to parental coping mechanisms.

Jo, Y. N. (2013) 'Psycho-social dimensions of poverty: when poverty becomes shameful', *Critical Social Policy*, 13(3), 514–520.

Commentators in poverty tend to give most attention to the material dimensions of living in economic hardship, but in this article, Yongmie Nicola Jo outlines the significance of non-material and social dimensions, particularly the shame and stigma of living in poverty and its impact on social relations.

Templeton, L. (2014) 'Supporting families living with parental substance misuse: the M-PACT (Moving Parents and Children Together) programme', *Child and Family Social Work*, 19(1), 76–88.

This article draws on qualitative findings of the evaluation of 13 M-PACT programmes in England. M-PACT programmes bring several families together, where at least one parent has an alcohol or drug problem and where there is at least one child aged 8–17 years old. The majority of families benefited from the programme, including by meeting others who were experiencing similar problems, gaining greater understanding of addiction and its impact on children and improving communication within the family. In some families there was a reduction of arguments and conflicts.

CHAPTER 4

BEING SUPPORTIVE

CHAPTER OVERVIEW

This chapter

- Argues that 'being supportive' requires appropriate attitudes and demeanour more than specific techniques.
- Looks at how best to react to the ambivalence associated with accepting help.
- Stresses the importance of developing good working relationships with family members.
- Explores the dynamics of power and difference when working with families.
- Examines issues and practices in engaging with mothers, fathers, children and 'wider family' members.
- Explains how understanding communication as a two-way process can increase the chances of effective communication.
- Highlights the importance of listening to and learning from family member narratives when helping families.

Introduction

Whether family members eventually experience contact with practitioners as supportive will depend on a number of factors, including the worker's attitude, demeanour and actions, and the efforts they make to engage family members. As the research of de Boer and Coady (2007: 40) suggests being supportive is not primarily a matter of learning techniques but more about 'ways of being'. As they state, 'specific techniques can augment an empathic, supportive and collaborative attitude and approach, but they cannot substitute for this'. If workers are to effectively support families and help them overcome the difficulties they face, they need to engage and build positive working relationships with family members. However, families and their members can understandably be ambivalent and wary of an outside agency coming into their family life.

Pearson (2009: 88) identifies a spectrum of uncooperative responses families can have to intrusion into their lives, ranging from ambivalence, through avoidance, and confrontation to violence. This chapter focuses on engaging families who experience the understandable ambivalence associated with accepting and receiving help from outside agencies.

The primary focus is supporting families that are under strain, as part of early help to prevent abuse and damaging neglect from occurring. Supporting such families remains a considerable challenge, particularly if the worker is to be a catalyst for family members to overcome the difficulties they face. Some families do engage in extreme avoidant, deceptive and violent behaviour, and Chapter 7, 'Remaining Vigilant', examines issues arising from a family member engaging in verbal abuse, intimidation or personal threats towards the worker.

The Llywelyn family

The Llywelyn family is what Smart (2006) refers to as a post-divorce family in which family membership and family life can get complex. The family consists of sole resident parent Meredith (29 years old), non-resident father Gareth (28 years old), son Dylan (7 years old) and daughter Catrin (5 years old). Meredith and Gareth separated 18 months ago. Gareth lives with a new partner and her three children from a previous relationship.

Meredith has a part-time job and the family live on a low income with considerable accumulated debt. Their maternal grandmother collects Dylan and Catrin from school on the days her daughter works, but Meredith feels she does this only begrudgingly. Meredith is experiencing problems with her neighbours calling her names, and is struggling to cope. There remains considerable animosity between Meredith and Gareth, with many arguments about his contact with Dylan and Catrin. Meredith perceives him to be undermining her parenting and paying more interest in his new family to the detriment of his own children. The head teacher of the children's school has a word with Meredith about the way Dylan has been behaving in class, his and his sister's erratic attendance, and their sometimes shabby appearance. When Meredith gets upset, the head teacher asks her if she would like someone to come and talk to her about her difficulties and discuss how her situation might be improved. At that moment, Meredith reluctantly accepts the offer of help, but she arrives home regretting that she agreed. A week later, Alishba, a family social worker based in the school, visits her.

Developing supportive relationships

First contacts

How Alishba initially interacts with Meredith will influence whether Meredith is able to overcome and move past her feelings of ambivalence, fear, stigma and lack of trust. Alishba's attitude, demeanour and actions will

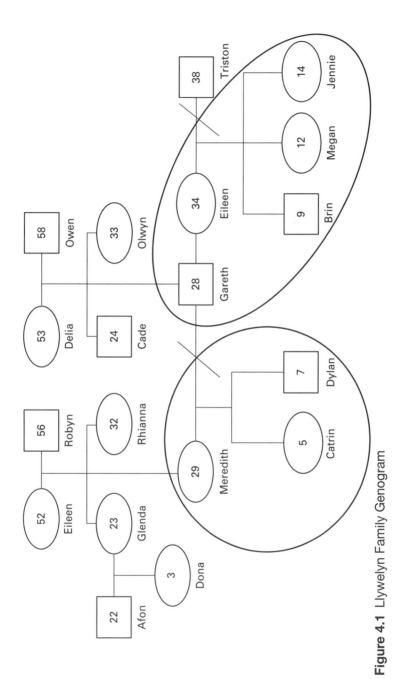

Figure 4.1 Llywelyn Family Genogram

either help or hinder the development of a constructive relationship. She needs to have an encouraging, supportive, non-punitive and non-judgemental attitude, and an empathic demeanour towards Meredith. Alishba's work with the Llywelyn family is an attempt at early intervention, before the situation gets worse. Alishba sees her first task as developing a good working relationship with Meredith and other family members, as this is one of the most important determinants of the outcomes of home-based family support (de Boer and Coady, 2007: 32). She is mindful of the idea that it is often not families who are hard to engage, but that families experience services as hard to engage with (Aggett, Swainson and Tapsell, 2015: 194).

At the doorstep, Alishba says who she is, where she is from and makes sure Meredith was expecting her visit. Alishba clarifies why she is visiting, that is, that the head teacher of Dylan and Catrin's school had asked her to visit. Meredith rather coolly invites Alishba in, muttering something under her breath that indicates she regretted speaking to the head teacher. Alishba takes care not to negatively react to Meredith's initial cool non-committal responses and makes a distinction between this and what her later response may be, as these can be quite different (Pearson, 2009: 90). As she interacts will Meredith, Alishba is careful to remember that Meredith's current coolness and defensiveness is likely to dissipate if she maintains an empathic listening stance.

To break the ice, Alishba endeavours to build a rapport with Meredith by talking about the weather and the photographs of the children. Eventually Alishba asks Meredith when things first started to get difficult. She carefully listens to Meredith's account, asking her to expand on some points. Alishba addresses Meredith's unrealistic fears of her coming to judge her and take her children away from her and does not prejudge the situation on the basis of the referral information. She listens to Meredith's story, pointing out strengths, and conveying respect and displaying a non-judgemental attitude. Alishba is aware of Meredith's perception of her as powerful and that her defensiveness and ambivalence are understandable. She believes her response to Meredith's negativity needs to be understanding and supportive, and not counter-hostility and exhortations.

Accepting and receiving help

Meredith has reluctantly agreed to the head teacher referring her and her family to the family support team. Her reluctance is likely to reflect the ambivalence that is characteristic of those seeking help (Broadhurst,

2003: 346). Potentially there are a number of factors that lie behind Meredith being in two minds about accepting help. On one hand, she feels in need of support and help, while on the other, she has some misgivings about accepting help. These include a fear of the social impact of receiving help, for example, the stigma associated with needing help, the negative perception of Alishba's agency and associated fears of losing control, of being negatively judged and of Alishba removing her children. In addition, accepting help from an outside agency, as opposed to family and friends, limits the possibility of mutual exchange, something that tends to make the help from informal sources more palatable than formal sources (Cutrona, 2000: 103).

Alishba frames the two sides of Meredith's ambivalence as, on the one hand, Meredith perceives her situation as getting serious, and that with the exception of her sister Rhianna, she experiences her own social network as unsupportive. On the other hand, Meredith is uncertain and ambivalent about accepting help, and somewhat wary and suspicious of Alishba, but believes turning down help will only heighten the head teacher's concerns. The important point is that Alishba recognises the ambivalence for what it is and does not put it down to a lack of motivation, for instance. Alishba judges that if she is to do productive work with the family, she will need to make careful efforts to engage Meredith from their very first contact. She responds to Meredith's negative attitude with respect and eagerness to listen to what Meredith has to say.

Developing good working relationships

There is considerable agreement that being supportive requires building good working relationships (Ruch, Turney and Ward, 2010). Using a multiple interview design to interview six worker–service user dyads drawn from child welfare agencies in Canada, de Boer and Coady (2007) researched 'good helping relationships'. They selected the dyads on the basis that both worker and service user felt they had developed a good working relationship. The purpose of the research was to see if good working relationships were possible in child welfare work and identify the characteristics of the workers' practice that managed to achieve such relationships. Alishba has already displayed some of the characteristics identified by de Boer and Coady (2007: 35), namely engaging in 'small talk' to establish comfort and rapport, seeking to get to know Meredith as a whole person and recognising and valuing her strengths and successes in coping.

In their work, de Boer and Coady (2007: 41) acknowledge that service user attributes and behaviour impact on the quality of any helping relationship and concede that it may not be possible to engage every child welfare service user in a positive relationship; however, they argue it is the worker's responsibility to persevere in doing so. They explain that

> Many of the workers in this study had interpersonal difficulties with their clients, particularly in the early stages of relationship development. These workers maintained their positive attitudes and actions, clients' strengths and abilities emerged and were nurtured, and, in a gradual, interactive process, mutual trust, respect, understanding, liking and collaboration continued to grow.
>
> (de Boer and Coady, 2007: 41)

Further, de Boer and Coady (2007: 39) claim that the results of their study illustrate that good helping relationships can be developed and maintained even when there are serious concerns.

Conversations with a purpose

Both the notions of 'interview' and 'assessment' have a tendency to provoke a defensive stance in the recipients, and the interrogatory style of interaction will do little to promote engagement, as they suggest one

---

Research Focus

Mason, C. (2012) 'Social work the "art of relationship": parents' perspectives on an intensive family support project', *Child and Family Social Work*, 17(3), 368–377.

To learn about the skills required for effective relationship-based practice, this article draws from the narratives of parents whose children had been assessed by workers as 'at the edge of care'. From the parents' descriptions of 'positive practice', Claire Mason identifies four key elements in building good working relationships:

1. Respectful communication, trust, honesty and feeling safe;

2. A shared goal;

3. Practical assistance and understanding parents' own needs; and

4. Reliability: being available.

person asking questions and another answering them. Ulvik (2015) argues for an exploratory mode of conversation in preference to an interrogatory one, and we can employ this idea of 'exploratory conversations' in working with families to explore their views and perspectives on family life.

This would involve engaging family members through the medium of 'conversations' rather than 'interviews', albeit a 'conversation with a purpose' (Burgess, 1984, cited in Morris, 2013: 200), with conversations being interactive two-way exchanges between two or more participants. However, it is wise to remember Smart's (2006: 158) caution that 'conversational style interviews' are still an 'unnatural technology' whose purpose is to elicit speech on given topics, no matter how conversational it is. These conversations can take place with individual family members on their own or in various combinations, including the whole family group, with the presence and absence of particular members making a difference to what family members say and do not say.

Relationship dynamics

Although generally the relationship between worker and family member is characterised as one of power imbalance, with the worker having more power than family members, in a number of ways things are usually far more complex and require a more nuanced understanding (Taylor and White, 2000: 126). One just has to consider the frequent claims of workers that family members will not cooperate, and workers feeling intimidated, to show family members can exercise considerable power. We cannot say that Alishba will have the most influence because she is the professional, or that Meredith as the service user, will have less influence. Each situation and each encounter requires its own analysis of power relations. Ideally each party would have the power to influence the topics of discussion and talk openly, and the other party would listen to what they have to say and take it seriously. This ability is relational, dynamic and contingent on the particular context and circumstances at the time. Power relations are dynamic in the sense that the balance of power between actors changes and develops over time in a context of each person occupying different structural positions in relation to the family, the situation and society.

Social identity is multidimensional and all professional workers need to be comfortable and skilled in 'working across difference', including having cultural awareness and sensitivity. All actors in a situation have their own social identities, occupying different positions in relation to the child welfare agency, the family and society. Alishba and each family member will bring to the encounters their own biographies, social identities and structural positions. The particular relationship dynamics of difference will depend on the various combinations of social identities between the worker and family members. In the dyads made up of Alishba and Llywelyn family members there will be various combinations of differences and similarities, including belonging to different gender groups, ethnic and racial groups, age groups and social classes. In many dyads there are likely to be commonalties, for example, common gender or age group membership. The playing out of these differences and similarities over time will influence the development of relationship dynamics between Alishba and individual family members.

To take the example of the relationship between Alishba and Meredith, there are similarities and differences between them in their social identities and social group membership. Both are nondisabled heterosexual females, who live in Wales with British nationality and are members of the same age group. Alongside these similarities are differences of social class and ethnicity, which means both of them are working across difference. Meredith is working class, while Alishba is a middle class professional. Meredith is White British and so a member of the ethnic majority, while Alishba is a British Asian and so a member of an ethic minority. In terms of ethnic identity, Meredith identifies with being Welsh, while Alishba identifies with Wales as the place she lives and Pakistan as the place of her cultural heritage. On occasion, service users and members of the public have subjected Alishba to racist comments and abuse, while Meredith can go about her day-to-day life not subjected to racial harassment. Consequently, there are some differences and similarities between them in social position, culture and ways of life that Alishba, like all workers, needs to be aware of and sensitive to.

Taking a whole family approach

It is tempting for Alishba to remain content and comfortable with working with Meredith as the key family member who has the most day-to-day responsibility for the care of the children; however, a whole family systemic approach requires her to have in mind the other family members, their relationships with each other and working towards engaging with them as individuals and as a family group. Such whole family practice is likely to be a challenge, and Alishba needs to work towards engaging the whole family from her first point of contact, which in this instance is Meredith. Alishba will want to develop some sort of relationship or connection with Dylan and Catrin, their father and members of the extended families.

At the initial contact, Meredith is to some degree the gatekeeper to the family, and Alishba will, where possible and appropriate, work at Meredith's pace. She does not want to alienate Meredith and for her to feel she is going behind her back.

Alishba will look for an opportunity to see if Meredith accepts that her wider family is a potential source of support and that she and Gareth need to relate to each other positively as parents of Dylan and Catrin. To some extent, Alishba will need to play it by ear and engage family members as her contact with the family develops. This will require Alishba to develop nuanced understandings of the routines of family life, family relationships and their family practices, recognising the particular ways they 'do family' (Morris, 2013: 205). Such a nuanced practice needs to be sensitive towards the sometimes subtle differences between the ways families 'do family'.

Alishba discusses with Meredith whom she includes in her family, and the relationships between her and Dylan, Catrin and Gareth. Emerging from this discussion are some concrete and tentative ideas of how making contact with family members might develop. She will arrange the next visit for when Dylan and Catrin are at home and Meredith seems comfortable with Alishba talking with them on their own. Alishba is happy about this, as she finds many parents are understandably somewhat reluctant about allowing a stranger to talk to their children on their own. Meredith appears to have a supportive relationship with her sister Rhianna and may welcome her involvement, but Alishba gets the feeling that Meredith will not be too happy about Alishba visiting Gareth and then meeting with Gareth and Meredith together as parents of Dylan and Catrin. Alishba has already picked up that Meredith is trying to keep her difficulties from her mother, so she needs to approach contact with her sensitively. At some later point Alishba hopes to include other family members in discussions with about who they see as part of 'their' family. Not only are there a rich variety of ways in which families are constituted, each member's construction of 'their family' is unique to them (Neale, 2000: 10).

Research Focus

Morris, K. (2013) 'Troubled families: vulnerable families' experiences of multiple service use', *Child and Family Social Work*, 18(2), 198–206.

Kate Morris's article draws on a small-scale study examining the experiences of 'highly vulnerable families with complex and enduring needs'. Her research ▸

shows gaps between existing practices and those that would successfully engage family members. She argues for the development of nuanced practice capable of recognising and working with how families 'do family' and the processes that support and inhibit professional interventions. The 'families wanted professionals to understand their realties and had a sense of fleeting professional visits not only meant they could mask risks, but also the challenges they faced were unrecognised' (Morris 2013: 205).

Working with diverse family members

In this section we consider a number of issues in engaging different family members including mothers, children, fathers and 'wider family' members. Societies are still a long way off from having democratic families, and gender, generation and age continue to structure families. Workers need to take into account current social arrangements in families, while remembering family members are unique human beings that occupy different positions in the family and have a number of identities, for example, Meredith's identities include woman, parent, mother, ex-partner, daughter, sister and worker. Engagement of mothers, fathers, children and 'wider family' members will need to take into account various factors, particularly that there is considerable diversity in the ways family members 'do' their family roles.

Mothers

Featherstone (1999) makes a number of important points about working with mothers and mothering, three of which are included here. First, Alishba can enhance her chances of engaging and supporting Meredith by recognising her as a whole human being with a number of identities and not simply a conduit for the promotion of Dylan's and Catrin's welfare (Featherstone, 2004: 157). This requires working with her in relation to how she sees herself and her needs at this particular stage of her life. Featherstone's (1999) argument is that recognising the importance of a mother's well-being not only helps the mother but is also central to her children's well-being. Second, Alishba could enable discussions about the difficult and contradictory feelings that motherhood can evoke, with the possibility that Meredith would experience relief in that it is possible to discuss the 'unacceptable' side of mothering. Featherstone, citing Parker (1995), states that

> Maternal ambivalence is an experience shared variously by all mothers in which loving and hating feelings for their children exist side by side. Much of the guilt which mothers are familiar stems from difficulties they experience in weathering these complicated feelings.
>
> (Featherstone, 1999: 48)

Featherstone concedes that while words like 'hate' may be too blunt, it does capture the contradictory and complex feelings of many mothers' experience. Third, Alishba should not assume that the relationship between mother and child flows in one direction but realize, rather, that it is an interactive process in which not only mothers change their children but children change their mothers.

There are a number of benefits of Alishba encouraging Meredith to give her account of mothering and supportively listening to what she has to say, including giving her the opportunity to tell her story and reflect on her experience. As Krane and Davies state

> Such a narrative might provide women the space to tell their own stories as mothers, to give voice to the actual daily physical and emotional caregiving labour and the context in which their mothering occurs.
>
> (2000: 43)

By listening to Meredith's account of mothering, Alishba will be better able to understand the physical and emotional demands of Meredith's motherwork and the conditions in which she struggles to care for her children (Krane and Davies, 2000: 43). It becomes clear that one of the demands and struggles for Meredith is sustaining her paid work and caring roles. In their review of research into lone parents and paid work, Millar and Ridge (2013: 564) refer to the 'family-work project' by which a lone mother's paid work is sustained by it becoming part of everyday and regular family practices involving all family members. Although many of the families in their sample managed the 'family-work project' well, others struggled with the demands of work and care on a low income.

Children and young people

Awareness of a number of factors may increase Alishba's chances of engaging Dylan and Catrin in conversations about their lived experience. Adults often take the limiting stance towards children and young people, seeing them only as 'adults in the making', hence 'incomplete'. Cross

(2011: 27) argues that sensitivity to 'temporal stances' taken by adults can make a significant contribution to practitioners' understandings of the relational work they do with children. 'Temporal stance' in this context is the practitioner's way of thinking about children and young people in relation to time. The dominant temporal stance towards children and young people is that of 'becoming', that is, 'adult in the making' (Lee, 2001: 38). The 'child becoming' discourse is explicitly future-orientated and places onus on what the child 'will be' in preference to what he or she 'is', that is, a future adult rather than a young human being in his or her own right (Uprichard, 2008: 304). Consequently, adults see children as incomplete adults and hence children are assumed to not be competent.

Lee (2001: 5), among others, puts forward an alternative stance, 'the being child', that emphasises children being knowledgeable active agents with no *presumed* shortfall in competence. Seymour and McNamee (2012: 92) make the point that given the power differentials that operate between parents and children, it is easy to overstate the extent of childhood agency within families. They argue that we 'can both recognise the unequal relations of power between adults and children but acknowledge that, in particular circumstances they are negotiated and changeable'. Alishba would increase her chances of engaging Dylan and Catrin by recognising them as young human beings, who are active agents in their social worlds, including their families, but operate within the family power structures in which they negotiate or resist.

Alishba also needs to explicitly recognise a number of complexities about 'being a child' and the social, cultural and structural context of their childhood. Children and young people are a diverse social group with individuals varying in a number of ways including age, gender, social class and ethnicity. There are obvious differences between age groups in terms of their social and cultural expectations, and their stage of physical, emotional and cognitive development. Equally, gendered understandings of childhood can inform engaging work with children and young people (Featherstone, 2004: 181), for example, more consciously seeing them as 'girls' and as 'boys' who will have their own agency and own way of 'doing gender' within structural constraints, including the powers of hegemonic femininity and masculinity. Also, boys and girls have multiple gendered identities in their family, for example, Dylan is a son, stepson, brother, grandson and cousin, and he also does gender in a number of social contexts outside his family, for example, at school, leisure facilities, social clubs and in peer groups.

Adults who want to engage children in exploratory conversations face challenges and difficulties, which are exacerbated when the adult is a professional and perhaps even more so a 'child welfare professional'. One of the biggest challenges workers face in enabling children to participate in 'conversations' with adults are their own 'professional practices'. As stated above, Ulvik (2015) argues for an exploratory mode of conversation rather than an interrogatory one. This is a call for a more democratic practice that stresses the interactive nature of conversations. Ulvik recognises that some children may have experienced less development support and

> Consequently, they may struggle in articulating clear views or wishes, as well as finding the words for their thoughts and experiences. It is an important task for the professionals in child welfare services to arrange conversations where children are assisted in forming views, articulate experiences and reflect upon what they want for their lives.
>
> (2015: 195)

Another challenge identified by Ulvik is how to explore everyday life experiences when it is likely the child's everyday life is unacceptable according to cultural norms that the child is well aware of and how it is important to find sensitive ways of allowing the possibility of alternative norms or deviation from these norms to be articulated (Ulvik, 2015: 203).

Children and young people can be ambivalent about talking to adults, particularly those perceived to be in authority. They may want help and to tell adults things, but are fearful and unsure whether to trust adults. Young people in a study by Hallett, Murray and Punch (2003, cited by Featherstone, 2004: 176) would rather consult friends, as they feared that adults would take over their problems and insist they do something against their will. They felt adults would trivialise and marginalise their concerns and the adult's response might exacerbate the problem. Dylan and Catrin are younger than the young people in Hallett's study and Alishba needs to be particularly sensitive to Dylan and Catrin's age and verbal competences, remembering that such competences do not always correspond to their age.

The work of Ulvik (2015: 201) gives some useful ideas that Alishba could use to encourage Dylan and Catrin to engage in exploratory conversation with her. She could involve them in some activity such drawing and carefully listen and watch for cues as to the direction they want the conversation to go. She can make efforts to anchor the conversation in the children's' concrete experiences by encouraging them to specifically place their lives and relationships in time, space, particular events and who does what when. She could try to guide the conversation towards their day to day experiences, asking them what they did that day and encouraging them to place them in time and place, and who else was there, which might create openings to develop the conversation. In this way Alishba might get some understanding to how Dylan and Catrin construct their lives and what day-to-day life is like for them.

However, she needs to be reflexively aware that her questions may inadvertently contain normative expectations of how a child's everyday life should be lived, which could make it difficult for Dylan and Catrin to process and express their own experiences if they deviated from these presumptions. For instance, that they should be receiving several meals in the day, and their mother should insure they brush their teeth each morning and night, and tuck them up in bed to say good night. To counteract this Alishba could endeavour to ask Dylan and Catrin concrete but neutral questions that are devoid of such expectations, for instance, what was the first thing they did when they woke up that day.

Fathers

Meredith paints a rather negative picture of Gareth, the non-resident father of Dylan and Catrin; however, Alishba needs to keep an open mind. Cameron, Coady and Hoy (2014: 15) believe there is a danger that Alishba allows Meredith's account of Gareth's involvement in the children's lives to increase his invisibility and that she will effectively allow Meredith to act as the family gatekeeper. There can be a tendency to see fathers as a potential physical threat to children and mothers, and although this will on occasions be true, there is danger that workers use this image as a stereotype and so deny fathers the opportunity to give their side of the story and make a constructive contribution to the care of their children. Cameron, Coady and Hoy (2014: 15) call for child welfare workers to be less fearful of men and more prepared to engage with them. As Alishba is taking a whole family approach, she is keen to hear Gareth's account of his involvement with his children and how he sees his role in their lives.

Featherstone (2004: 151) believes it can help practitioners to see fathers as falling into three categories, each of which presents them with opportunities and constraints to engage them in family work. The first category is men who are 'resources' for women and children, 'who wish to work alongside women and/or substitute for woman if the circumstances demand it'. The second category is 'vulnerable men', whose own needs in relation to mental and physical health and/or past experiences may preclude them being able to develop mutually agreed working parental partnerships and/or offer much to their children. The third category is those men whose violent or abusive behaviour poses considerable difficulties for women, children and practitioners. Featherstone (2004: 152) argues that the advantages of this division are that it can challenge the very influential construction within child welfare of men as 'risks' to children, remove some of the fear of engaging men generally and increase the chances that the needs of vulnerable men do not go unmet. However, she concedes that there is a danger that it obscures the complexities of men's lives and reinforces tendency not to engage with those men who are 'risks'. Also, it might imply that vulnerability is never a factor in male violence.

There is a danger that social workers may effectively exclude fathers by focusing on the mothers as the main carers of children and as a consequence ignore fathers as a potential resource. Alishba does not want to make this mistake, but when Alishba asks Meredith how Dylan and Catrin feel about contact with their father she becomes very vague and it becomes evident that Meredith feels the less contact Gareth has with them, the better. Meredith makes clear that she does not want Alishba to contact Gareth, as she does not want him to know a social worker is visiting her. Alishba realises engagement of fathers is fostered by a proactive approach and early involvement, but her judgement is that it is better to

Research Focus

Cameron, G., Coady, N. and Hoy, S. (2014) 'Perspectives on being a father from men involved with child welfare services', *Child and Family Social Work*, 19(1), 14–23.

This article reports the findings of life story research with 18 fathers involved with child welfare services in Canada and focuses on their perspectives on fatherhood and their relationships with their children. The authors' review of the child welfare literature found a strong tendency among child welfare workers to emotionally and physically avoid fathers and overlook their involvement with their families. The literature review for their research indicated that the majority of families involved men in fathering roles, but consideration of their capabilities and potential contribution to caring for their children was largely absent. The authors found that the stories told by the fathers in their research were much more complex and nuanced than typical characterisations of them, that many of the fathers were not only willing but capable of constructively engaging with their children and that child welfare workers need to be less fearful and open to fathers' points of view.

wait until she sees Dylan and Catrin before discussing it further with their mother (Maxwell et al., 2012: 160). Alishba is not looking forward to that conversation, as she is in dilemma about whether to accept Meredith's wish that she does not contact the children's father or take a proactive approach and make contact despite Meredith's objections. Alishba's attitude to the involvement of fathers will be important. Alishba has a generally positive attitude towards fathers' involvement and no reason to suspect that Gareth is a danger to the children or Meredith. However, in a Northern Ireland study of barriers to paternal involvement, all 22 social workers agreed that a potential barrier was practitioner attitudes towards fathers and that such attitudes often operated on a non-conscious level (Ewart-Boyle, Manktelow, and McColgan, 2015: 474)

Wider family

The very term 'wider family' conjures up an 'immediate family' usually consisting a parent/s and their dependent children and a more peripheral 'wider family'. Some families and some cultures may have problems with this idea of distinguishing between 'wider family' and 'immediate family', and I use these terms here only for convenience. Cutrona (2000) defines social support as 'behaviours that assist persons who are undergoing stressful life circumstances to cope effectively with the problems they face' and 'suggests that it is preferable to help those who lack support by improving the supportiveness of the individual's existing relationships' (Cutrona, 2000: 103, 104). Wider family are among Meredith's existing relationships and are potential sources of social support.

The chapter so far has only referred to the immediate family, Meredith and Gareth and their two children, Dylan and Catrin, the children's maternal grandmother and their aunt Rhianna, which leaves many other 'wider family' members unmentioned. Engaging 'wider family' members (sometimes referred to as extended family, relatives or kin) raises a number of questions on a number of levels, including who are the wider family members and who is to be included in whole family work. The usual response to this question is 'ask the family', but this begs the question, who in the family is Alishba to ask? Should she be content to ask Meredith, or should she include Dylan and Catrin in the discussion? Should Alishba work through Meredith as gatekeeper to 'the family' and effectively let her have a veto of who to include, or should she take the initiative and approach wider family members independently. Alishba proceeds with caution, as wider family involvement has the potential to create or exacerbate disharmony within families (Morris et al., 2015: 7).

There has been comparatively little written about the practicalities of engaging 'wider family' members; however, as Pitcher and Arnill (2010: 18) state, there is a great deal of practice wisdom in the work of family group conference independent coordinators and in the area of kinship care; however, in these areas 'wider family' members, particularly grandparents, have strong incentives to get involved, for example, in order to prevent their grandchildren being subjected to more severe forms of intervention if they refuse. Pitcher and Arnill's (2010) research into working with grandparents, when the plan is for children to remain in the care of their parent/s, identified a number of issues that grandparents may face. Among these is their uncertain role, the autonomy of the 'immediate family', expectations that grandparents and wider family should always be available, trying to walk the thin line between interference and support, and fears that further demands will be made on them.

There has been a growing recognition of the important role grandparents can play in kinship care but less recognition of the large number of grandparents who play important roles when their grandchildren do not live with them. Grandparents have always played an important role in supporting families, particularly at times of difficulties, but increased life expectancy, growing numbers of dual-worker households and higher rates of family breakdown mean grandparents are playing an increasing role in their grandchildren's lives (Griggs et al., 2010). Alishba needs to recognise the important potential supportive role Dylan and Catrin's maternal and paternal grandparents could be playing or are playing in their grandchildren's lives. She would obviously need to do this in the context of the relationships between both sides of the family.

Research Focus

Griggs, J., Tan, J.-P., Buchanan, A., Attar-Schwartz, S. and Flouri, E. (2010) 'They've always been there for me': grandparental involvement and child well-being, *Children and Society*, 24(3,) 200–214.

Griggs et al. (2010) found in their research of young people aged 11–16 and their grandparents that grandparent involvement was significantly associated with child well-being. They also found that grandparent involvement with their grandchildren's hobbies and interests, their education and schooling and being available to discuss future plans was strongly associated with child adjustment. A

▶

large number of their 'interviewees were very aware that when spending time with their parents they were not the sole focus of their attention. This was not the case when it came to spending time with grandparents, who were able to dedicate their time entirely to their grandchildren.' They found 'a particular strong theme for those who had close relationships with their grandparents was the role they played during times of difficulty', and this could be the case even when grandparent and grandchild lived some distance apart and the support took place over the telephone.

Communication and family narratives

It is through effective and respectful communication that Alishba will engage family members and build good working relationships with them. For this to occur, Alishba will need an understanding of communication as a process and have good communication skills, a crucial aspect of which is being able to respectfully and actively listen to what family members have to say. The existence of good communication is an important part of Alishba being supportive, leaving family members feeling that she has listened to them and understood their perspectives. Through this process, Alishba learns about family member perspectives, relationships and difficulties.

Communication as a process

We can usefully see Alishba's encounters with the Llywelyn family members as interactive processes of communication in which people exchange messages. To take the simplest case of an encounter between two people, each person is a sender and receiver of messages, and both are constructors of messages they send and interpreters of the messages they receive (Reder and Duncan, 2003: 87). Effective communication occurs when the listener gives a similar meaning to what the sender intended. Messages consist of both verbal and non-verbal elements, that is, the words spoken, how actors say the words and their accompanying body language. Alishba needs to be mindful that she is interpreting and giving meaning to what Meredith is telling her, and that Meredith interprets Alishba's utterances and the necessity of interpretation leaves considerable scope for misunderstandings to occur. How each person frames the situation will influence how they interpret what they hear and see. Alishba frames the encounter as her having a conversation with Meredith so as to get to know her and her family better. Meredith may be framing it as Alishba assessing her in order to judge her and her parenting.

Good listening

The experience of 'being listened to' is supportive in itself as well as in reducing the chances of misunderstandings occurring. Alishba can clearly communicate her genuine interest and respect through good listening practices that are a collection of well-known attributes and actions. The core attributes of good listening, as identified by Forrester, Westlake and Glynn (2012: 125), are positive empathic listening, non-verbal communication, use of open questions, affirmation of positives and using reflections. Empathic listening requires Alishba being interested in learning Meredith's point of view, wanting to understand her narrative account of family difficulties, how she has got to where she is and what she sees as the nature of the difficulties the family face and how both of them working together could overcome them. There is no reason why Meredith should trust Alishba and a lot of reasons why she should not. It is through good listening that Alishba can enable Meredith to overcome some of her reticence about telling Alishba the full extent of her difficulties.

In day-to-day communication, non-verbal communication occurs mostly on a non-conscious level with the 'message sender' being unaware of the non-verbal messages they are emitting. Likewise, the 'message receiver' can be unaware that much of the meaning they construct is through interpretation of the sender's body language and tone of voice. Other things being equal, if Alishba has genuine respect and interest in Meredith's account, her body language and tone of voice will express this and Meredith will sense it. There are a number of ways 'other things may not be equal', including Alishba being very nervous, her blushing very easily or being prone to particular habits like fidgeting with hands. Likewise, individuals vary as to how sensitive they are at picking up non-verbal communication, and so they may be prone to misinterpreting what the other person is meaning.

There is a danger that rather than feeling supported, Meredith feels Alishba is interrogating her. This is more likely if Alishba asks a series of relatively closed questions that restrict Meredith's responses (Lishman, 2009: 40). Empathic listening is associated with relatively open questions, that is, questions that invite a wide range of responses, leaving Meredith free to choose how she responds. 'Do you have difficulties getting the children to school in the mornings?' is a relatively closed question, while

'How did you feel when the head teacher had a word with you about Dylan and Catrin?' is a relatively open question. 'Affirmation of positives' is when Alisha takes every opportunity to encourage Meredith by openly and explicitly feeding back the positives contained in her account of family difficulties and relationships.

A simple reflection simply repeats or paraphrases what Meredith has just said. Complex reflection takes the form of lengthier summaries and may include some element of interpretation and 'connection making' for Meredith to accept or reject. When Alishba gives reflections back to Meredith, she shows that she has been listening and is interested in understanding Meredith's experience and feelings. They also give Meredith the opportunity to give feedback to Alishba if she has not understood or hasn't got things quite right. In brief, empathic supportive listening encourages Meredith to tell her story.

Family narratives

When family members give an account of their current situation and how they got there, they are constructing narratives. Riessman briefly describes narrative as when

> a speaker connects events into a sequence that is consequential for later action and for the meanings that the speaker wants listeners to take away from the story. Events perceived by the speaker as important, are selected, organised, connected and evaluated as meaningful for a particular audience.
> (Riessman, 2008: 3)

The above definition stresses the important role of the audience in the production of narratives. The importance of the audience means that it may be better to refer to the co-production of narratives. Alishba is obviously an important audience member, and on this first visit is the sole member, but she needs to have in mind that when more than one family member is present, the audience will be larger and the family member constructing their story will select, frame and sequence events, taking into account those who are present and those who are absent.

Alishba formulates questions that help Meredith construct a coherent account of how she and the family got to where they are. She is skilled in asking questions that help Meredith reflect on what she is saying, thereby helping her to re-evaluate and possibly reconstruct her narrative. Meredith experiences Alishba empathically listening to and acknowledging her story as very supportive. Constructing her account of family life and difficulties may have 'produced a degree of reflexiveness that might not otherwise have occurred' (Smart, 2006: 158). Constructing a narrative may also be part of making sense of past experiences by linking events and seeing patterns; narratives are therefore not necessarily just 'accounts', they may become part of the lens through which actors interpret events, as well as becoming part of the structuring of future events (Smart, 2006: 156, 158).

Helping family members construct narratives of family difficulties, how they arose and how they think they might overcome them is a supportive intervention in family life. Welbourne, discussing the nature of family narratives, points out narratives

> are about far more than sequences of events. They add detail such as motivation, and explanation for the way things happened, why they happened one way and not another. Different causal explanations may be considered, some more dependent on the choices made by the person telling the story, others emphasising lack of choice and environmental factors. Some make for more explicit reference than others to the idea of the 'self' as an active agent.
>
> (Welbourne, 2012: 74)

Alishba is particularly interested in how family members position themselves within their narratives. Smart's (2006) research into children's narratives of post-divorce family life found that some positioned themselves as 'victims of divorce', while others positioned themselves as 'successfully managing adversity'.

Raising concerns

One issue for Alishba is the potential tension between empathically listening to Meredith and raising concerns about the care of Catrin and Dylan. Specific challenges for her are how to be honest and clear without provoking hostility and how to remain emphatic without colluding with unacceptable behaviour (Forrester et al., 2008b: 24). Forrester et al. (2008a: 47) found varied levels of skill in workers raising concerns. Some raised concerns emphatically, while others were highly confrontational. The confrontational approach tended to create high levels of resistance, whereas the emphatic approach was associated with greater disclosure of information, less resistance and no reduction in clarity of concerns. Alishba has listened emphatically to Meredith's account of the difficulties she faces, including problems with her neighbours, the difficult relationship with the children's father, her debts and the difficulties in making ends meet. Meredith's account does not include the impact her stress is having on her care of Catrin and Dylan. Alishba hoped that Meredith would herself raise the concerns expressed by the head teacher but she does not, being preoccupied with her own difficulties. Having established some rapport between them, Alishba waits for an opportune juncture when she raises the school's concerns in a non-confrontational and clear fashion, namely, the reported deterioration in Dylan's behaviour, his and his sister's attendance, their punctuality in the mornings and their appearance.

When Alishba raises the concerns, Meredith breaks down in tears, saying she is under a lot of stress and knows that she has been neglecting the children somewhat lately. Alishba responds in a supportive manner when Meredith discloses there are times when Dylan and Catrin get very upset when she shouts at them, having got to the end of her tether. Alishba sensitively explores the reasons for Meredith's behaviour rather than jumping to conclusions. She continues to let Meredith at least partially set the agenda and talk about the stress she is under, but steers the discussion to the impact the stress is having on her and how this affects the children. She does this in an empathetic, non-judgemental and non-confrontational way, while being clear that there are concerns about the children's welfare and she is happy to work with her to bring about improvements in the family situation and the care of the children.

Congruence and incongruence

Platt (2007: 326) defines congruence as consistency between the workers understanding of the family's difficulties and that of family members. After this first visit there is a high degree of congruence between Meredith's understanding and Alishba's understanding of the family's difficulties and the impact Meredith's stress is having on her care to Catrin and Dylan. This bodes well for developing good working relationships and a high degree of cooperation between Alishba and family members. By cooperation, I mean an interactive process of two or more people working together to achieve the same goals rather than the alternative meaning of doing something that someone else asks or tells you to do. The congruence between Meredith's and Alishba's understandings may be threatened as Alishba widens her involvement and listens to the other family members' narratives of family life and difficulties.

There are occasions when workers cannot take at face value everything they are told by family members; however, Platt (2007: 334) argues 'that much could be achieved through workers, working to understand the family's perspective more fully or more empathically and by opening up their own analysis to further discussion'. Platt (2007: 332) points to the complexity and circularity in the interaction between congruence, cooperation and good working relationships. If the worker and family members are able to establish a shared narrative about the nature of the family's difficulties, 'then this congruence is likely both to support and contribute to good working relationships' from which cooperation can be developed. His analysis presents the important insight that cooperation is not simply a characteristic of family members but a feature of the interaction between the family and worker. An implication is that workers cannot solely blame family members for a lack of cooperation and they need to look at their own practice.

Chapter Key Points

1. Workers need to have appropriate attitudes and demeanour if family members are to experience contact with them as supportive.

2. To engage family members requires an understanding of family members' understandable ambivalence about accepting help from an outsider.

3. Supportive practice involves working with the dynamics of power and difference between worker and family members, and having critical awareness of issues involved with engaging with mothers, fathers, children and 'wider family' members.

4. Workers can increase their chances of them and family members understanding each other through appreciating communication as a two-way process involving the construction and interpretation of messages.

5. Helping family members construct narratives of family life and the difficulties they face is in itself a supportive intervention in family life.

6. Having an empathic stance enhances rather than impedes frank discussion of concerns.

7. Workers cannot solely blame family members for a lack of cooperation and they need to look at their own practices.

Reflective Exercises

1. Thinking about issues in engaging 'wider family' members, how would you proceed when a family member asks you not to make contact with a particular 'wider family' member?

2. To what extent do you agree or disagree that being supportive involves the worker's attitude and demeanour more than specific techniques?

3. Think critically about the argument that a lack of cooperation from family members is often the result of a worker's poor practice.

4. Think critically about what you would do if you did not agree with a family member's account of the reasons for the family's difficulties.

Putting into Practice

Identify a situation in which you tried to be supportive to a person or family, and think about whether they actually felt supported by you.

Identify the factors that you think contributed to that person feeling or not feeling supported by you.

Which topics from this chapter do you think are most important to you being successful in your efforts to support families?

Further Resources

Broadhurst, K. (2003) 'Engaging parents and carers with family support services: What can be learned from research on help-seeking?', *Child and Family Social Work*, 8(4), 341–350.

This is a review of the research into seeking help; it identifies issues of stigma and ambivalence associated with seeking help.

Morris, K. (2013) 'Troubled families: vulnerable families' experiences of multiple service use', *Child and Family Social Work*, 18(2), 198–206.

This is one of the few studies reporting on family perspectives on their experience of early intervention.

Chapter 5 'Narrative and understanding the family's world', in P. Welbourne, (2012) *Social Work with Children and Families: Developing Advanced Practice*, Abingdon: Routledge, 71–88.

This chapter looks in some depth at understanding family narratives.

SUPPORTIVE INTERVENTIONS

CHAPTER OVERVIEW

This chapter

- Explains how the ecological framework supplies a theory of change and a set of ideas which practitioners can use to combine more specific interventions together.
- Stresses the importance of practical and concrete support.
- Looks at interventions that focus on the family group, namely, family group conferencing, family therapy, family meetings and family tasks.
- Introduces some specific models or methods of intervention: Crisis Intervention; the 'Homebuilders Model'; Brief Solution Focused Therapy; and Multisystemic Therapy.
- Considers some services that are potentially supportive of families, including family centres, mediation, parenting programmes and 'short breaks'.

Introduction

The adjective 'supportive' in the chapter title is necessary because not all interventions are supportive. Intervention tends to mean an outside agency or person becomes involved in a situation in order to help, prevent or resolve difficulties, problems or concerns. The issue is that there are different categories of intervention that form a spectrum ranging from 'supportive' to 'coercive', with the term 'intervention' often associated with the latter. Featherstone, Morris and White (2014) rightly point to the difference between 'support' and 'intervention' and argue that 'the term intervention needs interrogation, as it suggests practices delivered to families rather than practices with families' (Featherstone, Morris and White, 2014:1740). This is not just a problem of terminology, as there is a real danger that 'supportive interventions' becomes something imposed *on* families rather than done *with* families. Consequently, care needs to be taken that 'supportive interventions' are done with families rather than done to families.

The previous chapter focused on being supportive and discussed the ways workers can be supportive through the manner they interact with family members, particularly in terms of their attitude and demeanour and their readiness to listen and understand a family's situation from their point of view. In other words, it stressed the importance of listening and understanding family narratives. It is not enough for the worker to believe they are being supportive; family members need to feel that the worker is listening to them and trying to understand their points of view. Being supportive in this way is one of the most important 'supportive interventions' and one of the most important components of the effective use of all the interventions explained in this chapter. As such, the chapter complements the previous one, by explaining a number of supportive interventions in the form of methods, approaches and ideas about helping actions that workers and families can engage with in a supportive way. These supportive interventions can be catalysts for families to engage in problem-solving, decision-making and actions that can mend family relationships, increase coping capacities and improve their social, material and institutional environments and generally make them stronger.

The Tomlinson family

The Tomlinson family household consists of Carol (31 years old) and her partner Leigh (29 years old), Carol's children from a previous relationship, Nadine (15 years old) and Raymond (13 years old), Leigh's son Jack (10 years old) and their half-sister Valerie (5 years old). Nadine and Raymond's mother and father, Simon, separated six years ago. Simon lives locally and Raymond visits him most weekends, while Nadine refuses to see her father. Simon lives with Amy, his new partner, with whom he has a child, Haley, aged 6. Leigh's daughter, Bella (11 years old), lives with her mother Emily (27 years). Raymond's visits to his father often result in tension and arguments with his mother and sister, while Simon accuses his ex-partner of turning his kids against him. Raymond has expressed a wish to go and live with his father, who has told him they have not got the room, and Amy is adamantly against it. In reconstituted families such as the Tomlinson family, relationship dynamics have an extra layer of complexity with the possible presence of stepfathers, stepmothers, stepchildren, half-siblings and stepsiblings posing challenges for family members and workers wishing to engage all family members. Family tensions can be particularly fraught during the period of family formation.

Carol and Leigh are both in low-paid employment and the family have no savings, a high level of debt and a weekly income that is wholly committed. Nadine is doing well at school, has a close relationship with her mother and gets on well with Valerie. Leigh's and Carol's employment mean that they regularly leave Nadine in charge of Valerie, Raymond and Jack, which usually results in Raymond hanging out with his friends. He gets into trouble in the neighbourhood for fighting and 'anti-social behaviour'. Raymond's school and his parents are concerned about him, as he plays truant from school and, when he is there, is disruptive in class, talking out of turn and being defiant towards teachers. A particular issue at school is conflict between him and a group of other students. At home he is disobedient and rude, and his mother, stepfather and sister all accuse him of stealing money from them. Carol and her partner report that Raymond is the source of rows between them. Leigh maintains a low profile in parenting Raymond, and keeps out of the considerable conflict between Raymond and his mother. Carol feels that her daughter Nadine is the only person she feels able to talk openly to about the stress she is under. Raymond's behaviour, at home, in the neighbourhood and at school, has had cumulative effect on his mother's coping capacity, with the last straw being his exclusion from school.

The chapter introduces a number of potentially family supportive interventions, which, in their own way, can help families overcome the problems they are experiencing. The interventions vary in the relative importance of timing and their scope, some being relatively narrow, others relatively wide. The prime focus can be family relationships, family solution-building, family decision-making, family communication, a family's material environments or a combination of these. This chapter is organised into five sections. The first section explains ecological theory as a set of ideas which practitioners can use to combine more specific interventions. Next we discuss the importance of practical and concrete support. This is followed by a section on interventions that focus on the family group, namely family group conferencing, family therapy, family meetings and family tasks. Then the chapter turns to some specific models or methods of intervention: crisis intervention, the 'Homebuilders Model', Brief Solution Focused Therapy and Multisystemic Therapy. Finally, some services that are potentially supportive of families are outlined, namely family centres, mediation, parenting programmes and 'short breaks'.

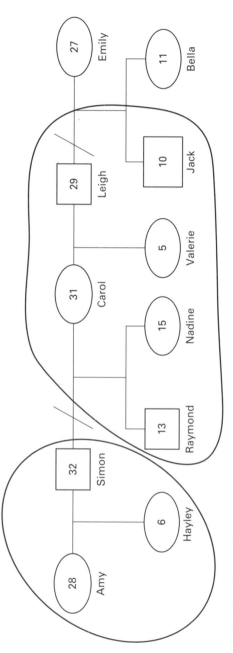

Figure 5.1 Tomlinson Family Genogram

Ecological framework

Chapter 2, 'Understanding Families', discusses the need to have an ecological understanding of families, and here the focus shifts to ecological
intervention. Bronfenbrenner's (1979) social ecological theory provides
the basis for ecological interventions which endeavour to simultaneously
intervene in a number of different domains or levels of reality, including
the individual, interpersonal, peer and family relationships, community,
neighbourhood, local agencies like schools, and society, including government policy. Researchers, theorists and practitioners use a number of other
terms to denote the idea of concurrently intervening in a number of
domains, including integrative or holistic approaches, multisystemic, mul-
tilevel, multicomponent and multidimensional interventions. In a particular family situation, the range of domains considered appropriate for
attention can vary considerably. In this chapter's case scenario, potential
relevant domains include family relationships, schools, the neighbour-
hood/community and the family's material conditions. In her research into
preventative services for adolescents, Biehal (2008: 458) found that concurrent work on child behaviour and parenting style, and mediation
between the generations, created a virtuous circle of more positive behaviour at home, which was strengthened by intervention in other environments, notably school.

The ecological framework also provides a theory of change. It recognises
that factors located on different levels interact together to bring about and
maintain family problems and difficulties, and that intervention in these different domains can also provide mechanisms of change. Such intervention
requires a good fit between the nature of the family difficulties and the
particular mix of interventions, which needs to have coherence and not be
a random hotchpot of activities that overload the family. There is a real danger that the sheer number of workers involved, making their own demands,
overwhelms families. The ecological approach to supportive intervention
presents opportunities for collaboration between agencies, professionals
and community groups and services, which the next chapter discusses.

As an indication of a multi-domain intervention within ecological
framework, a supportive ecological intervention in the chapter case scenario could combine work within the

- 'Family domain' on family relationships,

- 'School domain' on involvement of Raymond in his school's mediation
  project for resolving conflicts between pupils,

- 'Community domain' about the availability of community mediation for resolving the conflict between the Tomlinson family and other families in the neighbourhood, or

- 'Material domain', with the local credit union about debt counselling and a saving scheme so the family could save for unexpected items like a washing machine when it breaks down.

Focusing on material needs

The Tomlinson family struggle to achieve a reasonable standard of living and have trouble fulfilling the most basic material needs such as food, fuel and shelter. They live in a condition of poverty as set out by Townsend (1997: 31, cited in Callan et al, 1996: 6), with 'their resources so seriously below those commanded by the average individual or family that they are in effect excluded from ordinary living patterns, customs and activities'. On a day-to-day basis family poverty confronts workers, yet for them it can remain a rather vague background factor being part of the circumstances in which families live and not a target for intervention. Krumer-Nevo, Monnickendam and Weiss-Gal (2009: 227) explain that for social workers 'such a large segment of social work clients live in poverty, poverty becomes 'normal' or 'natural' and therefore considered to be belonging only to the context and not, in itself, as the problem'. Yet living with and coping with poverty and its consequences has a major impact on family life and family well-being.

There is a danger that workers overly focus on emotional support, family relationships and family practices, and neglect the material conditions in which families live. To combat this 'poverty blindness' there have been calls for a more 'poverty-aware practice' (Davis and Wainwright, 2005; Krumer-Nevo, Monnickendam and Weiss-Gal, 2009). Poverty-aware practice means being explicitly aware of the impact living in poverty has on family life and discussing with family members their ideas on how they could work together to improve their material conditions. It is one thing to explicitly recognise the poverty a family are living in and the effects it is having on family life, but another to know how best to help families increase their income.

Causes and solutions of poverty

Theories of poverty tend to be characterised as those that blame the poor for their poverty or those that blame the structures of the society they live in.

Strier (2009: 1072) divides poverty theories into three broad categories: individual, cultural/behavioural and structural. These theories are important, as they link the causes of poverty to its solutions. He identifies two subtypes of theories that focus on individuals – human capital theories and motivational theories – and explains that human capital theories portray poverty as a result of unequal distribution of education and technical and vocational skills, and portray its remedy as individual training and educational investments. Whereas motivational theories see poverty as a result of individuals lacking sufficient motivation and its remedy as changing attitudes, priorities and values related to work.

He points out that cultural/behavioural theories of poverty reflect the belief that poverty comes from *shared* non-productive values, norms and behaviours and its remedy is changing the culture of communities and families. While structural explanations see poverty as direct result of systemic barriers that severely reduce opportunities and access to resources, services and participation in society, with its remedy being changing the structure of the system. Professional workers are likely to find some of these theories more convincing and palatable than others. For instance, many social workers would be most comfortable with human capital theories at the individual level and structural theories at the societal level, but face the challenge of finding practical ways of helping families improve their standard of living.

Family and community agency

A good place for workers to start is recognising the agency of people living in poverty. Lister (2004: 130) identifies two dimensions of the agency shown by those living in poverty, a personal/citizenship dimension and an everyday/strategic dimension, giving four forms of agency in total. The agency shown in the *personal/everyday* form is 'getting by' living on a low income; the agency shown in the *personal/strategic* form is 'getting out of poverty'; the agency shown in the *everyday/citizenship* form is 'getting back at' the system through resistance; and the agency shown in the *strategic/citizenship* form is 'getting organised' with others in collective activities. Carol, Leigh, Nadine and Raymond show their *personal/everyday* agency through getting by on a low income, and show their *personal/strategic* agency through their ambitions to get out of poverty. However, they face many barriers, including 'getting by' sapping much of their time and energy, and them having received a poor education.

There is potential for family members and workers to collaboratively work together to improve the family's material position, particularly on an individual capacity-building level in terms of work skills and qualifications and overcoming other barriers to them getting a better job. At a community level, family members could get involved with and use community action and resources. If workers are to collaborate with families, even at a basic level, they need to have contact with and work with community workers, local resources and services such as credit unions, debt counselling services, basic skills classes, community food co-ops, local cooperative enterprises, resident groups and family literacy schemes. For example, Drakeford and Gregory (2008) argue that workers need to work with local credit unions, as they are local sources of low-cost credit, a convenient and acceptable means of saving and a source of assistance in dealing with debt and financial crises.

Family group

This section looks at interventions specifically focused on the family group, including family group conferences (FGCs), family therapy, family meetings and family tasks.

Family group conferencing

An FGC is a process of family decision-making mainly used when a child is at serious risk of harm. It is a potentially supportive intervention designed to promote wider family participation in decision-making, particularly when authorities are on the verge of starting proceedings to take a child into public care. It is not hard to imagine the Tomlinson family situation deteriorating to a point when a FGC would be appropriate. In principle, if not always in practice, important features are the inclusion of immediate and extended family members and significant others. The process was introduced to New Zealand's child protection legislation in 1989 (Connolly, 2006: 345) and since has spread to other jurisdictions including the UK, the USA, Canada, Australia and Sweden. Advocates of this model emphasise its empowerment base, the expertise of the family and the conferences' practical outcome of agreed plans (Holland and Rivett, 2008: 22).

Key elements of the process are:

- referral to the independent FGC organiser who helps the family organise the conference;

- an introduction stage in which the independent organiser explains the process and establishes 'private family time' ground rules including that the family members give each participant space to speak and be listened to, with particular emphasis on listening to children;

- an information stage where professionals set out their concerns and the resources available;

- 'private family time' in which the family develop their own plan to address those concerns unhindered by professionals; and

- the expectation that professionals agree the plan unless it threatens child welfare (Family Rights Group, undated).

Professionals and family members then implement and monitor the plan.

Internationally there are variations and modifications of the process (Ney, Stoltz and Maloney, 2011: 187), for example, Healy, Darlington and Yellowlees (2012) found in Queensland, Australia, that in only two of the 11 'Family Group Meetings' observed were the family offered private family time, an element widely considered to be the hallmark of family group decision-making. Research into user satisfaction and the immediate outcomes of conferences has consistently found high levels of user satisfaction among family members and professionals. The limited research into longer-term outcomes for child welfare using a comparison group have had inconclusive and more mixed results (Holland and Rivett, 2008: 23). Sundell and Vinnerljung's (2004) Swedish study compared three-year outcomes of FGCs with traditional child-protection investigations. They found less stability in the lives of FGC children during the three-year follow-up period, but the differences were small and give several plausible explanations for the results. Berzin et al.'s (2008) randomised control study in the USA found that there were no significant differences between family group decision-making cases and the comparison group receiving traditional services in terms of child safety, placement stability and permanence. Frost, Abram and Burgess's (2014) review of FGC outcome research found that some showed that they had more positive outcomes than 'service as usual', while others reported no difference. However, the research into the experience of the FGC process is overwhelmingly positive.

Holland and Rivett's (2008: 32) study of 17 FGCs found that as well as a practical plan, the actual process of family members meeting together appeared to have a therapeutic effect. Although family members expressed high emotions, they tended to be a source of catharsis, with conferences ending with a sense of resolution and usually antagonistic parties communicating more calmly and effectively. Healy, Darlington and Yellowlees's (2012) observational study of 11 Family Group Meetings in Queensland, Australia, found that professionals dominated the meetings, but only one of the meetings included private family time. The authors attribute the limited participation of family members to the 'tensions between the democratic ethos of family group decision making and the forensic orientation which dominates child protection services in Queensland and other liberal welfare states' (Healy, Darlington and Yellowlees, 2012:10). Their findings give further weight to the principle that private family time is a key element in family group decision-making. Connolly's (2006: 352) study involving four focus groups of care and protection coordinators across New Zealand found that while some of the coordinators put the success of a conference down to the 'magic of family time', it was also evident that they felt on occasions the 'private time' can also reinforce power dynamics within a family, with a particular family member dominating decision-making.

Research Focus

Frost, N., Abram, F. and Burgess, H. (2014) 'Family group conferences: evidence, outcomes and future research', *Child and Family Social Work*, 19(4), 501–507.

Nick Frost and colleagues review the relatively small number of outcome studies of FGCs and include studies from the UK, the USA, Canada, New Zealand and Scandinavia. They discuss the difficulties of implementing FGCs as well as researching them, particularly the way the different jurisdictions make changes to the process, and 'service as usual' used as a comparison can be markedly different in different countries. They report that those researching the outcomes of FGCs have difficulties in finding appropriate comparison groups and in recruiting participants, meaning sample sizes are small. The studies analysed had mixed results, some showing positive outcomes and others neutral outcomes. The authors argue that the evidence suggests that FGCs are no less effective than 'service as usual' but have the benefit of children and families experiencing them as family-centred, strengths-based and empowering.

Family therapy

Family therapy is effective for a proportion of cases of child behaviour problems and other child focused problems (Carr, 2014: 113); however, it is open to question whether a worker at this stage would refer the Tomlinson family for family therapy, likewise whether Raymond's parents would warm to such a suggestion and whether the receiving agency would give it sufficient priority. The term family therapy covers a broad range of approaches to helping families and most commonly takes place in a clinical setting, less often in a family's own home (Waisbrod, Buchbinder and Possick, 2012). One thing the various schools of family therapy have in common is that all family therapists highlight the role of the family in problem resolution (Carr, 2000: 3). The extent that families find family therapy a supportive intervention is open to question given that research into families' satisfaction is comparatively rare compared with outcome research. The term family therapy can put off many families, as it implies the presence of some dysfunction within the family, in contrast to a common parent perspective that the identified child is the problem, as is the case in the Tomlinson family. There is also a danger that families fear that family therapists will negatively judge them as a family and see them as part of the problem, which therapists counteract by emphasising the family as part of the solution. There can be a mismatch between what families want and what actually happens within sessions, for instance, families can assume they will receive advice, only to find that therapists focus on exploring family relationships.

Even if the Tomlinson family attended an appointment there is no guarantee that they will engage in the process. Raymond is not the main initiator of the family's attendance and engaging him in the process is likely to be a particular challenge for the family therapists (O'Reilly and Parker, 2013: 491). O'Reilly and Parker (2013) found that children identified by the family as 'the problem' employed both passive and active disengagement behaviours like inattention, ignoring direct questions and refusing to answer questions. They argue that for the therapy to be successful it is necessary to achieve more than just the physical presence of Raymond, and the therapist will need to recognise and manage his disengagement while maintaining alliances with his parents and siblings. The therapist would have to take some responsibility of engaging Raymond in the therapy sessions, something that is a complex task, especially when parents and siblings are vocal in presenting him as 'the problem'.

Researchers and practitioners have long considered a therapeutic alliance between family member and therapist as essential to therapeutic progress and positive outcomes across all therapies (Aspland et al., 2008: 699). In family therapy the therapist has the additional challenge of developing and maintaining such alliances with multiple family members in a context of pre-existing family dynamics (Friedlander et al., 2006: 215). The four dimensions of the observational rating system developed by Friedlander et al. (2006) sheds some light on the nature of such alliances. The rating system is designed to rate the strength of the therapeutic alliance in family therapy. The four dimensions are (i) emotional connection with the therapist, (ii) engaging in the therapeutic process (iii) safety within the therapeutic system and (iv) shared sense of purpose within the family. Safety within the therapeutic process includes 'safety in front of the family' and 'safety in front of the therapist'. This means each family member needs to feel safe talking in front of other family members and in front of the therapist.

Family meetings

The term family meeting is used for an informal meeting together of family members in their own home, not to be confused with FGCs or family therapy, which have been discussed. If the Tomlinson family could successfully hold such a meeting, it is likely to improve their situation. However, it is another matter whether they would meet together and use the meeting to resolve family issues. The so-called democratic family might make decisions, for instance, like where to go on holiday, or resolve issues by holding family meetings. Such meetings might involve all members of the household meeting together or include family members living elsewhere. The former would involve Leigh, Carol, Valerie, Raymond and Nadine, the latter would include Simon and possibly his current partner, and one or more extended family members. Family meetings might be part of some families' practices but it is highly questionable how common this practice is. Finch and Mason (1993, cited in Holland and Rivett, 2008: 28) found that families might like to think that they negotiate family caring responsibilities by meeting together around the kitchen table, but, in reality, discussion and decision-making tended to take place in a series of one-to-one conversations.

A second form of family meeting is one suggested by and perhaps facilitated by a professional worker to promote and strengthen family communication and problem-solving. If households and families rarely meet together to resolve issues, instigating such a meeting might be a challenge, and if it does take place, might prove to be emotionally demanding. There are usually practical difficulties in setting up family meetings, in terms of getting most family members in the same room at the same time and focusing on the issue at hand. There is little chance of such meetings taking place unless at least one family member is keen enough to organise and encourage or persuade others to take part. Family meetings are an opportunity for families to have some time together to resolve issues and engage in joint problem-solving and for workers to see at first-hand family dynamics, communication and relationships. They give the worker the opportunity to gain an understanding of

> who does the talking and who sits back and listens or seems left out; who feels [they are the] leader, who defers to the leader, who agrees or resents the leader; areas of agreement and disagreement, and some hint of how differences are managed.
>
> (Billings and Block, 2011: 1060)

Facilitation of a family meeting is a challenge and workers need a high degree of skill and confidence to promote family communication, negotiation and problem-solving. There is always the potential for family members to express high emotions and for conflicts to occur, as well as some members being disengaged and possibly not wanting to be present. The worker needs to give recognition and attention to family emotions and acknowledge the difficulties the family are facing. Facilitating or even being present at a family meeting requires a complex set of skills, particularly when the meeting involves conflict and/or high emotions. Family meetings are a relatively common practice in a number of settings, particularly in palliative and adult social care when families and professionals need to make difficult decisions, but appear less common in family support. From the practitioner's point of view, the main aim of the meeting is for family members to tell their own stories and effectively communicate and negotiate with each other. For this to happen there needs to be clear ground rules negotiated and a degree of trust established.

We can identify a number of different forms of family meeting, including those that might occur spontaneously when a worker visits a family and a number of family members happen to be present in the same room and start to communicate with each other about family issues. A worker might suggest a family hold a family meeting before their next visit or arrange to be present when the family hold the meeting. If the worker is present they can either try to be just another participant or take a facilitative role. Key issues in such meetings being successful are clear, negotiated ground rules agreed by family members and establishing a climate of trust, with someone taking a facilitative role. To some extent the family's usual dynamics will operate, and incorporating the five principles of moral discourse into their ground rules will support family communication (Blaug, 1995: 431; Hayes and Houston, 2007: 1001). These are:

- All must be allowed to speak;
- All must be listened to;
- All must be allowed to question others;
- All must strive for consensus; and
- The only legitimate force is the force of reasoned argument.

Family tasks

A relatively straightforward supportive intervention is negotiating practical tasks for family members to complete. Task-centred work has a long history in social work, with Reid and Epstein (1972) first setting out task-centred casework in the early 1970s as a structured approach within short time limits that uses the carrying out of specific tasks to alleviate a target problem. Family members and the worker explicitly identify and agree upon a specific target problem as the focus of work. Key features are a time-limited intervention, negotiation of explicit target problems and relevant tasks. The method consists of five phases: the initial contact, problem search and selection, the task selection, the work on tasks and termination (Butler, Bor and Gibbons, 1978: 394). Workers supporting families can negotiate a family task for them to complete before the next meeting. Family therapists also sometimes set tasks for families to complete between sessions (Carr, 2000: 260), and discuss at the following meeting how the task went or the reasons why the family found they could not carry out the task.

Reid (1985) gives the fundamental principle as concentrating on alleviating target problems through relatively simple, straightforward tasks. He identifies three major types of tasks: shared, reciprocal and individual. All or particular family members complete a shared task together, for example, Raymond and his stepfather doing some activity together. Reciprocal tasks plan for an exchange between family members, for example, when left with Nadine, Raymond agrees to tell her when he is going out, where he is going and when he will be back. In exchange, Nadine will give him some pocket money. Individual tasks do not require collaboration or reciprocation, for example, asking Leigh that when he and Carol are on their own, he would be more explicitly supportive towards her and her parenting efforts.

Strengthening informal social support

As stated in the previous chapter, Cutrona (2000: 103) defines social support as 'behaviours that assist persons who are undergoing stressful life circumstances to cope effectively with the problems they face'. Social relationships can be important sources of support; however, they can also be sources of stress. Immediate and 'wider family' members are important potential providers of social support but so are non-family social network members like friends, neighbours and work colleagues. As well as working on family relationships becoming more supportive, workers can focus on enhancing non-familial informal social support. Informal social support provided by people who are not family members has the potential to improve well-being alongside other types of social support. Workers have a potential role in enhancing opportunities family members have to develop such relationships.

Sheppard (2004: 940) points out that there is good evidence that the presence of a trusted confidante to share feelings protects against depression, particularly when the person uses that support. A person outside the household is sometimes in a better position to provide such support. Carol at present feels socially isolated, and a worker could initiate a conversation about social support by asking Carol whom she feels most able to confide in and, if appropriate, continue by discussing opportunities to make friends. They start by identifying the kinds of venue where people meet people that might become friends, including their workplaces, leisure facilities, adult education venues, school gates and pre-school provisions like playgroups, children's centres and other places.

Raymond is also in need of supportive relationships at this difficult time, and peer relationships are a potential source of that support. Peer relationships are an important part in adolescent well-being and have a prominent role to play in positive development (Sanders et al., 2014: 1). Such relationships can also be challenging and stressful, and a root to problematic behaviour; however, there could be some room for supportive interventions, such as involving Raymond in community youth initiatives like five-a-side football and youth clubs.

Specific models

Crisis intervention

Caplan (1964), building on the work of Lindemann (1944), first set out crisis theory and crisis intervention in the early 1960s. Within crisis theory, a crisis occurs when a person or family perceive demands outstripping their resources and their usual coping abilities suddenly fail. According to the theory, families in a state of crisis are more open to change and more inclined to accept intervention (Al et al., 2011: 992). Within the theory a state of crisis is time-limited, and typically lasts something like four to six weeks, with the crisis having to be resolved in one way or another. Rapid timely intervention means the person or family are more likely to resolve the crisis in a positive rather than negative way. During a crisis there can be a high, but temporary, level of dependency on others. Hence, crisis intervention is an intensive, short-term intervention with the limited aim of returning the individual or family to their pre-crisis state, sometimes referred to as their steady state. Strictly speaking, crisis theory is only applicable when a family or family member is in a state of crisis, so whether crisis intervention is appropriate in the Tomlinson family situation depends on whether one or more of its members has experienced a crisis event and are in a state of crisis.

Crisis intervention theory does not specify what happens face-to-face with the family or individual but rather is a framework concerning timing, intensity and resolution of the immediate crisis. Staudt and Drake (2002) are critical of the way workers and projects can use crisis intervention theory in situations where the primary goal is to enhance family functioning rather than to re-establish a pre-crisis state, or where family member/s are not in a state of crisis. As above, they argue that at least one family member needs to perceive an event or situation as a crisis, that is, perceive the resources available to them are not adequate to cope (Staudt and Drake, 2002: 788). They are critical of agencies and projects inappropriately using crisis intervention theory to justify short interventions, even though families require more long-term help with deeply entrenched chronic problems.

Golan (1987: 365) postulated that a crisis can be precipitated in two ways, either a 'shock crisis' through the occurrence of a shock event or an 'exhaustion crisis' when an individual or family have previously been able to cope effectively but are faced with a series of stressors which through their cumulative effect become overwhelming. Golan (1987: 365) explains that in an exhaustion crisis, the person or family may have previously coped with a series of stressful events but eventually their coping abilities weaken and the person or family reach a point of crisis when they no longer have the resources to cope. The Tomlinson family could fit with the definition of 'exhaustion crisis' as the family is having increasing difficulty in coping with the challenges that Raymond is presenting them, with his exclusion from school being the final straw. In such circumstances, returning to the immediate pre-crisis state may not be enough, and family and worker need more time to move beyond the immediate pre-crisis situation and deal with underlying issues that have been present for some time.

The Homebuilders Model

As well as individual workers and teams using crisis intervention when working with situations in which a family or family member is in an acute state of crisis, crisis intervention has commonly been used as the theoretical basis of family preservation and family intervention projects and services (Al et al., 2014; Forrester et al., 2014; Van Puyenbroeck et al., 2009). Many family intervention projects and programmes are based on 'The Homebuilders Model' (Kinney, Haapala and Booth, 1991), the characteristics of which are brief (four–six weeks) intensive in-home intervention that starts immediately, with specially trained and supervised workers who have high availability and small caseloads and can develop a strong therapeutic alliance with the family and provide concrete services, advice and referral to aftercare. Although the Tomlinson family might benefit from taking part in a Family Intervention Project based on the Homebuilders Model, they are unlikely to meet high eligibility criteria thresholds.

The most important feature of the families of the original Homebuilders programme is that they were experiencing one of two crises. They were experiencing a crisis either because child protection services had said that the family were not providing adequate childcare and were planning to remove one or more children, or parents were so exasperated with a child or children that they were refusing to allow them to continue to live at home. The basic components of the approach were flexibility, intensity, low caseload and brevity. Sessions took place when the family wished and lasted as long as they wanted, enabling the worker to stay long enough to hear their whole story. Workers had a low workload of only two families at a time. The intensity of contact enabled the duration of the contact to be brief, from four to six weeks. A single worker, supported by a team, worked with the family for the duration of the service.

Research Focus

Al, C. M. W., Stams, G. J. J. M., Asscher, J. J. and van der Laan, P. H. (2014) 'A programme evaluation of the Family Crisis Intervention Program (FCIP): Relating programme characteristics to change', *Child and Family Social Work*, 19(2), 225–236.

Al et al. (2014) evaluate a Dutch Family Intervention Programme based on the Homebuilders Model (Kinney, Haapala and Booth, 1991) in which the presence of a crisis and concern about safety of a child were intake criterion. After intervention, the crisis had decreased and child safety increased, family functioning had improved, as had levels of 'parental stress' and parents reported improvements in child behaviour problems. The researchers related these positive features to particular programme characteristics, namely extended duration, therapeutic alliance, analysis of family situation and a solution approach. Al et al. (2014: 232) state 'the results tend to favour an approach in which the … worker invests in a good relationship with family members, analyses the family situation, and approaches the family as the source of change and solutions'.

Brief solution focused therapy

Lethem (2002) nicely sums up the main thrust of the Brief Solution Focused Therapy (BSFT) as 'therapist and client collaborate to clarify the best ways to build on existing strengths and resources in order to move towards a future that the client would prefer'. The method was first developed by De Shazer (1995), and key assumptions are as follows: it not being necessary to understand the causes of a problem to find a solution to it; that successful therapy depends on knowing where the family wants to be; there are always times when the family are already doing some solution building, however fixed the problem pattern seems to be; only the smallest of changes are needed to set in motion a solution to the problem; and problems do not represent underlying pathology or deficits (George, Iveson and Ratner, 2000, cited in Lethem, 2002: 189). The approach firmly focuses on solutions, but the worker needs to let the family tell their story and recognise the distress the problem is causing and show the family that they fully understand.

BSFT could well be appropriate in the Tomlinson family situation, one reason being that at present family members centre their talk on problems, and BSFT gives the worker techniques to change the focus to solutions. The key skills in BSFT are asking questions to elicit examples of exceptions to the problem, that is, examples of when a particular difficulty is less, absent or easier to cope with (Lethem, 2002: 189). The idea is to build on partially successful attempts to reach a solution. There are a number of different categories of questions, including questions about the family's preferred future, questions about exceptions, questions about scales and questions about periods of coping with the problem. For example, the miracle question is designed to elicit the family's or family member's vision of their preferred future. It takes the form of, 'If you wake up one morning to find a miracle had happened overnight and the problem has disappeared, what will be different that will tell you that a miracle has taken place?' How would others notice the problem had gone? Scaling questions ask family members to rate the current situation using a scale of 0 being the worst things have ever been and 10 being the situation after the miracle has happened. If the family rate the present situation as, say, 2, the worker could ask them what got them from 0 to 2 and what needs to happen for them to get to 3. Before the next session, the therapist asks the family or individual to do more of what they were doing when there was an exception to the problem.

Corcoran's (2006) research investigated the effectiveness of BSFT for child behavioural problems by comparing BSFT with 'treatment as usual' with no random assignment of subjects. She found no significant differences between the two forms of treatment in terms of effectiveness, but, interestingly, the BSFT group had a significantly lower dropout rate. Gingerich and Peterson's (2013) review of controlled outcome studies included quasi-experimental studies, that is, studies with a control group but without random assignment of subjects. They concluded that 74% of 43 studies reported significant positive benefits for BSFT. Corcoran and Pillai's (2009) review of research on BSFT had a strict inclusion criteria of including only research studies that had a control group and random assignment of subjects. Of the hundreds of studies screened, only 10 studies passed this test. The conclusion of their research was that, overall, the effects of BSFT were ambiguous and it needs more rigorous research design to establish its effectiveness.

Multisystemic therapy

Multisystemic Therapy is an example of an intervention that adopts an ecological framework and is family and home-based. The 'standard' form of Multisystemic Therapy, known as 'Standard Multisystemic Therapy' is an evidence-based intervention specifically for young people with serious anti-social behaviour and designed to reduce reoffending and out-of-home placement. One of the main assumptions of Standard Multisystemic Therapy is that the caregiver is the primary catalyst for change (Fox and

Ashmore, 2014: 3) and working through with the caregiver the intervention endeavours to address the multi-determined nature of serious anti-social behaviour, including individual young person factors, family factors, school factors, peer group factors and neighbourhood factors. As Fonagy et al. explain,

> Therapists work primarily with the caregiver to improve his or her parenting skills, enhance family relationships, increase support from social networks, encourage school attendance and achievement for the young person, and reduce young person's association with delinquent [sic] peers.
>
> (Fonagy et al., 2013: 3)

Developed specifically for young people aged 11–17 years with serious anti-social behaviour, Standard Multisystemic Therapy is being adapted for specific use with other issues, including abuse and neglect of children, substance misuse and problem sexual behaviour (Fox and Ashmore, 2014: 5).

There is a strong emphasis on implementation fidelity, that is, practitioners implementing the intervention strictly as designed by the developers. One key feature is 'intervention intensity', with a small team of three to four therapists working flexibly on-call 24 hours a day, seven days a week. The intervention is strictly over a three-to-five-month period, with no possibility of extension. There is a strong emphasis on current family strengths and peer supervision. Fonagy et al. (2013: 3) identify 20 randomised controlled trials of Standard Multisystemic Therapy, that is, evaluation research with young people being randomly allocated to either a Multisystemic Therapy or a control group such as 'service as usual'. Sometimes Multisystemic Therapy worked exceptionally well, but it did not do so consistently. Littell, Popa and Forsythe (2005) explain how there are a number of possible explanations for inconsistent results, including variability in intervention fidelity, 'service as usual' being of variable quality in different national contexts and that when the developers carry out the programme, they are more likely to be highly motivated to achieve success.

In their systematic review, Littell, Popa and Forsythe (2005) found eight randomised controlled studies conducted in the USA, Sweden and Norway that met their inclusion criteria and found that it is premature to draw conclusions about the effectiveness of Multisystemic Therapy compared with other services. They report that results are inconsistent and the studies varied in quality and context. Butler et al. (2011) completed the first UK trial and found that although young people receiving Multisystemic Therapy and YOT (Youth Offending Teams) both had reduced reoffending, the Multisystemic model significantly reduced the likeli-hood of non-violent offending during the 18-month follow-up period. On the basis of these promising results, a multicentre UK-wide ran-domised trial known as the Systemic Therapy for At Risk Teens (START) trial is being taken (Fonagy et al., 2013: 3). The main strength of Stand-ard Multisystemic Therapy is its proven effectiveness when implemented in accordance to its nine principles (see MST-UK, undated). Its effective-ness most likely rests on the following: a high level of implementation infidelity; high intensity intervention; practitioners specifically trained in Multisystem Therapy; its ecological focus; and working through the car-egiver. Among its main weaknesses are the low capacity of teams to take on cases due to low caseloads and the five-month cut off if the interven-tion is not successful. This low capacity of teams to take on cases and the targeting of *serious* anti-social behaviour means that a Multisystemic Therapy team is unlikely to accept Raymond Tomlinson for intervention.

Research Focus

Butler, S., Baruch, G., Hickey, N. and Fonagy P. (2011) 'A randomized controlled trial of multisystemic therapy and a statutory therapeutic intervention for young offenders', *Journal of the American Academy of Child and Adolescent Psychiatry*, 50(12), 1220–1235.

This article argues for evidence-based interventions for all children at risk of care or custody and presents Multisystemic Therapy (MST) as a theory of change and describes the current models of practice. It gives an overview of MST and goes through its present barriers and strengths. The barriers are identified as MST not targeting every child at risk of care, MST sites needing to be licenced and staff trained in the model, intervention being limited to three months, the case having to be closed if the young person is away from their usual carer for more than four weeks, the demanding role for MST professionals and families, staff needing to be on-call around the clock and each team having a low capacity to take cases due to low caseloads. Strengths are that it has a strong evidence base, strong empha-sis on implementation fidelity, cost savings, stresses the engagement process and is a flexible process aligned with family. Families do not feel judged or blamed, and MST is focused on the present, provides a comprehensive assessment and can work alongside social work; also, different professionals can provide the intervention and a maintenance and sustainability plan is put in place pre-discharge.

Other services

Children's centres

Children's centres and family centres are a potential source of family support offering a variety of activities and services, and may employ a wide range of staff. The range of activities and services might include parenting classes, health clinics, crèches, job advice, links with training and employment agencies, support for child minders, support for parents of children with special needs, groups and courses including self-help groups, counselling and family therapy. Over the years, there have been tensions in the focus of centres, including tension between universal and targeted services, and between direct support for families and an indirect support through community, neighbourhood and environmental development and action (Sheppard, 2012; Warren-Adamson, 2006). The working through of these tensions means that children's centres change over time and can be very different from each other in terms of their users, orientation and the activities and services they offer.

Children centres in England cater for families with younger children, and Carol attended her local centre with Raymond and Nadine when they were younger. Whether a family with young children attends a children's centre depends on a number of factors, including whether there was a centre close to them, whether it offers activities or services that fitted with their family situation and whether one or more of its members were willing to or interested in giving the centre a try. The 2010–2015 UK Coalition Government policy was to increase the focus on the 'neediest families' while still offering open access. This signalled a shift towards targeted services and potentially a move away from universal services. However, there have been issues in reaching families most in need of support. Many centres engage in outreach activities and home visiting and offer targeted groups designed to 'ease the transition from first contact, or one-to-one support in their own home, to feeling confident enough to access other services' at a centre (Barnardo's, 2011: 14).

The Evaluation of Children's Centres in England (ECCE, 2015) found that providing support to a growing number of vulnerable families while continuing to run open-access services was resulting in overstretched centre staff. The report states that 'the main conclusions from this report are that staff and managers in Children's Centres are working very hard to meet the needs of their communities. However, their overall capacity to reach those needs is by their own admission, overstretched. Staff reported an expectation of serving more families with complex needs with reduced agency input and without the specialist qualifications to meet such needs.'

Mediation

Conflicts and disputes within families, and those with family outsiders, can generate family strain, for example, the conflict between Simon and Carol, and the dispute between the Tomlinson family and other families in the neighbourhood and conflicts between Raymond and his fellow pupils. Mediation is an approach to resolving conflicts and disputes that involves an impartial independent mediator sitting down with both parties and helping them achieve an agreement that both sides are happy with. It is a non-confrontational method of resolving conflict, particularly relevant when there is a continuing relationship between the disputants (Liebmann, 2000: 9). The idea is to facilitate negotiation and reach an agreement that is mutually beneficial to both parties. Underpinning the process is the belief that people have the capacity to find their own solutions if provided with a safe environment that encourages the sharing of responsibility (Griffiths, 2013: 175).

Liebmann (2000: 10, citing Moore, 1986) identifies a continuum of dispute resolution methods, ranging from avoidance to aggression, with negotiation, mediation, arbitration and litigation in-between. She identifies mediation as the least interventionist of the dispute resolution methods that involve a third party. This is because the intervention by the third party is limited, and the decision-making remains with the parties themselves. Mediation takes place in a wide variety of contexts, and the most relevant to the Tomlinson family situation include 'family mediation' to support separated families, 'peer mediation' to resolve disputes between pupils in schools and 'community mediation' to resolve neighbourhood disputes. It is open to question whether Simon and Carol using a family mediation service, at the time of their separation, to reach agreement would have prevented unresolved post-divorce parenting issues reverberating through family relationships over the past five years. In her study of divorcing parents using court mediation in Israel, Cohen (2012: 227) found reaching agreement, as opposed to not reaching agreement, reduced inter-parental hostility but did not change parental behaviour.

Parenting programmes

A practitioner may suggest that Raymond's parents attend a parenting programme to increase their parenting skills and confidence. Parenting programmes single out parenting skills and confidence as the target of intervention, and usually consist of evidence-based, standardised, off-the-shelf manualised activities, often but not always delivered in organised classes (see, for example, Hutchings et al., 2008; Sturrock et al., 2014). Two of the best-known programmes that are used and researched internationally are 'The Incredible Years' programme developed in the USA (Webster-Stratton, 1989) and the positive parenting programme (Triple P) developed in Australia (Sanders et al., 2000). Programme developers have designed a multiple-component programme that addresses more than one area of need. These have tended to be more effective than single-component designs that focus solely on parental behaviour (Moran and Ghate, 2005: 333). Non-completion of programmes is a major problem, which programme evaluation research does not always take into account when interpreting findings. Completion rates vary and are considerably less than 100%, for example, Fox and Holtz (2009: 188) refer to completion rates of 43%, 50% and 67%. One issue in non-completion is the inappropriate use of parenting programmes to address the difficulties of families experiencing a wide range of complex problems, when this is something programme developers did not design their programme to do.

Whittaker and Cowley (2012: 140) make the point that 'for programmes to stand a chance of working it is logical that at the very least parents need first to attend and second to engage in the sessions'. For programmes to be successful, those organising and delivering the programme need to identify how to get parents to attend, keep them attending and engage them in the course material (Whittaker and Cowley, 2012: 144). Researchers find that parents generally welcome these types of programme, but there is a significant proportion who either drop out or whose difficulties remain entrenched despite having completed the programme (Moran and Ghate, 2005: 331). These parents tend to live in poverty and experience associated issues such as poor housing, social isolation and marital conflict, suffer poor physical or mental health and have children who have behavioural and emotional problems at the more severe end of the spectrum. Equally, some ethnic minority families and fathers are hard to recruit and retain.

Whittaker and Cowley (2012: 140) identify factors that might predict parents' response to a programme, including 'structural barriers' that parents experience as real events blocking access, 'perceptual barriers' that concern how parents perceive the programme, and 'programme factors' concerning how parents experience the content and delivery of the programme. Structural barriers include inconvenient timing, busy personal schedule, home-to-venue distance and provision of childcare. Perceptual barriers include perceiving a programme as not relevant, too demanding and being more of a burden than help. Programme factors include staff not being clear about the programme's theoretical base. Whittaker and Cowley (2012: 145) argue that there needs to be a proactive stance on improving programme take-up, and suggest that it starts at referral but preferably sooner. When there are links between programmes and broader family support services, workers can work with parents on perceptual barriers and identify structural barriers such as lack of transport.

Short breaks

Borenstein and McNamara (2015: 51) point out that there is no universally accepted definition of 'short breaks' but propose 'a short term alternative care arrangement that assists in supporting and maintaining the caring role'. Short breaks can take many forms, including one-off or regular planned stays with another family and one-off relief care in a family crisis. Agencies use a variety of names for the service, including support breaks, support foster care, support care, family link placements, relief care and respite care (Roberts, 2015a). Roberts (2015b: 13) points to the lack of meaningful and practical support to families and highlights regular breaks with family support as an example of meaningful concrete support for families in a context where there is a dearth of practical supportive interventions available to workers.

Children may stay with 'wider family' members or other social-network members, when they are available and willing, and local authorities and voluntary agencies may link families with foster parents. A distinction needs to be made between short breaks being provided purely to give parents some relief from their caring role, a service generally only offered to parents of disabled children, and short breaks offered with the expectation of family change (Roberts, 2015a). The latter is usually strictly time-limited and is accompanied by a plan for parents to make constructive and purposeful use of time away from their caring responsibilities to bring about positive changes. In this way, short breaks can benefit the whole family, including the child, their siblings and their parent/s, but in some circumstances can exasperate existing problems. Barriers to the provision of short breaks include fears of such arrangements promoting dependency or them becoming long-term, limited availability and strict eligibility policies to ration a scarce resource. No matter what form and who provides the shorts breaks, a well-thought-through plan needs to accompany them.

Sheppard's (2004) study of social support work carried out by workers in relation to depressed mothers found the only statistically significant intervention associated with more adequate support was 'relief care' for children. Outcome research of short breaks is relatively scarce, but generally finds positive outcomes. Aldgate and Bradley's (1999: 141) study of the outcomes of short breaks found that 81% of the placements in all four agencies ended as planned or were continuing satisfactorily by the end of the study. Of the 11 which ended prematurely, only two were categorised as failures by workers, in that they did not prevent breakdown and they needed to accommodate the children. Whether the whole Tomlinson family household would benefit from Raymond and his mother having short breaks from each other for a period depends on a number of factors, including the meanings Carol and Raymond place on this suggestion and the use they make of the periods apart.

Chapter Key Points

1. Workers can employ supportive interventions to help families solve problems, make decisions and take actions to resolve their difficulties.

2. An ecological theory provides a framework for developing concurrent interventions in different domains of reality and a theory of change.

3. Practical and concrete support in relation to families' material environments is a neglected and important intervention in supporting families.

4. There are interventions specifically focused on the family group, including FGCs, family therapy, family meetings and family tasks.

5. There are specific models of intervention, for example, crisis intervention, the Homebuilders Model, Brief Solution Focused Therapy and Multisystemic Theory, that can potentially support families.

6. The provision and utilisation of family support services, such as children's centres, mediation, parenting programmes and short breaks have an important role to play in supporting families.

Reflective Exercises

1. Do you think it is practical for workers to intervene in the material context of families, for example, help them improve their income and housing conditions? Explain your reasoning.

2. What do you think are the best ways of improving family relationships? If it helps, think of the Tomlinson family.

3. What would be the challenges for family members and workers in using the services outlined in the last section of this chapter? Choose one service if you wish.

Putting into Practice

Think about the Tomlinson family and the difficulties they face, or another family you know that faces challenges. Place their difficulties within an ecological framework and identify which domains could usefully have attention and what models of intervention multi-professional and multi-agency teams could employ.

Identify some challenges that workers face in adopting an ecological approach to supporting families.

Pick one of the models of intervention identified in this chapter and describe its main features and how workers could implement it in a family supportive way.

Further Resources

Fox, S. and Ashmore, Z. (2014) 'Multisystemic Therapy as an intervention for young people on the edge of care', *British Journal of Social Work*, Advance Publication, 1–17.

In this article Fox and Ashmore present current models of practice with young people on the edge of care and puts forward Multisystemic Therapy (MST) as an evidence-based theory of change. They give a good overview of its main features, including its barriers and strengths.

Holland, S. and Rivett, M. (2008) '"Everyone started shouting": Making connections between the process of family group conferences and family therapy practice', *British Journal of Social Work*, 38(1), 21–38.

This article presents the findings of a qualitative study of 17 FGCs in Wales. It focuses on the reported communications between family members during private family time.

Krumer-Nevo, M., Monnickendam, M. and Weiss-Gal, I. (2009) 'Poverty-aware social work practice: a conceptual framework for social work education', *Journal of Social Work Education*, 45(2), 225–242.

Krumer-Nevo and colleagues are very critical of the ways poverty is treated as a rather vague, almost marginal, factor in social work education and go on to explain a conceptual framework of poverty-aware practice for teaching and learning 'poverty' on social work courses.

McLeod, A. (2012) 'What research findings tell social workers about family support' in D. Davies (ed) *Social Work with Children and Families*, Basingstoke: Palgrave Macmillan, 53–73.

In this chapter Alison McLeod discusses and evaluates the evidence from the findings of research into family support. She covers parenting programmes, direct interventions with children, prompting access to finance and services.

Roberts, L. (2015b) 'Using part-time fostering as a family support service: advantages, challenges and contradictions', *British Journal of Social Work*, Advance Publication, 1–17.

This article examines the use of regular short breaks, accompanied by family support work, as a means of supporting families. Louise Roberts bases the article on a qualitative study of 10 families who receive such a service. The article highlights many broader issues of supporting families.

CHAPTER 6

WORKING COLLABORATIVELY

CHAPTER OVERVIEW

This chapter

- Points out that there are different degrees of working together.
- Explains how collaboration involves individuals from different professions, agencies or specialisms working together on the same project or case.
- Stresses the importance and challenges of family members participating in interprofessional collaboration.
- Discusses the role shared theoretical frameworks can have in achieving effective collaboration.
- Examines how effective communication requires workers to have a 'communication mindset'.
- Identifies a number of factors that facilitate or hinder effective collaboration.
- Considers how interprofessional network members can work as a team.

Introduction

It is not uncommon for a number of workers, agencies and services to be involved in supporting a family. For example, child welfare concerns rarely occur in isolation from other issues and require both interprofessional collaboration and inter-agency cooperation. It may not be easy for members of the professional network to imagine how family members experience having so many workers involved with them. Workers need to have in mind that families can find the experience daunting, chaotic and exhausting, and there is a need for interprofessional teams and networks to achieve a balance between 'too many cooks spoil the broth' and 'many hands make light work' (Morris et al., 2015: 8). It is widely accepted that those involved need to work together in a coordinated way for the benefit of the family and its members. This chapter will use the term 'collaboration' to denote workers working closely together on a particular case in a joined-up way. Collaboration can occur in loosely connected networks of workers who come from different agencies, or a team of workers within a common agency structure with common goals and common decision-making processes.

It is important to clarify that there are two levels of collaboration: lower-level collaboration between front-line practitioners and higher-level collaboration between agencies. The main focus of this chapter is inter-professional collaborative practice between front-line practitioners working on a particular case; however, inter-agency relationships are a very important context within which this practice takes place. The focus on joint casework with a particular family means that important front-line issues, like how referrals between agencies are dealt with, will not be directly addressed, save for the recognition that inter-agency relations is an important context of interprofessional practice.

The Ward family

The Ward family household consists of Danielle (12 years old) and Martin (8 years old), who live with their mother, Kim (28 years old). Other members of the family are their non-resident father, Ian (27 years old) with whom the children have contact, and their maternal grandmother, Susan (49 years old), and maternal great-grandmother, Edith (71 years old). The maternal grandfather and maternal great-grandfather died some time ago and the family have no contact with the paternal grandparents. Danielle takes on a caring role in respect of her mother who has poor mental health and suffers from depression. Danielle also does a considerable amount of looking after her younger brother and makes supportive visits to her great-grandmother who has physical disabilities. Susan, the children's maternal grandmother, helps out when she can but is struggling with her own life. Their father, Ian, is of little help and having difficulty in looking after himself. Danielle and Martin are absent occasional days from school but are doing reasonably well. At school Danielle feels left out and different and unable to make friends. The family rent a house from a local housing association and are experiencing problems with a neighbour who torments Kim for relying on her daughter to carry out her responsibilities.

This chapter is about professionals collaborating with each other to support the Ward family. Members of the family have contact with a good number of professionals including Fatima, family social worker, Jason, young carer project worker, Paulina, school pastoral worker, and Karl, adult mental health social worker, who form the core collaborative network team. A housing officer, adult care social worker, psychiatrist and general practitioner are part of the wider network working with the family.

This chapter concerns interprofessional practice, and a brief clarification of the terminology used in this field is required.

Thylefors, Persson and Hellström (2005) use the term 'cross-professional teamwork' as a generic phrase to cover different types of team. There are three terms frequently used to describe different types of cross-professional team: multi-professional, interprofessional and transprofessional. Thylefors, Persson and Hellström (2005: 104) explain that '"Multi" as a prefix to professional or disciplinary simply announces that several or many professionals are involved but tells nothing about the work process. "Inter", on the other hand, denoting between, among, reciprocal or together indicates a type of collaboration. "Trans", meaning across and beyond, refers in this context to the professional roles'. D'Amour et al. (2005: 120) describe the transprofessional team as 'a type of professional practice in which consensus-seeking and the opening up of professional territories play a major role. As a result, boundaries become blurred or vanish. A transdisciplinary team is characterised by a deliberate exchange of knowledge, skills and expertise that transcend traditional discipline boundaries'. The focus in this chapter is interprofessional teamwork, in which workers from different professions and specialisms, who can be from different agencies, work together on the same case.

Working together

The case scenario identifies eight workers and seven agencies working with the Ward family. The workers would most effectively support the Ward family if they all took a whole family focus in carrying out their roles and tasks and worked collaboratively together. However, professionals do not always find working together easy, with an understandable tendency for each worker to focus on 'their client' and align themselves with them. In their research into professional responses to families with adult mental health and child care needs, Stanley et al. (2003) found that 90% of the professional workers showed a lack of whole family perspective when they agreed that they saw it as their task to advocate on behalf of a particular family member. Devaney (2008: 251) found that the majority of 28 experienced child welfare professionals interviewed cited the need for better working relationships between children's services, adult mental health and addictions services, and had the perception that adult service workers identified their role as being solely about their adult patient/service user, on whose behalf they often advocated.

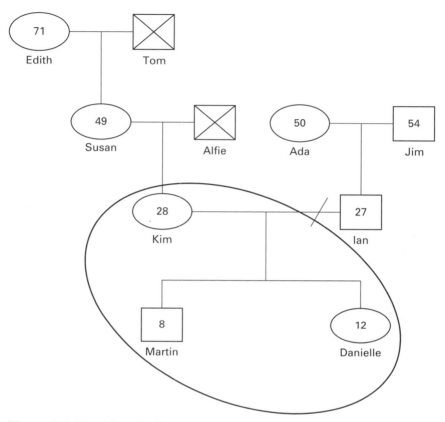

Figure 6.1 Ward Family Genogram

Degrees of working together

There is no agreed language to denote varying degrees of different professional workers working together; however, there is a spectrum of ways of working in an interprofessional context, with complete isolation at one end and working as a highly integrated team member at the other. D'Amour et al. explain as follows:

> At one end of the spectrum, professionals intervene on an autonomous or parallel basis, thus creating a *de facto* parallel practice. At the other end of the spectrum, professions have a narrower margin of autonomy but the team as a whole is more autonomous and its members are better integrated.

(2005: 120)

In the case scenario there are two arrangements for working together operating: the loosely connected network of the nine identified workers and a closer core network consisting of family social worker, adult mental health social worker, school pastoral coordinator and young carer project worker who meet together and endeavour to work as a team. Two members of the network are members of the Community Mental Health Team (CMHT), a co-located single agency multi-professional team, which consists of community psychiatric nurses, adult psychiatrists, adult mental health social workers and clinical psychologists. The particular focus of this chapter is the core network of four professionals working together on a particular case. When the work with the Ward family is complete the exact grouping may not come to work together again, so the network's life is limited and focused on a particular project.

Working collaboratively

Collaboration is a type of professional practice in which professionals work together on the same project. The term has the connotation that those collaborating do not normally work together, as they are members of different professions and/or from different agencies. Collaboration is required when a single professional or a number of professionals working in isolation are unlikely to be effective in achieving the support required. As Darlington, Feeney and Rixon state,

> Collaboration enables the bringing together of knowledge, skills and values of different professions and agencies to generate creative solutions for ... families who would otherwise be beyond the scope of any one worker or agency'.
>
> (2005: 239)

Collaboration is an activity that requires particular working-together attributes, including collaborative skills, knowledge and values, some of which are similar to those required to support families. These include interpersonal skills, knowledge of group, team or network dynamics, appreciating different perspectives and valuing the opinions of others.

The Ward family are experiencing multiple issues, including Danielle facing the challenges of being a young carer, Martin facing similar issues at school as his sister, particularly name-calling and teasing, one parent experiencing mental distress and the other proving to be largely ineffective, poor relations with their neighbours and a great-grandmother living on her own with physical disabilities. The workers collaborating with each other will bring the knowledge, skills and values of different professions and agencies to effectively support the family. The way services are organised and the specialist skills required mean a number of workers are involved with the Ward family and if the workers do not work closely with each other, family members will experience a fragmented, disjointed, contradictory and ineffective service. If they join together in a collaborative project to support the Ward family, with a joint coordinated plan to achieve agreed goals, the workers greatly increase the chances of successful supportive intervention.

Involvement of family members

There is a danger that a professional collaborative project excludes family members, whereas the aim should be family members being active members. With the exception of the family social worker, each member of the interprofessional network is likely to have the most contact with a *particular* family member and the core network team are likely to need to meet together to engage in interprofessional discussion. However, family members are unlikely to achieve participation through their attendance at such meetings, shown to be dominated by interprofessional talk (Hall and Slembrouch, 2001: 145; Bolin, 2015). It might be better for the interprofessional network to meet together to engage in interprofessional discussion and in a separate meeting meet with family members at which the dominant talk is between family members and professionals. So from time to time Fatima, Jason, Paulina and Karl meet with Kim, Danielle and Martin to review the family situation and the family support plan so that they all can work together.

Achieving effective interprofessional collaboration is difficult enough, let alone joint collaboration between family members and the professional workers. To achieve such collaboration, workers need to see family members as active participants in a collaborative project rather than as passive recipients. In theory this should be easier to achieve when there are no serious concerns about a child's safety; however, a good number of barriers still exist. At the beginning of contact each family member of the Ward family, in their own way, was highly suspicious of the various workers collaborating with each other. Over time a level of trust and respect between professionals and family members has developed, allowing for open communication and discussion in meetings. Workers earned this trust and respect through initial patient engagement work with family members. As well as respecting other workers' expertise, the workers had

---

Research Focus

Bolin, A. (2015) 'Children's agency in interprofessional collaborative meetings in child welfare work', *Child and Family Social Work*, Advance Publication.

Danielle has no trouble taking a full part in the meetings with the core network team but this is by no means typical. Martin is more typical; he remains very quiet. Anette Bolin reports on a Swedish study of how children exert influence in meetings involving collaborating professionals. Researchers interviewed 28 children who were in receipt of social support services. The findings reveal that the children perceive professionals' talk and language as restricting their opportunities to contribute to meetings. The children believed they had the capacity to exercise agency in three ways: first, conforming to expectations and feigning boredom and seeming disengaged, but at the same time paying close attention to what is being said; second, using exit strategies to exist the meeting, like simply leaving the room; and third, by staying and using strategies to speed up the end of the meeting, for instance, by asking if it was over. She stresses that practitioners need to look beyond the surface behaviours of children at meetings and adopt a bilateral, opposed to unilateral, approach to relations with children. This entails having conversations *with* children rather than talking *at* them.

---

respect for the expertise of family members, who are the only participants with lived experience of the Ward family life. Each worker made explicitly clear that they would be exchanging information, communicating with each other and collaborating together to support the family effectively.

Shared theoretical frameworks

One thing that can facilitate professional workers effectively collaborating with each other is holding a common overarching theoretical framework. There are several such frameworks that the interprofessional network members could potentially share. The previous chapter discussed the ecological framework (Bronfenbrenner, 1979) as a theory that workers can use to combine specific interventions and that provides a theory of change. It can also provide a common framework for interprofessional network members to connect their different approaches and roles in supporting the Ward family. Another potential framework is the biopsychosocial model of mental distress (Pilgram, 2002), which can reconcile the mental health social worker's and adult psychiatrist's different approaches to Kim's mental health difficulties. The biopsychosocial model of mental distress constructs the origins and recovery of mental health problems in terms of an interplay between biological, psychological and social factors. Here, we discuss a 'family perspective' and 'social exchange theory' as providing potential common frameworks for the interprofessional network members to work together to support the Ward family.

Family perspective

Workers can increase the chances of overcoming barriers to effective collaboration by adopting a whole family perspective. However, there is a danger that each worker narrowly focuses on 'their client' and the issues they face within their area of expertise. Such a single-minded focus makes working collaboratively more difficult, which in turn makes it harder to support a family effectively. For example, many of the interventions for adult family members affected by mental health issues tends to focus on only one member of the family. Adult mental health agencies tend to focus on the parent with mental health problems, while child welfare services focus on the child (Reupert, Green and Maybery, 2008: 39). Walter and Petr (2000: 494) argue that successful inter-agency collaboration requires commitment to a shared value base and that family-centred principles provide an appropriate framework. Each worker would see 'their client' as a member of their family and understand their predicament within a family context. This would mean understanding 'their clients' issues as embedded within family relationships, living conditions and family ecology, and recognising that plans to support the individual family member and resolving issues affecting them had to be set within these contexts. If each worker, no matter what profession or area of expertise, held this perspective, it would provide a common framework within which to collaborate with others.

Research Focus

Maybery, D., Reupert, A. and Goodyear, M. (2015) 'Goal setting in recovery: families where a parent has a mental illness or dual diagnosis', Child and Family Social Work, 20(3), 354–363.

Maybery, Reupert and Goodyear (2015) give recognition to how the mental health specialism has not always commonly acknowledged the parenting role and contribution to family life of adults with mental health issues. They explain how mental health teams can adopt a family perspective and outline a 'family recovery planning model' that explicitly incorporates the individual's parenting role and their involvement in family life. Examples of some of the goals are for the parent to support children going to school, put aside money for family activities and demonstrate respect and an ability to negotiate with children. The educational programmes for children of parents with mental health issues described by Reupert and Maybery (2010) are examples of adult mental health services taking a family perspective. Such programmes aim to increase the child's understanding of their parent's mental health problems, and address the young person's misconceptions and issues of self-blame.

Social exchange

Some knowledge of social exchange theory can also help workers understand that successful collaboration between members of different professions, specialisms or agencies at least partly depends on successful exchanges. The theory is concerned with the exchange of resources between people and the development of good working relationships. Cropanzano and Mitchell (2005: 890), in their helpful review from which this section draws, explain that 'social exchange comprises actions contingent on the rewarding reactions of others, which over time provide for mutually and rewarding transactions and relationships'.

When viewed through the lens of social exchange theory, interprofessional collaboration involves participants exchanging 'information', 'ideas' and 'services'. If a member of an interprofessional network shares important information or offers to provide a service, this might be accompanied by an *expectation* that others will reciprocate, if not straight away, at some unspecified time in the future. In addition, those receiving the information or benefiting from the provision of the service might feel a sense of *obligation* to reciprocate in some unspecified way in the future.

Social exchange is characterised by a norm of reciprocity, a standard of how one should behave and those who follow the norm feel obliged to return a benefit. If parties abide by the 'norms' of exchange, social exchange relationships evolve over time into trusting, loyal and mutual commitments. When Karl responds positively to Jason's request for help in Danielle gaining a greater understanding of her mother's mental health problems, Jason feels a sense of obligation to reciprocate at some unspecified point in the future. When Karl gives his positive response, he had an expectation that Jason or another member of the network would reciprocate at some point in the future. If in the future Karl asks for help from Fatima but her agency is unable to provide it, this could be a source of resentment and conflict.

The source of motivation to participate in social exchange is both internal to the person and voluntary, so more likely to result in the development of positive working relationships. However, interprofessional work is not context-free and external factors can have a negative impact (Farmakopoulou, 2002: 52). For instance, when a third party, like upper management, requires professionals to collaborate, the motivation is external and involuntary and so less likely to lead to positive working relationships. Resource scarcity can result in the pursuit of self-interest, causing conflict, negotiation and bargaining rather than social exchange (Farmakopoulou, 2002: 53). Social exchange theory, based on principles of reciprocity, is different from these negotiated exchanges which incite more use of power and less equality, while reciprocal exchange engenders better working relationships and the development of more trusting relationships.

Interprofessional communication

Members of the interprofessional network need to effectively communicate across professional boundaries if they are going to work successfully together to support the Ward family. For instance, Fatima and the adult care social worker need to communicate effectively with one another

Research Focus

McLean, S. (2012) 'Barriers to collaboration on behalf of children with challenging behaviours: a large qualitative study of five constituent groups', *Child and Family Social Work*, 17(4), 478–486.

This study highlights the dynamics of information exchange and shows how poor interprofessional relationships have a negative impact in social exchange within an interprofessional network. McLean (2012: 482) researched the experiences of a diverse group of workers who work with children in out-of-home care, including teachers, foster parents, child welfare workers, child mental health professionals and residential workers. Her thematic analysis of qualitative data revealed four tensions that she argues are inherent in collaborative work: attitudes towards others' knowledge and approach, power imbalances, tensions in information exchange and resourcing. She reports that one of the central ways in which workers played out issues of power were in the dynamics of information exchange. There were times when workers did not volunteer important information and waited until other workers sought it, and other times when they actively withheld information.

around the level of support Danielle can give her great-grandmother. Reder and Duncan (2003: 84) consider communication 'as a person-to-person activity in which individuals speak, write, and gesture or otherwise attempt to convey messages to each other'. Interprofessional collaboration requires, at a very basic level, that workers have some sort of contact throughout the life of the case. No matter what form this contact takes, communication is an interpersonal process that involves sending and receiving of messages. As explained in Chapter 4, effective communication, requires the receiver of a message to give a similar meaning to that intended by the sender. Opportunities for misinterpretation are great. Messages contain both factual information contained in words, and emotional information contained in an array of nonverbal and non-vocal features including body language, tone of voice, tone of writing and facial expressions. The crucial point is that the receiver needs to interpret the message, that is, infer or construct meaning, and a host of factors can impact on that construction, including the context in which the communication episode takes place.

Reder and Duncan (2003) say that for successful communication to occur, workers need to develop a 'communication mindset'. This entails a degree of reflectiveness, with parties being mindful of communication as an interpersonal process in which they need to construct messages in a way that the receiver can accurately interpret the sender's intended meaning, and when receiving messages from others, being mindful that they need to engage in an interpretation process within which there is a constant danger of misunderstandings occurring. Face-to-face communication gives more opportunity for parties to monitor mutual understanding, as the message sender can monitor the reaction of the 'message receiver' to check whether they have interpreted the message accurately. Indirect communication, like messages taken by third parties and other forms of non-face-to-face communication or some form of textual communication such as letters, text messages or emails, do not have nonverbal cues of face-to-face communication to help receivers interpret the message, and therefore such messages require particular precision and an absence of ambiguity.

The contexts in which communication occurs can influence how people construct and interpret messages. Members of interprofessional networks belong to different professions/specialities and have different home agencies that form a multilayered context within which interprofessional communication takes place. This context forms a lens through which workers approach collaborative work and impacts on how messages are constructed and interpreted (Reder and Duncan, 2003: 82). This includes the working practices of the worker's home agency, its prevalent belief systems and degree of support provided. A worker's usual working practices, belief systems and the degree and kind of support they receive can facilitate or hinder effective communication depending on whether or not these contexts are orientated around good interprofessional practices. Workers also bring with them professional ideologies and personal beliefs that, depending on their content, can hinder or facilitate effective communication. There are differences in the core interprofessional network about Danielle's caring role in the family. These differences have the potential to positively contribute to discussions or result in negative conflict.

Facilitating and hindering factors

Researchers and theorists have identified a number of factors, the presence and absence of which workers believe facilitate or hinder effective collaboration. Darlington, Feeney and Rixon (2005: 241) found that workers believed four sets of factors assisted effective collaborative process: communication factors, knowledge factors, role clarity, and resource

Research Focus

White, S. and Featherstone, B. (2005) 'Communicating misunderstanding: multi-agency work as social practice', *Child and Family Social Work*, 10(3), 207–216.

This article reflects on the findings of an ethnographic study of interprofessional communication and social relations in an integrated child health service, during and after the relocation of different parts of the service to a single site. White and Featherstone (2005: 207) found that workers had taken-for-granted robust professional identities and engaged in 'the kinds of professional narratives that maintain ritualised ways of working and reinforce professional boundaries' which hindered collaborative work. Their conclusion is that co-location does not straightforwardly lead to more or better communication, but proximity did make practices of others more visible. They argue that professionals cannot communicate with proper openness to other professionals, while professional narratives that maintain ritualised ways of working remain underexplored. They argue managers and workers need to find ways whereby everyday practices are open to scrutiny and challenge, while not creating the condition for indecision.

factors. This section will briefly discuss a selection of factors concerned, namely workers' knowledge of and respect for other professions, network dynamics and power imbalances, management of conflict, inter-agency relations, and resources.

Knowledge of and respect for other professions

There is always the danger that workers fall back on stereotypes and have negative attitudes towards other professions; however, a facilitating factor for interprofessional collaboration is workers having basic knowledge and appreciation of the other professionals' practice areas. Suter et al. (2009: 41) found that the 60 health care professionals in their individual and group interviews identified two core competences for effective collaborative practice: (i) appreciating professional roles and responsibilities of others and (ii) effective communication. They see the absence of appreciation of the role, knowledge and skills of other professions as a hindrance to the development of collaborative practice. If Fatima, the family social worker, lacked basic knowledge of mental health she would not be able to engage in effective interprofessional communication with Karl, the adult mental health social worker. Equally, to effectively participate in the interprofessional project to support the Ward family, all the workers will need confidence in their own professional identity and expertise. This includes being clear about their own role, responsibilities and boundaries as well as that of the other workers.

Sloper (2004: 576) also found respecting and valuing each other's knowledge, professional identity, role and expertise, alongside positive attitudes towards collaborative work, as important facilitating factors for collaborative practice. This involves workers being able to appreciate 'difference' in terms of professional cultures and values. As previously discussed, workers sharing a family perspective and appreciating the importance of family participation may help workers work across these differences. Initially there may be a lack of trust; however Horwath and Morrison (2007: 64) point to the emergence of trust between network members as an important ingredient for successful collaborative practice, including workers having a belief and expectation that other members will carry out agreed tasks.

Network dynamics and power imbalances

Interprofessional networks are connected but geographically dispersed sets of individuals, and, like other human groups, they have particular dynamics that develop over time. Network members relate and interact with each other in particular ways, creating specific group dynamics and interpersonal relationships that impact either positively or negatively on collaborate processes and outcomes. Network dynamics include the ways members communicate with each other, their emotional connections and the forces acting between them. Like with family relationships, we can analyse networks in terms of dyadic relationships between two members, triadic relationships between sets of three members or whole group dynamics, including processes such as scapegoating and the formation of coalitions and alliances. One of the main issues identified by those critical or cautious of greater collaborative work between professionals is its potential to increase the power of professionals to control families and keep them under surveillance rather than support them. The concern is that the combined power of professionals working together can be used for or have the unintended effect of subjecting families to greater control (Smith and Anderson, 2008: 763). In effect, the argument is that working together can result in 'collusive power' rather than 'cooperative power' (Tew, 2006).

It should not be surprising if 'differences of opinion' about the case occur within interprofessional networks, where members belong to different professions, have different specialist knowledge and skills, and work for different agencies. The existence of different perspectives and opinions is one of the benefits of collaborative work and 'uniformity of view' is a potential hazard. It is the ways members manage and respond to such differences that determine whether they enhance or hinder collaborative practice. Differences of opinion can have an important role in developing deeper understandings of families and developing well-thought-through interventions. As stated by Abramson and Mizrahi (1996: 279), 'whereas similar perspectives can facilitate working relationships, optimum collaboration occurs when interprofessional interaction adds previously unrecognised perspectives or additional options to resolving the situation at hand'.

From time to time issues occur within the core interprofessional network, around balancing the sometimes seemingly conflicting needs of parents and children. To move forward, group dynamics need to create a climate in which reasoned discussion can take place and participants listen to each other, work towards deeper understandings of the situation and develop ways forward. Some members of the interprofessional network hold the dominant view of young carers like Danielle having too much responsibility for her age and that her caring role is depriving her of her childhood (O'Dell et al., 2010). Others hold a more nuanced view of caring not being a wholly negative experience for children. They would recognise that Danielle does not view herself as a tragic victim of circumstances and wants to care for her family. It gives her a sense of agency and the opportunity to gain skills and fulfil felt obligations to brother and mother. They would judge that Danielle was managing to balance her caring duties with her education and social life outside her family.

Management of conflict

Payne (2000, cited in Brown et al., 2011: 5) differentiates between two sources of conflict within teams: substantive issues to do with the case and interpersonal/emotional issues to do with relations between workers. Differences of opinion about substantive issues to do with the case have the potential to develop into covert or overt conflict; however, interpersonal/emotional issues between workers have greater potential of developing into tension and conflict. Leever et al. (2010) developed a conceptual model of the sources of such conflicts and their management. In their research they found that each of the participants developed clear expectations of how colleagues should behave in a situation of collaboration. Adapting their model somewhat, conflict or friction between team members occurs when a worker perceives another as not meeting their expectations of collaborative practice. These expectations fall into five categories: effective communication, mutual respect, professionalism, good working-together manner and competent practice. The weight given to each expectation varies from person to person, and workers may vary in what they perceive as 'good collaboration'. When the other worker does not meet their expectations, the worker with the expectations can either ignore the violation or engage with it. If they engage with the conflict, they will either directly or indirectly confront the violating worker.

If they deal with the conflict *indirectly* they ask a third party to intervene; if they deal with the conflict *directly* they can adopt one of two conflict management styles. The first is 'discussing' the issue with the other person, the second is 'forcing' the issue by making clear what their position is, in such a way that there is little room left for the opinion of the other person. Whether it is best to avoid or engage conflict is not a question Leever et al. (2010) address, but they do identify five categories of factors which play a role in participants choice of 'engaging' or 'avoiding' conflict. These are 'factors of self', like personality, self-confidence, level of knowledge and experience;

'characteristics of the other person', like their personality, attitude, expertise and experience; 'nature of the conflict', its seriousness and urgency, whether violation is isolated or part of a pattern; 'context of the conflict', factors linked to the moment and atmosphere in which the conflict arises; and 'personal motives', whether it is improving collaboration, avoiding escalation, changing practices or creating learning opportunities.

Inter-agency relations

An important context for interprofessional work at the field level is inter-agency relations at management levels. However, it does not automatically determine what happens on the ground between practitioners, as there can be instances of effective interprofessional collaboration with families when inter-agency relations at the management level are poor or non-existent. Likewise, there can be instances of poor levels of joint-working between front-line practitioners even when there are good levels of cooperation between agencies at a higher level. However, good working relations between agencies are an important enabling factor in interprofessional collaboration. Practical ways agency management can work together to promote joint-working between practitioners include negotiating joint protocols; providing sufficient time and services; and joint training events and programmes.

Joint protocols can provide a practice resource, details of procedures, clarity about respective roles and lines of communication, giving workers more confidence in communicating across professional boundaries. They can promote a family perspective and, for instance, greater understanding of the interrelation between parental mental health and children's needs (Webber, McCree and Angeli, 2013). Local joint-work-based training events and programmes in interprofessional collaboration have the potential to improve the effectiveness of interprofessional collaboration (Zwarenstein, Reeves and Perrier, 2005). These can be linked to the introduction or updating of joint local protocols to promote more positive interpersonal and interprofessional relations and a collective ability to work together to support families. Copperman and Newton (2007: 147) identify the importance of developing 'collective efficacy', that is, 'the necessity of groups members to believe that the combined efforts of the group are not only necessary to obtain the desired shared goal but also that each member is capable of and willing to do their share of the work'.

Resources

Another facilitating factor is agencies providing sufficient resources to their workers, including manageable workloads, supportive supervision, time to attend meetings, family support services and training resources (Darlington, Feeney and Rixon, 2005: 243). 'Time' in particular is a vital resource for the initiation and maintenance of collaborative projects, time to work face-to-face with families and time to attend collaborative meetings. Darlington, Feeney and Rixon (2004: 1177) point out that collaboration can occur with limited resources, and sufficient resources alone do not ensure effective collaboration. However, inadequate resources or competition for the same resources can hinder both collaborative relationships and outcomes of collaborative efforts. Conflicts, disputes and ill feeling can occur within interprofessional networks when agencies do not or cannot provide their workers with sufficient resources. High workloads and poor support can mean that workers cannot meet the expectations of their interprofessional colleagues, and frequent changes in personnel disrupt collaborative work. It is frustrating for interprofessional colleagues when agencies do not provide a worker with sufficient time to attend meetings or have enough contact with family members. Ill feeling can arise when a worker cannot provide needed services or has to close cases prematurely (Harlow and Shardlow, 2006: 66).

Working as a team

The term 'team' is used in many different ways, from a grouping of people who simply carry out the same functions or cover the same geographical area, to a group of people who may have different roles but work together to achieve the team's goal. There is considerable potential overlap between the concept of teamwork and collaboration as defined above. Both apply to a group of people working closely together, but both interprofessional networks and multi-professional teams may or may not work as a 'team'. For instance, the core members of the chapter scenario network can work together as a team, while the scenario CMHT members, which has the word 'team' in its title, may not work as a team.

There is more to being a team than being organised into a group of workers. It is not uncommon for sports commentators to put a football team's defeat down to the players not working together as a team or a team's victory being due to players working well together as a team. Teamwork requires each member to know and carry out their role and to understand and appreciate the roles of other team members in achieving the team's objective. Teamworking revolves around team members having a sense of joint responsibility, a commitment to a shared purpose and developing and acting upon plans to achieve this purpose. Interprofessional networks work as a team when they move beyond information sharing to the joint analysis of the issues facing the family and sharing ideas about how to move forward.

Improving teamworking

Team effectiveness in achieving a team's objectives has been associated with a positive team climate (Thylefors, Persson and Hellström, 2005). Team climate is the shared perceptions of the conditions and atmosphere within a team. A positive team climate would include members feeling able to express their opinions freely within a supportive atmosphere of respect for differing opinions. Jones and Jones (2011) carried out a qualitative study of the introduction of a service improvement programme designed to promote better teamworking on a medical rehabilitation ward for older people. The programme introduced three changes, including relocation of the therapy workforce and social work services to the ward, introduction of weekly team meetings, and a series of staff workshops on contextual factors that enable teamworking. Four themes emerged from the study that give some insight into the development of interprofessional teamworking: the emergence of collegial trust within the team; the importance of team meetings and participative safety; the role of shared objectives in conflict management; and the value of autonomy within the team. Trust in colleagues took time to develop and entailed trusting each other's judgement and believing that other team members would do what they said they would do. It was felt that the face-to-face interaction within meetings promoted the development of trust and a feeling of being able to contribute to meetings without fear of recrimination from other team members. The existence of the shared objective of improved interprofessional teamworking focused on the patient, made the management of conflict within the team easier and, despite the development of a strong team ethos and some shared roles, individuals valued maintaining their own professional identities.

Collective preferences

Rose (2011) puts forward the concept of 'collective preferences' as useful in understanding a group of interprofessional workers successfully working together as a team. 'Collective preferences' are preferences of a 'collective' such as a team or family that are not reducible to the personal preferences of their members (Gilbert, 2001). Collective preferences involve a degree of professional self-sacrifice and having obligations to the collective. Rose (2011: 152) explains the concept of 'collective preferences' brings together 'ideas about shared purposes, joint responsibility for and commitment to these purposes, and for finding strategies to progress these purposes'. Her argument is when people manage to achieve and enact collective preferences, it indicates that they have resolved professional dilemmas in some way. She defines dilemmas as situations where there is a difficult decision because all available options have disadvantages.

Her description of these professional dilemmas and their resolution represents a move towards the development of transprofessional teamwork rather than interprofessional teamwork. She identifies three types of professional dilemmas in engaging in interprofessional collaboration that need to be resolved if interprofessional networks are to work together collaboratively. These revolve around 'role', 'identity' and 'control'. Role dilemmas concern the appropriateness of the role undertaken by an individual. Identity dilemmas are about how an individual sees themselves and how others see them. Control dilemmas centre upon professional disagreement in collaborate decision-making. According to Rose (2011: 154), when workers accept collective preferences over their own they have accepted some level of disadvantage for the sake of the team. Resolving role, identity and control dilemmas may mean adjusting to a conceptualisation of themselves as non-specialists; accepting achieving team goals may not always entail using their specialist knowledge; coming to terms with carrying roles that would traditionally fall to someone else; or coping with someone else being given disproportionate decision-making power.

Chapter Key Points

1. Professionals having contact with one or more family members need to collaborate together to effectively support the family and its individual members.

2. Professionals do not always find working together easy, with an understandable tendency for each worker to align themselves with 'their client'.

3. Members of an interprofessional network need to consider how family members can best participate in the collaboration so it becomes a joint project between professionals and family members.

▶

4. The interprofessional team using a common overarching theoretical framework can help develop effective collaborative work.

5. Professionals may find it easier to work together if each network member places their work in a whole family context.

6. Professionals working together need to develop a 'communication mindset' that entails being mindful that communication involves both the construction and interpretation of messages and that miscommunication can easily occur.

7. The presence of a number of factors can facilitate the development of effective collaboration, including members having an understanding of the other workers' practice areas, being aware of and understanding network dynamics and power relationships, and possessing the ability to positively manage conflict.

8. Teamwork involves each member knowing and carrying out their role and understanding and appreciating the roles of other team members in achieving the team's objective. The degree for teamwork within an interprofessional network can range from none to well-developed.

Reflective Exercises

1. Think of an instance of miscommunication occurring either in your personal life or work life. What reasons would you put the misunderstanding down to?

2. Social exchange theory is about expectations and obligations. Think of an instance when you felt let down by someone who did not reciprocate a favour you did for them. What effect did this have on your relationship with them?

3. Do you think there are any dangers in professional workers working closely together? If you do, explain what these dangers are, and if you do not think there are any dangers, explain why this is.

Putting into Practice

Choose a profession different from your own that you have worked with in the past or are likely to do so in the future, and research the basics of its professional role within a multi-professional team or network.

What distinctive contributions could you make to a multi-professional network or team?

What challenges do you think you face, or would face, if you were a member of a multi-professional team or network?

Further Resources

Keeping, C. (2014) 'The Processes Required for Effective Interprofessional Working' in J. Thomas, K. C. Pollard and D. Sellman (eds) *Interprofessional Working in Health and Social Care: Professional Perspectives: Second Edition*, Basingstoke: Palgrave Macmillan, 22–34.

This chapter discusses the active ingredients of collaboration under the headings knowledge, attitudes and relational skills.

McLaughlin, H. (2013) 'Motherhood, apple pie and interprofessional working', *Social Work Education*, 32(7), 956–963.

Hugh McLaughlin gives a critical commentary in which he argues that commentators on social work have framed much of the debate about interprofessional working in an uncritical and benign way.

Morrow, G., Malin, N. and Jennings, T. (2005) 'Interprofessional team working for child and family referral in a Sure Start local programme', *Journal of Interprofessional Care*, 9(2), 93–101.

This paper examines issues such as emotional impact and professional anxiety that arose in the setting up of an interprofessional Sure Start programme.

CHAPTER 7

REMAINING VIGILANT

CHAPTER OVERVIEW

This chapter

- Considers some potential errors in reasoning and thinking that can negatively impact on a worker's ability to effectively support families.
- Highlights the importance of keeping an open mind and being prepared to change one's mind when new information comes to light.
- Explores attitudes and stances needed by workers if they are to form an accurate understanding of family situations.
- Discusses the tensions between remaining vigilant and families feeling under surveillance.
- Examines the necessity for the effective management of emotions if workers are to successfully support families and cope with strong emotions.
- Stresses the importance of engaging in self-care actions and activities so as to remain resilient to the pressures of supporting families.

Introduction

This chapter concerns the tensions and challenges of workers remaining vigilant towards their own thinking, emotions, actions and behaviour when working with families. You need to read this chapter in conjunction with the following chapter, 'Supportive Supervision', as supervision has an extremely important role, among others, in promoting reflexive thinking and self-care within the worker. This chapter concerns self-vigilance which is akin to self-awareness and self-reflectiveness. It overlaps with being self-reflexive, which Chow et al. (2011: 142), drawing from the Chambers English Dictionary, take to mean 'the action of the mind by which it is conscious of its own operations'. Among other things, such vigilance entails being alert to the various cognitive biases and processes that can get in the way of forming a more accurate understanding of family situations.

The Rahman family

The Rahman Family household consists of Zahara (19 years old) and Farha (18 months old). Farha's father, Samar, left the family home soon after she was born. Zahara emigrated from Bangladesh three years ago to marry Samar. Their marriage was not a happy one, with Zahara experiencing a destructive and sometimes violent relationship with her husband. She and Farha find themselves socially isolated because of stigma and shame of being divorced, and have very little support in the UK. Zahara has telephone and internet contact with her family back in Bangladesh but they do not know about the break-up of her marriage or the conditions she is living in. She has virtually no contact with the local community, as she perceives herself as being of a higher class than other Bangladeshi families living locally. Zahara can speak and understand English to a reasonable degree and is hoping that Farha learns to speak Bengali and English. The family suffer the hardships of living in poverty and social isolation. Zahara

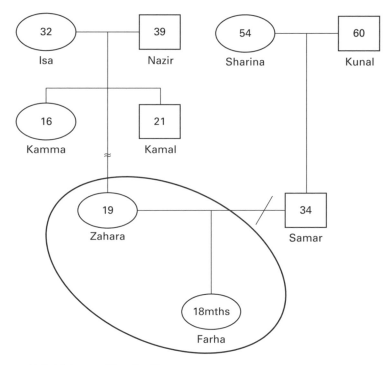

Figure 7.1 Rahman Family Genogram

has poor relationships with Farha's paternal grandparents and feels she cannot rely on them for support.

The health visitor currently has no specific concerns about Farha's care and development but has concerns about the family's living conditions and lack of support. She also has an uneasy feeling that something is not quite right in the household but cannot put her finger on it. An allocation meeting assigned the case to Afifah, a newly qualified social worker half-way through her first year in employment. She has spoken to the health visitor and visited the family once, and made an appointment to visit again when she would continue to build a working relationship with Zahara and Farha. She hopes to start working on various issues, including the distress caused by abusive telephone calls from Farha's father, poor relations with his parents, the family's poor living conditions and the lack of social support. On her first visit she found Farha playing contentedly with her bricks and Zahara being reasonably open about the difficulties she was facing but becoming momentarily very distressed about her current situation. The family were living in a cramped, dingy privately rented flat that had a very depressing feel to it. When Afifah got down on the floor to play with Farha she caught a fleeting glimpse of a change of Zahara's demeanour that hardly registered with Afifah. Afifah felt sorry for Zahara being so young in the circumstances she was living in, with a young child to look after on her own and no social support in a strange country.

Over time, Afifah will develop an understanding of the Rahman family and their situation, including the difficulties they face. She constructs the picture, starting with the referral information and allocation meeting discussion, her initial contacts with the family, including any assessments that she undertakes, and her contact with the other professionals involved with the family and discussions with her supervisor and colleagues. She knows that the family has had no previous contact with Children's Social Care and since coming to this country have always lived in the area. Coming away from her first visit, Afifah has formed an initial picture in her mind of a mother with a positive relationship with her daughter, caring for her in difficult circumstances. This chapter will look at potential errors in reasoning and thinking that could get in the way of Afifah constructing accurate understandings of the Rahman family situation. It will also discuss the attitudes and stances that can help her counteract these errors, and the effective management of her emotions and feelings so they do not get in the way of her effectively supporting families.

Errors in reasoning and thinking

Constructing a picture of the Rahman family situation will involve Afifah interpreting what she hears, sees and smells on her visits and conversations with family members. Worker self-vigilance is necessary because of the potential gaps between Afifah's understandings of the family situation and the realities. She can only construct pictures of the family situation and try to make this as accurate as possible, but these can never fully reflect the lived realities of family life. Interpretation involves putting meaning on the raw data from our senses. This is not a neutral process but involves mostly the non-conscious processing of information by the mind. Workers try and make this as a reflexive and deliberative process as possible; however, the processes are subject to potential errors in reasoning and thinking. Afifah needs to be alert to these errors, as they hold the potential of distorting her understanding of the Rahman family. This section discusses some of the pitfalls workers are vulnerable to, namely constructing superficial pictures that lack depth, clinging to beliefs despite contrary evidence, falling foul of confirmation bias, holding unjustified assumptions, being unrealistically optimistic and being a victim of the 'start again syndrome'.

Surface over depth

Afifah needs to be vigilant towards simply collecting surface information, rather than developing in-depth understandings of the Rahman family and the difficulties they face. In an influential paper published as the 20th century was drawing to a close, Howe (1996) argues that there was a new political and cultural context in which social work practice had become more shallow and concerned with the 'surface' manifestations or appearances of situations rather than their inner workings. It is an open question whether or not, over two decades later, developing countercurrents, such as ecological approaches (Jack, 2000) and relationship based practice (Ruch, Turney and Ward, 2010), have enabled workers to produce deeper understandings. There remains a danger that Afifah is content with the 'visible surface' appearance of the Rahman family and not the inner workings of its members, their relationships with each other, their family practices or the context in which they live, including their living conditions, communities and society. What is required is the development of in-depth understandings that draw from psychological and sociological theories.

In their study of family centre support, Whittaker et al. (2014: 483) quote a parent saying 'that staff need to understand their lives' and what it means 'to be a single parent living on a particular estate, responding to their children's needs and managing relationships with ex-partners and family members'. What this parent seems to be asking for is staff to develop deeper understandings of her family and life. The surface approach is not only associated with superficial descriptions of situations that lack depth of analysis, but also interventions that correspondingly only respond to the surface features of situation and not their underlying complexities. Whittaker et al. (2014: 479) explain that much of the work of the children's centre dealt with the immediate pressing needs, which was gratifying for both parent and staff and supported immediate engagement. However, staff and parents did not address the more complex family issues. Whittaker et al. (2014: 483) argue that practitioners need to work with families to 'problem solve immediate issues', while developing deeper understandings and seeking to resolve the more complex issues that family members face in their lives.

Confirmation bias

Confirmation Bias is a tendency of human beings to seek out, emphasise or interpret information in such a way that it confirms their initial impressions. Confirmation bias could affect both Afifah's interpretation of information and what type of information she seeks or selects. It is not a deliberate but a non-conscious process of selecting, seeking or interpreting information in a way that supports her existing beliefs, expectations or hypotheses (Nickerson, 1998: 175). Afifah would seek or select confirmatory information at the expense of potentially falsifying information. She would either ignore or re-interpret information that might shed some doubt on the existing hypotheses. Outsiders forming pictures of family situations might be particularly prone to this unwitting selectivity. Nickerson (1998: 192) suspects it is especially prevalent in situations that are inherently complex and ambiguous, where there are 'interactions among numerous variables, in which the cause-effect relationships are obscure, where data tends to be open to many interpretations'. There are a number of things Afifah can do to guard against confirmation bias in her picture building. According to Nickerson (1998: 211), crucial first steps are to be aware of its existence and pervasiveness, to be somewhat cautious about making up her mind quickly, to continually consider reasons why her judgements might be inaccurate and to actively seek information that does not support her current hypothesis.

Unjustified assumptions

Elder and Paul (2002: 34) define 'an inference as a step of the mind, an intellectual act, by which one concludes that something is true in the light of something else being true'. The 'something else that is true' are assumptions which are part of our belief systems. On the arranged home visit there is no answer and Afifah infers that Zahara has let their appointment slip from her mind, rather than her deliberately not answering the door or avoiding the visit in another way. She is making this inference on the assumptions that Zahara is not the kind of person that would feign being out and the doorbell is working properly. If both Afifah's assumptions are sound ones, her inference seems reasonable. The trouble is, Afifah is not explicitly conscious that she is coming to her conclusion based on assumptions. Afifah might understandably regard assumptions as a bad thing, although professional work and daily life would not be possible without making them. The inevitability of assumptions means that Afifah needs to be explicitly aware of any assumptions and inferences she makes in developing a picture of the Rahman family. She needs to check that she can convincingly justify any assumptions she is making, as it is unjustified assumptions that she needs to avoid.

Afifah, like all human beings, holds assumptions about the nature of human beings and society, and as a professional social worker will have particular theoretical predilections. These beliefs and predilections are constructs that will influence her thinking, for better or worse. Osmo (2001: 210) stresses the importance of Afifah making these assumptions explicit to herself and for her to engage in both an internal dialogue with herself and discussions with colleagues and supervisors so she and others can be explicitly clear about the positions she holds. Elder and Paul (2002: 34) explain that 'an important part of critical thinking is the art of bringing what is subconscious in our thought to the level of conscious realisation'. As will be seen in the next chapter, colleagues and supervisors asking questions like 'What is the basis of you thinking that?' can promote such critical thinking. Asking and answering such questions of ourselves promotes the reflexivity that is necessary to make explicit what is implicit. Bringing underlying assumptions and inferences to conscious thought enables the examination of their validly.

Unrealistic optimism

Optimism is a valued quality in social workers and forms part of professional culture and social work's professional identity. Generally, theorists regard 'optimism' as a positive emotion and link it to coping and resilience (Collins, 2008: 1183; Houston, 2010b: 366). However, we need to draw a distinction between the concepts of 'dispositional optimism', 'unrealistic optimism' and 'realistic optimism'. 'Dispositional optimism' is an 'enduring tendency to expect positive outcomes' (Shepperd et al. 2013: 396) and so is a personal trait. 'Unrealistic optimism' is an erroneous belief in a particular situation that a positive outcome is more likely than justified by the evidence available (Shepperd et al., 2013: 396). It involves overestimating the likelihood of a favourable future outcome and underestimating the likelihood of an unfavourable one (Bracha and Brown, 2010: 33). Family social workers need to be vigilant about being unrealistically optimistic, as well as about heeding the lesson from inquiries that when workers became optimistic about a family's progress they become slower to notice and recognise evidence that challenged their optimism (Munro, 1996: 806).

Realistic optimism is when the belief that positive outcomes are more likely is justified by the evidence available. Kearns and McArdle (2012: 387) argue for a balance between optimism and realism, which involves evaluating 'what is' against 'what could be'. They use the term 'managed optimism' for achieving an effective balance between idealism and realism within professional identity. Along a similar vein, Cree et al. (2014: 5) use the term 'critical optimism', meaning social workers need to remain optimist but in a critical way. For instance, Afifah needs a degree of justified optimism if she is to transmit hope to Zahara that things can get better, but there needs to a reasonable prospect of success. Lazarus (1991: 282) refers to hope being the antidote for despair, and if this is true, Afifah needs to transmit some hope to Zahara that her family's situation can improve. However, Afifah needs to recognise that hope is not a panacea, and without concerted action and a reasonable prospect of success it can do more damage than good.

Research Focus

Kearns, S. and McArdle, K. (2012) '"Doing it right"? – accessing the narratives of identity of newly qualified social workers through the lens of resilience: "I am, I have, I can"', *Child and Family Social Work*, 17(4), 385–394.

Kearns and McArdle found that among the prominent sources of resilience and strong identity was 'managed optimism'. Using 'narrative enquiry', they explore

▶

resilience in three newly qualified social workers in the children's services of a semi-rural area near a Scottish city. The researchers were interested in 'storying' the positive ways in which the social workers developed sustainability through resilience in first year. The authors wished to avoid using a deficit-based model of the children services role and used Grotberg's (1995) resilience framework as an analytical tool. The three dimensions of the framework are, 'I am', 'I have' and 'I can'. 'I am' concerns identity formation, 'I have' concerns supportive relationships and 'I can' concerns doing and knowing. The authors conclude that 'I am' and 'I have' were more important than the skills and knowledge dimension of 'I can'. Prominent sources of resilience and strong identity included managed optimism as well as positive role models; trust; flexibility of support; and, vitally, self-efficacy and space for reflexivity – self-efficacy in the form of a belief in their ability to achieve the intended result though collaboration with others, and reflexivity in the form of self-reflexive questioning.

Start again syndrome

One phenomenon that is unlikely to affect Afifah when working with the Rahman family is what Brandon et al. (2008a: 11) refer to as 'the start again syndrome'. Unlike many families needing support, the Rahman family do not come with a long history of contact with Children's Social Care. When there has been a long history of contact and there is a need for a new worker, either because of re-referral, staff turnover or sickness, there is a danger of the new worker being tempted with the idea of a fresh start. Brandon et al. (2008a) refer to this as the 'start again syndrome', which is particularly damaging in cases of chronic neglect, where they argue the dimension of time does not get the emphasis it needs. Children's Social Care often know families of neglected children over many years, often generations, and their family histories are complex, confusing, and often overwhelming for practitioners. One common way of dealing with overwhelming information and feelings of helplessness generated in workers by a family's long history of contact is to put aside knowledge of their past and give the family a fresh start. However, workers and their supervisors need to find other ways of coping with feelings of helplessness. Brandon et al. (2008a: 105) argue that effective and accessible supervision is crucial to help workers place a family's history within a critical, holistic and analytic understanding of the case. They emphasise that the 'start again syndrome should not be confused, however, with the benefits of a fresh perspective on a case which can allow professionals to think differently and reconsider and revise their judgements' Brandon et al. (2008a: 73).

Attitude and stance

Effectively supporting the Rahman family will partly depend on Afifah's attitude and stance towards developing an understanding of the Rahman family situation. This will include her ability to keep an open mind, have an attitude of respectful uncertainty and to maintain a whole family focus. Afifah tries to make her understanding of the Rahman family as accurate as possible, but there will always be a degree of uncertainty about its accuracy. For example, as we have seen, there are cognitive processes operating that can make it difficult for her to change her mind when new contradictory information comes to light.

Keeping an open mind

Afifah cannot rely on the fact that 'intake' has classified the case as 'child in need' requiring 'family support', as serious harm or death can occur through abuse or neglect in families not classified as needing 'child protection' (Lord Laming, 2003: para 17.106; Brandon et al., 2008b). Those working with families need to be vigilant in relation to the possibility that they have an inaccurate picture of what is happening and that a family member or members are being harmed; this is particularly true in relation to child members. There is always a possibility that there is hidden harm occurring within family situations classified as 'family support', as the classification of cases, 'family support' or 'child protection', is not an exact science and thresholds can move up and down for sociopolitical reasons. Equally, the harm caused by neglect may not be fully recognised or may be seriously underestimated.

Afifah has formed a picture of the Rahman family as Zahara being a young single mother caring for her daughter, Farha, the best she can, while being harassed by Farha's father, Samar, and many miles from her own family. Despite having this picture, she needs to keep an open mind and be prepared to adjust it or radically change it if additional information emerges that point to inaccuracies. According to Munro, one of our most pervasive biases is our tendency to cling to existing beliefs (Munro, 2008: 8). This is particularly important, as Munro's (1996) analysis of 45 inquiry reports found one persistent issue was that social workers were slow to revise their judgements.

There is a danger that Afifah's present picture of the situation becomes a prism through which she interprets what she sees and hears. Her present understanding forms a 'knowledge frame' that Goffman refers to as 'frameworks or schemata of interpretation' that are available to 'locate, perceive, identify, and label' occurrences (Goffman, 1986: 21). This is 'a cognitively available pattern used in perception in order to make sense of the perceived material by "imposing" that pattern and its known features on that material' (Ensink and Saucer, 2003: 3). Reframing involves making a conscious effort to put a different interpretation of the situation. Developing reframes or alternative hypotheses may unsettle her present comfortable thinking and help her keep an open mind.

Respectful uncertainty

If Afifah is to effectively support the Rahman family, she will need to develop trusting relationships with family members. Such relationships require a degree of mutual trust between the parties, which will include, for example, Zahara and Afifah trusting each other. However, there is a tension between Afifah remaining alert to the possibility that Zahara is not telling her the whole truth about what is going on and Afifah's need to listen to and respect Zahara's narrative of her situation. In his report on the death of Victoria Climbié, Lord Laming refers to 'respectful uncertainty' (Lord Laming, 2003: 205, para 6.602). This is in the context of accepting that while social workers are not detectives, they should not unquestioningly accept all that family members tell them. Respectful uncertainty means that Afifah would interact with Zahara in a respectful way while at the same time not unquestioningly accepting all that she says. Turney (2012: 152) discusses how workers like Afifah need to 'be skilled in developing trusting relationships with children and families while at the same time being aware that things may be other than they appear'. There is obviously tension between 'respectful uncertainty' and developing a supportive relationship, and Turney (2012: 155) talks about 'qualified trust' which acknowledges that what Zahara says and the picture she presents may be accurate but 'there may be better or equally compelling explanations'. Turney positions 'qualified trust' somewhere between an uncritical acceptance of what is said and 'a slide into cynicism'.

'Respectful uncertainty' arises from the inevitable uncertainty surrounding whether family members are telling the full story. As such, it operates in the background, in the form of keeping an open mind. Afifah needs to sensitively manage the tensions such vigilance can create if she is to form effective working alliances with family members. Developing a working alliance through empathy, listening skills and a non-judgemental stance is likely to fail if family members feel they are the objects of surveillance. Barnard and Bain (2015) carried out research into a small number of families receiving voluntary family support that included opportunities to increase oversight of families with substance-misusing parents. This was on the basis that parental substance misuse exposes the children to elevated risks of harm. However, fear of the consequences of that oversight inhibited the parents from meaningfully engaging with services. Such monitoring coupled with the power to intervene to protect children created 'resistance', with the most common form of resistance being concealment (Bloor and McIntosh, 1990: 176). In theory, we can make a distinction between 'respectful uncertainty' and having a dual agenda of support and surveillance. In practice, this distinction may be hard to maintain, but concepts like 'respectful uncertainty' and 'qualified trust' can help to positively manage the tensions involved.

Emotions and feelings

As we have seen, Afifah's thoughts and thinking are important processes in her work with the Rahman family. Equally important are her emotions and feelings. Kinman and Grant (2011: 264) state that 'the capacity to manage emotions of oneself and others effectively … is central to the role of a social worker'. This section will discuss the need for workers to be on the lookout for the following: over-emotional involvement; the avoidance of mental pain; ignoring gut feelings; the impact of personal threats; and the lack of the self-care that workers need in order to prevent burnout and emotional exhaustion.

Over-emotional involvement

Compassion is a valued quality in social workers, and qualifying social workers in England have to 'demonstrate the ability to engage with people and build, manage, sustain and conclude compassionate and effective relationships' (COSW/BASW, 2012). Compassion entails an acute awareness of the suffering of others and a desire to relieve it. For Lazarus (1991: 289), compassion involves 'feeling personal distress at the suffering of another and wanting to ameliorate it', and identifies its core relational theme as 'being moved by another's suffering and wanting to help'. Compassion for those experiencing hardship is rightly an important requirement to carry out effective social work, but there are potential negative effects of such compassion. Some workers in some situations may not be able to 'regulate their compassionate feelings and become overinvolved with another person's suffering, so much so that not only do they experience severe distress themselves, but they may be unable to offer useful help' (Lazarus, 1991: 291).

There are two aspects of this: first, an increased risk of emotional exhaustion and, second, intense feelings of wanting to help a family overriding thought and reasoning. Hordern cites O'Donovan, saying that

> Compassion is the virtue of being moved to action by the sight of suffering … It is a virtue that circumvents thought, since it prompts us to immediate action. It is a virtue that presupposes that an answer had already been found to the question 'What needs to be done?' a virtue of motivation rather than reasoning.
>
> (Hordern, 2013: 92, citing O'Donovan, 2006)

Although this variant of compassion may have little in common with the controlled compassion of social workers, it does allude to potential dangers. Koeske and Kelly (1995: 282) refer to 'detached concern' that is somewhere along 'a continuum from overinvolvement to dehumanisation' and that they say is difficult to achieve in practice. In a similar vein, one of the casework principals in Biestek's (1961) classic text is 'controlled emotional involvement', and Butrym (1976) states this involves avoiding the two dangers of over-emotional involvement and under-emotional involvement.

Avoidance of mental pain

Workers and their supervisors need to be aware of the potential operation of defence mechanisms protecting them from the mental pain involved in witnessing, thinking about or contemplating the human suffering that may be occurring within the families they are working with. Cooper (2005) refers to how inquiry reports into child deaths have on a number of occasions referred to how 'evidence for what is happening to children was both seen and not seen by professionals'. Rustin (2005) uses her reading of the Laming Report to explore why professionals working with Victoria Climbié found it impossible to see what was happening, despite the evidence being available. She observes the number of occasions that the Laming Report uses such phrases as 'if she had applied her mind to the matter' (Lord Laming, 2003: para 13.41). She points to the understandable difficulties workers had in allowing themselves to think about what might be happening because of the unavoidable anxiety and mental pain such thinking would involve. She states that 'understanding the way mental pain is faced or avoided is crucial to making sense of defensive evasion by large numbers of professionals which the report details' (Rustin, 2005: 11).

Another example of workers 'seeing but not seeing' is not taking sufficient notice of the impact of a family's living conditions on family life. The process operating could be the avoidance of the mental pain that comes with being explicitly aware of deprivation and the limitations of the material and human resources available to respond to the needs of families (Waterhouse and McGhee, 2009: 485). Despite the prominence of taking an ecological perspective on family difficulties, practitioners tend to downplay a family's standard of living in assessments (Jack and Gill, 2003). Hence, disadvantage does not figure highly in their understanding of causes of a family's problems or how they, with the family, could tackle the family's poor living conditions. Part of the reason for this blindness may be the very high proportion of families on social workers' caseloads which have high levels of deprivation (Winter and Connolly, 2005). The danger is that social workers become so accustomed to families living in poverty that 'they see but do not see'; they take it as a given. Welbourne (2012: 114) captures this phenomenon well in the phrase 'poverty can become part of the wallpaper'. Rustin (2005: 17) accuses society of leaving frontline workers in the community to face the 'pressures of being aware of their limitations and the extent of distress and deprivation' without the provision of sufficient resources and support.

Ignoring gut feelings

We use the terms gut feelings, gut instinct, and intuition for sensing rather than consciously perceiving, among other things, the atmosphere of the family home or visit. There is a danger that workers ignore or put to one side these feelings and as a consequence valuable information is lost. On one level, coming away from her first visit to the Rahman family, Afifah formed a positive impression of Zahara and Farha's relationship, but on another level, she, like the referring health visitor, had an uneasy feeling that things were not all that they seemed. Wilińska (2014: 609) neatly illustrates this sensing phenomenon when she describes her experience as a non-Japanese, White researcher visiting the homes of older people when researching old age in Japan. She describes how accompanying her visits were the type of 'gut feelings' that sends opposite signals to her body than those perceived by her eyes.

Though there were many smiles, and the visit appeared to be extremely pleasant, I left the place carrying a huge load. I saw myself shrink and drawing inward. My eyes were seeing happy faces, but my body was not accepting that image.

(Wilińska, 2014: 609)

The mood of the family home when workers visit may resonate within the worker and physically affect them. Ferguson (2009: 476) argues that 'it is essential to use and rely on these intuitions and trust their "gut feelings," to make sense of the experiences that are swirling around and unconsciously entering the mind and body'. If Afifah's body was saying the same thing as her mind she would not have an uneasy feeling after a seemingly positive visit. As it is, she might put the feeling to one side, as such feelings 'are liable to cause trouble in the sense they are demanding more thought and more work if they are taken seriously' (Rustin, 2005: 17).

Impact of personal threats

Workers need to remain vigilant in relation to any danger to themselves and the impact fear can have on their thinking and actions in relation to the case. A sense of threat might not always result from overt statements but, rather, an unspoken feeling of danger. A sense of threat can generate fear within the worker which can have an important protective function, with an 'action tendency' of avoidance or escape (Lazarus, 1991: 238). It can also impact on a worker's actions and thinking, lessening their ability to support families and protect family members from harm. The fear and anxiety generated by personal threats relate to the threat of future harm and entail an anticipation of the future and, as such, are 'prey to the workings of the imagination' (Smith, McMahon and Nursten, 2003: 664). The importance of social workers reporting and discussing personal threats and fearful feelings with their supervisor and colleagues cannot be overemphasised.

In his research into the stress arising from threats of violence, Littlechild (2005: 63) found that a particular issue is the impact of personal threats can have on social workers' well-being and practice. He states that 'the available evidence suggests that threats of violence are as, if not more, important in producing fear in the victim, than actual physical violence' and it is important that the effects of behaviours that are *perceived* as being threatening are included in any definition of violence. He found that some family members appear to use personal threats 'as a strategy to deflect the worker/agency from focusing on the matter in hand, i.e. on the protection of children' (Littlechild, 2005: 72). Littlechild gives examples of family members saying to the worker that they knew which car was theirs, or knew where they lived, or workers noticing someone following them in a car. The workers that encounter these types of indirect threats found them particularly intimidating. Littlechild identifies the need for workers to be encouraged to report threats, and for policy-makers and managers to develop policies and protocols to ensure workers, supervisors and managers deal with threats appropriately.

Research Focus

Koritsas, S., Coles, J. and Boyle, M. (2010) 'Workplace violence towards social workers: the Australian experience', *British Journal of Social Work*, 40(1), 257–271.

This Australian study investigated six forms of violence potentially experienced by social workers, namely verbal abuse, property damage/theft, intimidation, physical abuse, sexual harassment and sexual assault. The researchers sent 1,000 questionnaires to a random sample of members of the *Australian Association of Social Workers*, of which 250 respondents returned theirs completed, giving a completion rate of 22%. The respondents worked in a wide range of settings. The questionnaire asked whether they had experienced any of the six forms of violence over the last 12 months. Analysis revealed that the majority of social workers (67%) had experienced a least one of the six forms of violence over the past 12 months. The most common form of violence was verbal abuse, followed by intimidation. Sexual assault was the least common form. The number and proportion of social workers experiencing the different forms of violence were as follows: verbal abuse, 122 (57%); intimidation, 101 (47%); property damage/theft, 39 (18%); sexual harassment, 31 (15%); physical abuse, 19 (9%); and sexual assault, 3 (1%). What is distinctive about this research is that it paid particular attention to the different forms of violence social workers can experience and confirms that verbal abuse is the most common, followed by intimidation. As discussed in this section, the experience of behaviour perceived as intimidating can affect workers and their practice profoundly, and workers, their managers and agencies need to take it seriously.

Self-care, burnout and emotional exhaustion

Few would disagree that social work is a personally and emotionally demanding job and that social workers need to be emotionally resilient. Given the personal and emotional demands of the job, there is a danger of them experiencing 'burnout'. Burnout is the exhaustion that results from excessive demands on energy and personal resources (Evans et al., 2006). Maslach and Jackson (1986) conceptualised 'burnout' as having three component parts: emotional exhaustion, depersonalisation and reduced personal accomplishment. Emotional exhaustion is 'the depletion of emotional resources, leading to workers to feel unable to give themselves at the psychological level', depersonalisation is 'negative, cynical attitudes and feelings about clients' and reduced personal accomplishment is 'evaluating oneself negatively, particularly with regard to work with clients' (Evans et al., 2006). Burnout has negative consequences for the worker, their employing organisation and, in particular, the work they do with families. Afifah needs to be on the lookout for the contributory factors to burnout, commonly identified as having little latitude in decision-making, high psychological job demands and limited or no social support in the workplace.

Managers, supervisors and workers have responsibilities to prevent worker burnout and emotional exhaustion; however, workers also have responsibilities to engage in personal and professional self-care. Professional bodies and regulators recognise this responsibility that workers in the helping professionals have to engage in such self-care. For example, the professional capability framework in England (COSW/BASW, 2012) at a qualifying level states that 'with support, take steps to manage and promote own safety, health, wellbeing and emotional resilience'. Self-care is 'any action or experience that enhances or maintains' worker well-being' (Bradley et al., 2013: 456). Grant, Kinman and Baker (2014) nicely express the need for workers in the helping professions to engage in self-care in the flight safety announcement phrase, 'put on your own oxygen mask before assisting others'. Among the many self-care actions and experiences that workers can engage in are the following: maintaining a clear boundary between home life and work; creating a healthy work–life balance; engaging in (not just attending) supportive supervision (when it is available); participating in case discussions with colleagues; having a supportive network both inside and outside the workplace; and having a sense of achievement when families accomplish small improvements in their lives.

Research Focus

Mandell, D., Stalker, C, Wright, M., Frensch, K. and Harvey, C. (2013) 'Sinking, swimming and sailing: experiences of job satisfaction and emotional exhaustion in child welfare employees', *Child and Family Social Work*, 18(4), 383–393.

Stalker et al.'s (2007) study of Canadian child welfare workers unexpectedly found that there was a group of research participants that scored high on 'emotional exhaustion' but continued to have high 'overall job satisfaction' – a relationship that is counter-intuitive and goes against previous research findings. As a consequence, the same research group directly investigated this phenomenon by comparing three groups of social workers (Mandell et al., 2013), those that were 'sinking' (high on *emotional exhaustion*, low on *job satisfaction*), those that were 'swimming upstream' (high on *emotional exhaustion*, high on *job satisfaction*) and 'those that were sailing' (low on *emotional exhaustion*, high on *job satisfaction*).

Sailing workers had a sense of personal confidence, clear personal boundaries between work and their personal lives, tended to articulate realistic and attainable objectives and appreciated small changes. Swimmers tended to be younger than the other two categories and had a personal investment in and identification with the mission of improving family welfare. This sometimes made it difficult for them to disengage emotionally, achieve a sustainable balance between work and their personal lives and derive satisfaction from small changes. However, it also helped them persist despite the challenges. They also had a sense of work demands fluctuating according to the time of week or time of year, and of 'time off' giving a sense that no matter how bad things were, they would get better. Those that were *sinking* described themselves as overwhelmed, defeated and out of steam and saw problems as relentless and themselves as not having the capacity to survive. They had a weak personal boundary, reported little time for their personal life outside work and gained little satisfaction from small changes. The most significant differences between those *sinking* and those *swimming upstream* was the latter's sense of work demands fluctuating, giving a sense that no matter how bad things were, they would get better, while those *sinking* expressed a sense of defeat. *Swimmers* had a clear sense of mission that those *sinking* lacked.

The researchers speculated that some of the *swimmers* may start *sinking*, while others may begin to *sail*. The research suggests that for swimmers to become *sailors*, they would need to develop clear achievable goals with families, cultivate a sense of achievement from families succeeding in making small improvements and develop a clear boundary between personal life and work life, which will require them to disengage constructively sometimes in the interests of self-care.

Chapter Key Points

1. Remain vigilant for errors in reasoning and thinking, including having superficial understandings of family situations, falling victim to confirmation bias, holding unjustified assumptions, being unrealistically optimistic and ignoring a family's history.

2. Manage the tension between having respectful uncertainty or qualified trust towards family narratives and families becoming resistant to help because they feel under surveillance.

3. Manage compassionate feelings and work/personal life boundaries so you do not get over-emotionally involved.

4. Be vigilant towards the dangers of not seeing what is in front of your eyes so as to avoid mental pain, ignoring your gut feelings and not openly acknowledging the sense of personal threat you feel when working with families.

5. Engage in self-care both inside and outside work, so that you do not become emotionally exhausted, suffer undue stress and, eventually, burnout.

6. Actively participate in supervision to promote self-awareness, reflexive thinking and self-care.

Reflective Exercises

1. Think critically about the idea of having respectful uncertainty or qualified trust when working with families. To what extent do you think they can have a detrimental effect on forming a working alliance with family members?

2. What weight should workers place on their intuitions, compared with deliberate and thoughtful analysis? Should they have an equal weight or should one be more important than the other?

3. Think of a situation either in your work or private life where you regretted ignoring your gut feelings.

Putting into Practice

What self-care activities do you employ or plan to employ to cope with the pressures and emotional demands of practice?

What place should optimism and hope have in supporting families? Do they do more harm than good? If you can, give examples from experience.

What would you do if you felt intimidated by family members?

Further Resources

Chapter Eight 'Minimising Mistakes' in Munro, E. (2008) *Effective Child Protection,* second edition, London: Sage, 125–152.
  This chapter gives an in-depth look at the various ways errors in thinking come about and how workers can reduce the chances of them occurring.

Barnard, M. and Bain, C. (2015) 'Resisting your good intentions: substance-misusing parents and early intervention to support and monitor children in need', *Child and Family Social Work,* 20(2), 171–180.
  This article reports on a qualitative pilot study of a Scottish early intervention project offering voluntary support to substance-misusing parents where there were no current concerns that the children were at risk of serious harm. The project allied support with the intention to monitor the family situation to keep a watch on the children's welfare. The article is of particular interest, as it highlights how surveillance produces family resistance.

Grant, L. and Kinman, G. (eds) (2014) *Developing Resilience for Social Work Practice,* Basingstoke: Palgrave Macmillan.
  Part Two of this book focuses on developing techniques to build resilience. There are chapters on maintaining a work–life balance, on the role of reflective supervision and on personal organisation and time management.

CHAPTER 8

SUPPORTIVE SUPERVISION

CHAPTER OVERVIEW

This chapter

- Explains the role supportive supervision can play in supporting families.
- Discusses how the organisational context in which supervision takes place has strong influence on the kind of supervision that occurs.
- Explores how peer supervision can provide a safe space for deeper thinking and reflection on work with families.
- Considers the nature of the supervision session and the supervisory relationship.
- Examines the nature of the relationship dynamics of supervision including those around the micropolitics of supervision and mirroring processes.
- Stresses the importance of supervision providing a reflective space to promote critical thinking and emotional support.
- Argues that the quality of supervision will determine whether its outcomes are beneficial or detrimental to practitioners, the organisations they work for and the families they work with.

Introduction

Supporting families can be a stressful, complex, challenging and emotionally laden activity, and if practitioners don't get sufficient support in doing their job they will not be able to support families effectively. Workers that feel unsupported can develop low morale and burnout and may leave their profession or change jobs (Mor Barak et al., 2009: 6). The usual vehicle for practitioners to receive support is through one sort of supervision or another. However, in England and other countries there can be a gap between the rhetoric of providing effective quality supervision and the reality. Only a quarter of the 28 social workers undertaking a post-qualifying childcare award programme at a university in the north-east of England felt satisfied with the supervision they currently received, with a much higher proportion clearly dissatisfied (Turner-Daly and Jack, 2014: 1). When workers don't receive effective supervision there are likely to be negative consequences for the worker, the families they work with, their collaborative colleagues and the agencies they work for.

The Nowak family

The Nowak family household consists of Karolina (34 years old) and her two children, Lukas (12 years old) and Monika (10 years old). Six years ago Karolina and Dawid migrated from Poland to England with their two children. For two years Karolina, Lukas and Monika have had no contact with Dawid, the children's father, and he is unaware of their present location. Karolina fled intimate-partner violence three years ago, taking Lukas and Monika with her. She and the children have been living a relatively settled life in their present home for two years. Karolina and the children have made some new friends, but their Polish friends still live in the area that the family fled from and do not know their location for fear Dawid locates and intimidates them. Karolina has thought about returning to Poland but fears that Dawid will learn of their presence there. She has not been in a relationship since leaving her ex-partner and works 30 hours a week in a local care home. Her children attend their local school where they have presented no particular problems. Family social worker Melissa started working with the Nowak family two weeks ago, when Karolina requested the local authority to take her son Lukas into care because she could not cope with his attitude and behaviour towards her anymore and fears he will become violent. So far, Melissa has made two visits to the family home and had conversations with Karolina, Lukas and Monika.

Melissa is experiencing a range of emotions in her work with the Nowak family. She has a degree of anxiety about the decision as to whether having a break from the family is in Lukas's interests. She feels compassion for Karolina, with all that she has been through and the severe difficulties she is now experiencing with Lukas. She also feels for Lukas, who seems polite and sensible, on the surface at least, during her visits, but who does show a negative attitude towards his mother. In front of his mother he says he would like to get away from her, but his non-verbal communication tells a different story. Monika is a bit of an enigma, as she seems happy and unaffected by the fraught relationship between Lukas and his mother. Melissa has managed to contain the situation for now and is working with the family to help them resolve the difficulties they are facing. Melissa has formed the distinct impression that Karolina has never talked with the children about the period they lived together with their father. Winston is Melissa's new team leader and supervisor.

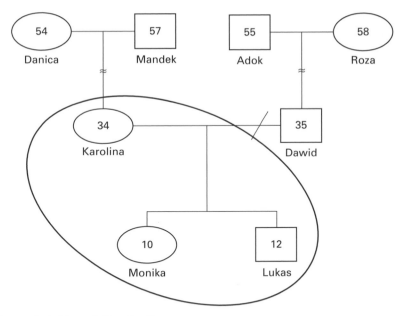

Figure 8.1 Nowak Family Genogram

The chapter will use this family scenario to explore the ingredients of effective supervision. It concentrates on supervision as an interpersonal process by which colleagues, line managers or more-experienced practitioners support workers in terms of their emotions, thinking, decision-making and practice. We will examine what the supervision process between Melissa and Winston needs to look and feel like for Melissa to feel supported in terms of her emotions, her thinking and her practice, and for Winston to satisfy himself that Melissa is doing competent and effective work with families. The chapter begins with the organisational and societal contexts of supervision and the tensions they can create for those trying to provide effective supervision.

Organisational context

Winston occupies a space between the worlds of upper management and his team of front-line workers. He is immersed in the culture of the organisation and subjected to the shared behavioural expectations and normative beliefs that constitute its organisational culture (Glisson and James, 2002). Part of these behavioural expectations and normative beliefs will concern the priority he should give supervision and what form it should take. This will include what the appropriate balance between the managerial aspects and professional aspects of supervision should be. Hence, the organisational context in which supervision takes place has a strong influence on the kind of supervision that he gives. Two broad characteristics of supervision are professional supervision and managerial supervision. Professional supervision prioritises helping practitioners work effectively with families and cope with emotional demands of working with families under strain. Managerial supervision prioritises organisational and administrative oversight, giving pre-eminence to checking that procedures and bureaucratic requirements are met.

There can be considerable disquiet about the availability and quality of supervision, particularly the growth of managerial supervision at the expense of professional supervision. Organisations do not operate in a vacuum but within political, economic and social contexts, and changes in these wider contexts impact on supervision practices. A growth in managerial supervision has been one of consequences of the widespread growth in managerialism, associated with monitoring worker performance, appraisal, audit and work outputs (Noble and Irwin, 2009). In addition, the global economic crash of 2008, the following economic recession and austerity policies have resulted in severe reductions in government welfare spending. These contexts can force organisations to restrict supervision to monitoring worker performance and 'to do more for less', with an inevitable consequence of reduced quality and scope.

Research into what actually happens in supervision sessions is comparatively rare, as opposed to participants' self-reports of their experience. An exception is Bourne and Hafford-Letchfield's (2011) small-scale qualitative study involving video recordings of actual supervision sessions and the managers' own reflective accounts of the effectiveness of their supervision skills. The authors report that it was evident from the audio-visual recordings that some supervisors showed intense interest and concern to prioritise administrative and managerial responsibilities which at times conflicted with staff's professional and individual needs for reflection and space to acknowledge the uncertainty, fear and anxiety associated with working with families under strain.

Munro (2011: 87) cites Oakeshott (1989: 33) who 'draws attention to the limitations of a "crowded life" where people are continually occupied and engaged but have no time to stand back and think'. This chapter will be concerned with 'reflective supervision' that, when carried out by the worker's line manager, is equated with achieving an appropriate balance between managerial and professional aspects of supervision. Such supervision would provide a reflective space where workers could step back and think. Workers in agencies where supervisors do not provide this type of supervision, and alternatives do not exist, need to do what they can to get the reflective supervision they need. One thing they can do is organise peer supervision or case discussions, which have an important role to play in providing a reflective space where they can find the room and time to develop their thinking about their work with families.

Peer supervision

Golia and McGovern (2015) identify three types of peer supervision: facilitated peer supervision, planned peer supervision and ad hoc peer supervision. Peer supervision usually takes the form of case discussion and needs to be distinguished from group supervision when a supervisor facilitates a group supervision session. Peer supervision potentially provides a safe thinking space, free from surveillance, which potentially enables critical reflection that promotes thoughtful practice informed by emotions. The various forms of peer supervision can be important supplements to one-to-one supervision with line managers, or make up for the lack of such supervision. As noted above, there is considerable concern about the high proportion of workers that are not receiving reflective supervision from their line manager, and some doubt that in the present organisational and politico-cultural contexts that they ever will. Even in these circumstances, Ingram (2015), in his research into the opportunities social workers had to explore the emotional content of their practice, had not anticipated that participants' most-cited forum for feeling safe to express their emotions was informal contacts with colleagues.

Effective practice involves both 'doing and thinking', but in pressurised environments there can be a lack of spaces in which to 'think', coupled with a reluctance to think more deeply about the nature of concerns. Ruch (2007a) points to an inability to tolerate anxiety generated by emotionally charged situations, with workers ending up frantically 'doing' without engaging in deep thinking. She argues that workers need time and space to stop doing and engage in emotionally informed thinking and that the capacity of existing teams to offer such a space has been under-recognised. The space provided by peer supervision needs to be a safe space and, like all groups, the dynamics, atmosphere and climate of the group is crucially important. These need to be collegiate, supportive and respectful if members are able to openly and non-defensively communicate with each other.

Ruch (2007b) describes a case discussion model that consists of three stages. In the first stage, a practitioner outlines a case and their current preoccupations. The remaining group members simply listen without taking notes or asking questions. In the second stage, the group engages in discussion about what struck them about the presentation, while the presenter observes and listens but does not participate no matter how difficult this is. The final stage involves the whole group, including presenter, engaging in reflective discussion on the aspects of the case that caught the attention of the group. Ruch emphasises that it is important at this final stage that the group does not prematurely resort to their problem-solving/action mode by trying to resolve rather than explore the discussed issues. She argues that the three-stage model creates an open space in which thinking and reflecting are encouraged.

Co-working and joint-working are further ways of promoting reflective discussion and analysis. Co-working involves sharing responsibility for a case, which requires workers to engage in reflective discussion concerning their work with families. This means the co-workers consider and reflect upon the case from at least two points of views and are likely to find the experience of co-working supportive (Wilson et al., 2008: 24). Wilson et al. (2008) stress that co-working is not a replacement for supervision and requires joint supervision.

There are models of working where a team holds joint responsibility for the case. Some local authorities in England have introduced 'pods' which are small teams with reduced caseloads and a team leader (Somerset County Council, 2007). Although each case has a named worker, the whole team have joint responsibility for the work, with flexibility as to who does what. Effectively, the whole team works with the family, with members viewing the team caseload as a joint responsibility. Typically, the team would meet each morning to update and agree priorities, with tasks allocated for that day. Whether such meetings are forums for reflective discussion will depend on, like in other forums, the environment the group provides and what actually occurs within the meetings. Melissa is

---

Research Focus

Lietz, C. A. (2008) 'Implementation of group supervision in child welfare: findings from Arizona's supervision circle project', *Child Welfare*, 87(6), 31–48.

Group supervision is very different from peer supervision, but they have the group dimension in common. Group supervision is when the supervisor meets with their

▶

supervisees in a group. In the above paper, Lietz reports on research into a project that introduced group supervision in a state-wide child welfare agency in
Arizona, USA. The project had three phases: the first involved the collection of
data on the current levels of perceived critical thinking within supervision; in the
second, supervisees attended five training sessions on group supervision, after
which the supervisors were expected to begin implementing group supervision
with supervisees. The final phase was the collection of post-test data on perceived levels of critical thinking in supervision. The findings support the idea that
group supervision can create as atmosphere where dialogue, questioning and
creativity can be initiated (Lietz, 2008: 45). Lietz argues that discussing cases in
a group can foster critical thinking when the process brings together supportive
critical questioning and multiple perspectives (Lietz, 2008: 35). The findings highlight the continued importance of the supervisory relationship in group supervision, with the supervisor needing to set a tone of respectful dialogue. Lietz states
that without establishing trusting relationships, group supervision may not be
effective and, in fact, may increase anxiety in supervisees who do not feel
respected by their supervisors.

currently not involved in any form of peer supervision or co-working, but
she has a new supervisor that has a strong belief in the importance of
reflective supervision and the supervisory relationship.

The supervision session

The most common form of supervision consists of a supervisor meeting
with a supervisee in a dedicated session. O'Donoghue (2014) reports on
a qualitative research study that explored the inner workings of 'the
supervision session' from both sides of the interaction. The aim of the
study was to produce an interactional map of the supervision session by
analysing data obtained from interviewing 16 supervisees and 18 supervisors from across New Zealand about their experience of a supervision
session. After analysing the interview data, the researcher produced an
interactional map showing both parties following five *stages*: (i) preparation, (ii) beginning, (iii) planning, (iv) working and (v) ending. Each *stage*
consisted of a number of *phases*, some of which were common to both
parties, and others different. The parties interacted with each other, navi-
gating the session through a process of cooperative engagement with
each party playing their respective parts. O'Donoghue (2014) explains

how the interactional map helps both parties to supervision become mindful of the process and their contribution to it.

For Melissa, the *preparation stage* includes two phases: *'continual consideration phase'* which includes noting in her diary on a day-to-day basis issues she wished to raise in supervision and a *'session preparation'* phase, when before the supervision session she would go through her dairy and make a list of the items she wished to raise. For Winston, the *preparation stage* consists of three phases: *'reviewing records'* of the previous session, *'thinking about the forthcoming session'*, what he needs to raise and what needed to be followed up from the previous session and *'attending to the setting'*, preparing the room in which supervision was to take place.

For both Melissa and Winston, the *beginning stage* also consists of two phases. For Melissa, there is a *'social engagement'* phase, including exchange of greetings and a brief catch-up, followed by an *'orientation'* phase which marks the transition to focusing on supervision. For Winston, the *beginning* stage consists of a *'starting'* phase and *'checking-in'* phase. In the *starting* phase, Winston asks how Melissa was, and if he had not seen her for a while there would be a *checking-in phase* consisting of a social catch-up.

The *planning stage* consists of the same two phases for Melissa and Winston: *agenda setting* and *prioritising items*. They would each go through the items they wished to raise and prioritise them in order of importance.

The *working stage* consists of Melissa telling the story or presenting an item, while Winston clarifies and explores the story or item raised. In the second phase, Winston *facilitates decision-making and task-setting*, with Melissa *interactively processing* her thinking about the case.

For Melissa, the *ending stage* consists of two phases: *a summary and review* phase and *the practicalities of next session phase*. For Winston, the *ending stage* consists of three phases: *reviewing what they covered, finishing up the session* and *finishing the notes*. Within his paper, O'Donoghue (2014: 67) also includes a very useful practical checklist for supervisors to use within their sessions.

The supervisory relationship

Simmonds (2010: 216) refers to a serious clash of cultures that has arisen between those that identify supervision as a relationship-based activity and those who identify it as an audit-based activity where the qualities of the people involved and the relationship between them are largely irrelevant. It is the position of this chapter that a key component of the effectiveness of Winston's supervision will be the quality of the supervisory relationship between Melissa and him. Winston aims to create an open and trusting climate in which Melissa feels safe enough to share her thoughts and emotions, and be open about any confusion or misgivings she has about her work with the Nowak family. Like Noble and Irwin (2009: 346), he believes that social work supervision needs to 'mirror the helping relationship in that the supervisory relationship, like the helping relationship is built on a trusting, confidential, caring, supportive and empathic experience which sets the atmosphere for "the professional work" to be undertaken'.

The supervision literature recognises a number of ingredients that are required if Melissa is to receive effective supervision. In her review of contemporary discussion of the practice of supervision, Beddoe (2010: 1289) identifies the theme of 'trust, support and openness' underpinning a culture of critical reflection in which mistakes are per-ceived as opportunities for learning and where strong emotions and frustrations can be explored within high-trust relationships. Effective emotional and thinking support requires open communication which is not possible without first establishing trust. So Melissa and Winston need to develop a degree of trust before they can openly communicate about how they think and feel. From her previous supervisory experi-ence, Melissa started off with a degree of suspicion and guarded com-munication, but a degree of trust is growing through the way Winston interacts with her.

In an effective supervisory relationship, Winston and Melissa would form a working alliance, with both participants working together to effec-tively support families and help them overcome their present difficulties. Both Winston and Melissa need to contribute to the development of such a working alliance. Noble and Irwin (2009: 347) argue that 'in the main, supervision is seen to be most effective when the supervisee engages in the process as a proactive participant interested in her/his own learning'. For Melissa to make a positive contribution to the supervisory relation-ship, she needs a willingness to play a full part in the interaction, have the courage to ask for assistance or help, appreciate the importance of self-reflection, be open to learning, listen and accept help (Beddoe, Davys, and Adamson, 2014: 124). In addition, she needs to be open to chal-lenge, avoid becoming defensive and refrain from engaging in guarded communication.

Supervisory styles

Winston pays attention to the quality and dynamics of their supervisory relationship, recognising that it requires time to develop into a working alliance between the two of them. This involves recognising that his style of supervision will have a considerable impact of his supervisory relationship with Melissa. Wonnacott (2012: 73) identifies three styles of supervision: the 'active intrusive supervisor', the 'active reflexive supervisor' and the 'passive supervisor'. She describes the 'active intrusive supervisor' as predominantly task-centred, restricting supervision to actively making sure that visits are made, family members are seen and reports completed, while showing little interest in their supervisee's casework.

In contrast, the 'active reflective supervisor' displays an active interest in their supervisee's casework, as well as being conscientious in ensuring required tasks are completed. They facilitate critical reflection by challenging the supervisee's thinking, while having an active interest in the emotional impact of the work. Most importantly, they are aware of the effect they have on the supervisory relationship and constantly evaluate their own supervisory practices. The 'passive supervisor' is so keen to be responsive to their supervisees that they allow them to dictate the supervision agenda. They are unaware of the detail of their supervisee's work, show little interest in task completion, provide little challenge and are more interested in ensuring that their supervisees felt supported. Winston clearly has 'active reflective' style of supervision, so there is a good chance that his supervisory relationship with Melissa will develop into an effective one.

Relationship dynamics

As with other relationships, particular dynamics will develop within Winston and Melissa's supervisory relationship. These dynamics can be complex and not only affected by their personal characteristics but also the structure and processes of their supervisory relationship. As Winston is Melissa's line manager, their relationship is likely to be an asymmetrical one, with Winston being in a relatively powerful position in relation to Melissa. There is also a chance their supervisory relationship mirrors the dynamics of Melissa's relationship with the Nowak family. In this section, we will take a brief look at these two aspects of supervisory dynamics: power and authority, and mirroring processes.

Power and authority

Leung (2012: 159) argues that both supervisee and supervisor would benefit from developing an understanding of the micropolitics of supervision. Theorists use the term micropolitics to describe the political interactions that take place between social actors within organisational settings (Potrac and Jones, 2009: 225). This involves Leftwich's (2004) perspective on power, that we find 'politics' whenever two or more human beings are involved in some form of collective activity, whether formal or informal, public or private. He considers micropolitics as the activities that occur between people who often have different resources, power, interests, preferences and ideas. It is important to remember that micropolitics concerns not only conflict but also cooperation between social actors, and so supervision will always be a site of micropolitics.

An important factor in establishing an effective supervisory relationship is the way participants handle power (Turner-Daly and Jack, 2014: 3). Wonnacott identifies four ways supervisors can exercise their power; two of them involve them abdicating their responsibilities by being either permissive or neglectful, and in the remaining two ways, supervisors use their power either in an authoritative or authoritarian manner. The authoritarian supervisor is overly directive and unresponsive to their supervisee's emotional and learning needs, whereas the authoritative supervisor is able to balance the use of their authority and power by being clear about expected standards of practice while being responsive to their supervisee's needs.

Winston has authority through his position in the organisation and his professional knowledge, experience and skill. This asymmetrical relationship impacts on the dynamics of the supervisory relationship and creates a power imbalance between him and Melissa, particularly as he is her line manager. That is not to say that Melissa is completely without power; she, while not having the formal power of Winston, has informal power to fully or only partially participate. Such informal power is demonstrated by Leung's (2012: 159) finding that supervisee's adopted micro-strategies in reaction to a perceived negative supervisory relationships that included limited disclosure of information.

Winston's and Melissa's attitudes to authority will impact on the dynamics between them. Hughes and Pengelly (1997: 168) maintain that most significant to the supervisory relationship is 'a person's attitude to authority that permeates her/his way of exercising professional and role authority and responding to that of others'. Hughes and Pengelly (1997: 168) identify three sources of authority: role authority, professional authority and personal authority. His supervisory role provides Winston with delegated authority to oversee Melissa's work, while Melissa's role requires her to acknowledge Winston's delegated authority. Winston has to earn professional authority through demonstrating professional knowledge and expertise, and he could grant Melissa professional authority if he judges that she has demonstrated sufficient professional expertise. Personal authority refers 'to the capacity of some people, by their demeanour and the way that manage themselves, to establish a natural authority and communicate it to others' (Hughes and Pengelly, 1997: 168). From the above, we can appreciate that the different forms of authority interconnect and play out within supervision, and will impact on the supervisory relationship. A key question is whether Winston is comfortable with his authority and whether Melissa respects it.

Mirroring dynamics

Dynamically there are three, not two, participants in supervision, with Winston and Melissa joined by the Nowak family (Hughes and Pengelly, 1997: 41). A process known as mirroring occurs when 'the processes at work currently in the relationship between family and worker are ... reflected in the relationship between worker and supervisor' (Mattinson, 1975, cited in Hughes and Pengelly, 1997: 83). Winston and Melissa are in danger of re-enacting the dynamics between Melissa and Karolina in their supervisory relationship. Winston might find himself feeling sorry for Melissa as she struggles to make sense of Lukas's behaviour. This would mirror Melissa feeling compassion for Karolina having gone through so much in a violent relationship with the children's father and now having to cope with Lukas treating his mother so badly. Wonnacott (2012: 38) explains a converse process that can occur when aspects of the supervisory relationship are re-enacted in the relationship between supervisee and family. She points to the possibility of the supervisor's style of supervision being re-enacted in the relationship between Melissa and Karolina; this would be a positive process because Winston's style of supervision is 'active reflective', but it would be negative if it was either 'active intrusive' or 'passive'.

Reflective supervision

The purpose of reflective supervision is to help Melissa think critically about the Nowak family situation, her work with the family and the impact it is having on her. The overall purpose of reflective supervision is to enable

Melissa to support the Nowak family effectively, and we will discuss five interrelated processes that potentially help her to do so: critical thinking, emotional support, containment, reflective learning and mediation. Reflection concerns engaging in deeper rather than superficial thought about something. The idea of reflective supervision reflects the importance of providing a safe thinking space for workers, where the supervisor can help the worker develop their thoughts about families and the work they do with families, including the emotional dimensions of that work.

Critical thinking

The best way for Winston to enhance Melissa's thinking about the case is through reflective supervision that prompts critical thinking and develops her analytical skills in responding to complex situations (Lietz, 2010: 68). Such critical thinking requires an enquiring attitude, curiosity and creativity. Winston endeavours to help Melissa critically think about and examine the relationships she is building with Nowak family members, her developing understanding of the Nowak family's relationships and their situation and her thinking on how she is going to support the family. These elements require Melissa to engage in critical thinking, analysis and sound decision-making. Winston can prompt and develop Melissa's critical thinking by asking Melissa questions that require her to explore, examine and question her present understandings of the Nowak family and their situation. When Winston asks Melissa why she thinks the relationship between Lukas and his mother is so fraught, she replies that he blames his mother for losing contact with his father. Winston responds by asking her a series of questions such as 'Why does she think that?' and 'What assumptions is she making and has she developed any alternative hypotheses?'

The aim is to promote critical thinking through asking questions designed to deepen Melissa's thinking about the case. Such an approach involves Winston listening to what Melissa has to say, and mutual respect between the two of them. Such questions such as 'Why do you think that?' or 'What is your reasoning behind that?' at first flummoxed Melissa, but with Winston's help she becomes better able to articulate and examine her reasoning. Winston is asking these questions in a supportive manner to encourage Melissa to critically examine her current thinking about the case. Melissa is being encouraged to reflect on her own thinking and be open to alternative explanations. They work together to generate an alternate hypothesis and discuss the aftermath of intimate partner violence, including the need to recognise that the intimate partner abuse can involve undermining the mother–child relationships (Humphreys, Thiara and Skamballis, 2011). Winston reminds Mellissa that the family situation is multidimensional and she needs to have in mind the family's relative social isolation, their experience of migration and being Polish in England. The discussion continues as Winston asks 'why now?' in relation to the timing of the referral. They continue to discuss how Melissa needs to keep an open mind and test hypotheses, and be prepared to abandon them when there is clear evidence that they do not fit.

Emotional support

There are significant and complex emotional dimensions to supporting families, and these emotional dimensions operate alongside and interact with the intellectual dimensions. In order to achieve and maintain

---

Research Focus

Lietz, C. A. (2010) 'Critical Thinking in Child Welfare Supervision', *Administration in Social Work*, 34(21), 68–78.

The above paper reports findings of research into the prevalence of activities that indicate critical thinking in facilitated supervision in a large state-wide public child welfare agency in Arizona, USA. I have chosen this paper because it is comparatively rare for research into critical thinking in supervision to be attempted. The authors constructed a scale of nine items to measure the level of critical thinking in supervision. The research used an online self-report survey emailed to 600 administrators, supervisors and caseworkers using a Likert Scale of levels of agreement or disagreement with a series of statements, with a response rate of 64%. Examples of the statements used are 'My supervisor asks me questions that make me think' and 'My supervisor helps me think about all aspects of a case'. The arithmetical mean of workers' impressions that critical thinking occurs during supervision was between 'somewhat disagree' and 'somewhat agree', indicating that there were some critical thinking activities occurring in supervision sessions. Another finding was that variables measuring quality of the supervisory relationship and supervisor availability are significant predictors of the presence of perceived critical thinking within supervision. The findings also suggest the availability of supervisors and open and respectful communication make it more likely that critical thinking will occur. It is interesting to note that in response to the findings, the agency introduced a new group supervision process to increase the level of dialogue and critical thinking in supervision.

successful and meaningful relationships with Nowak family members, Melissa needs to engage with the family members at an emotional as well as professional level (Leeson, 2010: 483). Winston needs to be willing to engage in these emotional aspects of Melissa's practice, while Melissa needs to feel safe enough to share her feelings about the case. They both have important contributions to make to providing space for the emotional dimensions of practice; however, as discussed above, Winston has more power and authority to set the supervision agenda. Supervisors have the potential to dictate what can and what cannot be included in supervision and Ingram (2013: 15) would recommend that each party explicitly identify where they believe the balance of supervision between the emotional aspects and managerial aspects of Melissa's work should be. Ingram suggests that supervisors and supervisees explore and discuss any divergence of view so as to reach an agreement.

These emotional dimensions of supporting families are part and parcel of the processes of practice, and case discussions need to include exploring and articulating these emotions (Ingram, 2015: 899). Supporting families places a number of emotional demands on workers, including those associated with forming working relationships with family members and coping with family suffering, conflict, emotional upset and anger. Workers can be feeling emotional turmoil on the inside while they give the appearance of orderly calm control on the outside (Mann, 2004: 209). Such 'emotional labour' (Leeson, 2010) requires an outlet, which, arguably, supervisors should provide within supervision. Emotional information will not be available in their discussions if Winston does not give Melissa

---

Research Focus

Ingram, R. (2015) 'Exploring emotions within formal and informal forums: messages from social work practitioners', *British Journal of Social Work*, 45(3), 896–913.

The above paper reports on the findings of a research project into the views of social workers across a Scottish local authority about their ability to explore the emotional content of their practice in formal and informal forums. The researcher sent questionnaires to staff by the internal intranet, with 112 returned completed, of which he interviewed 17 using semi-structured interviews. Ingram found there were different experiences across the authority, with some seeing supervision as safe and supportive forums where they could discuss all aspects of practice,

▶

including emotions. For others, it was an unsafe setting where discussion was restricted to caseloads. It was not uncommon for respondents to highlight issues of time pressure, supervisory paperwork and the skills of the supervisor as being pivotal factors in determining the quality and focus of supervision. A key finding was the role that informal support from peers played in terms of discussing their emotions. Important aspects of this source of support were shared expertise, it being unrecorded and accessible, and that they could use it for preparation for formal supervision.

the space to express her emotions in relation to her work. The organisation and the family will experience the negative consequences of her suppression of emotion if she does not feel safe enough to share them.

Containment of anxiety

Ruch (2007a: 660) uses Bion's (1962) concept of containment to explain how Winston could contain Melissa's feelings so as to not allow them to disrupt her thinking. Facing Karolina's emotional turmoil and pleadings to take Lukas into care has generated considerable anxiety within Melissa as she struggled with how to respond and do what was best. Wonnacott (2012: 84) quotes the conclusion of Menzies's (1960: 118) study into the high levels of stress and anxiety among nurses, stating that 'the success and viability of a social institution are intimately connected with the techniques it uses to contain anxiety'. Supervision should provide a process by which Melissa's supervisory relationship with Winston provides a safe container for her anxieties. If Winston is to support Melissa and her work with the Nowak family, he needs to contain her anxieties and not let her emotional turmoil draw him in.

The supervisory relationship has the potential to provide a container for unmanageable feelings that make it difficult to think coherently about a situation. Hence, Winston has the potential to provide such a container of Melissa's emotions, if he listens to her attentively, tolerates her expression of emotions and helps her explore them in a non-threatening manner. Hughes and Pengelly (1997: 178) identify the feeling of being contained 'as a sense of being in a bounded, safe place' which provides 'the capacity to apply understanding to anxiety-laden experiences, in order to give them shape and meaning' so that they can be contained. Attending to Melissa's feelings, as part of her working experience, 'is not

merely to be supportive but to explore them in order to discover the information they provide'. This affords understanding not only about Melissa
but about her work. 'Putting words to the situation prevents the build-up
of "nameless dread" which would either paralyse' Melissa or catapult her
'into action as a means of avoidance' (Hughes and Pengelly, 1997: 178).

Reflective learning

There is the potential for supervision to provide a supportive environment
in which learning takes place. Although Winston can usefully provide guidance and information from time to time, here the emphasis is on Melissa's
learning through her participation in reflective supervision. We can define
'reflection' simply as a process of thinking about and examining something
in a deep rather than a superficial way. Dempsey, Halton and Murphy
(2001: 632) cite Dewey's (1933: 12) definition of reflective thought as
'active, persistent and careful consideration of any belief or supposed
knowledge in the light of the grounds that support it'. Reflective learning
is a product of engaging in critical or reflective thinking, hence it is a process by which we learn from engaging in reflective or critical thought.
Through this process we gain new knowledge and thinking skills that are
available to us in the future. The point is to recognise that this learning will
only take place in supervision if Winston facilitates Melissa's engagement in
critical or reflective thought about her work with the Nowak family.

When discussing her thinking in terms of helping the Nowak family,
Melissa explains that she is contemplating discussing the issue of communication with Lukas and his mother. Winston thinks he already knows
why Melissa is thinking along these lines and asks why she is planning to
take this approach. Melissa cannot answer this question beyond the question of how else can she get Karolina to talk with Lukas about the time
they lived with his father. After some more critical discussion around the
issue of raising this difficult period in their lives, Melissa thinks more deeply
about her plan. She then works out a tentative outline plan of a series of
meetings with different combinations of family members, with the intention of reviewing her hypothesis and plan after each meeting. First she
intends to meet with Monika, Lukas and their mother to get to know
them better as a family and encourage a family discussion about how they
live together as a family – what Chapter 2 refers to as their 'family practices' and family life. She hopes that family communication patterns and
processes emerge and are discussed during the session. Melissa will then
consider meeting with Karolina to discuss how she feels about having

conversations with Lukas and Monika about when they lived with their father, and if she agrees, work out a plan with Karolina as to how to take this forward. Melissa learnt from this that she needs to think more carefully about plans and think things through in terms of possible consequences of her actions, recognising potential sensitivities involved and the need to work out things *with* family members.

Responsibilities and accountabilities

Winston has certain managerial responsibilities and is accountable to upper management for carrying them out. Melissa also has responsibilities to her employing organisation and is accountable to Winston for fulfilling them. Among other things, Melissa is responsible for carrying out her work role in a competent and ethical manner, implementing and following agency policy and procedures, and fulfilling professional and bureaucratic requirements. It is Winston's right and responsibility to satisfy himself and upper management that Melissa is fulfilling her responsibilities. It is the way he and the organisation do this that can be controversial, as when managerial responsibilities dominate supervision to the exclusion of reflective supervision. Managers and others need to pay attention to how supervisors can carry out their administrative and managerial responsibilities without creating a surveillance culture that breeds a climate of mistrust within the supervisory relationship (Beddoe, 2010).

Wonnacott (2012: 138) identifies the need for supervisors to recognise their responsibility for creating a work environment within which their staff can successfully carry out their work, and she includes team and interprofessional network dynamics in the work environment. She points out that supervisors cannot be solely accountable for these conditions, and stresses the importance of their role in working with wider systems to improve the working environment and providing feedback to the wider organisation, for example, about the impact organisational policies and procedures are having on work with families and worker morale. The Social Work Reform Board (2010) include 'caseload and workload management' as one of four key elements of effective supervision, and a recurring issue for Melissa is not enough time to see families and build relationships with family members. The Board state that supervision should include an analysis of caseload and workload management and address any issues relating to the time available to work directly with families.

Like many workers, Melissa is feeling under considerable pressure at work, related to both the number of cases she is working with and the actual work she is doing with families. As the representative of the organisation, Winston has a particular responsibility for Melissa's welfare and needs to recognise these pressures, discuss them with Melissa and work out with her a manageable and sustainable workload. Shier and Graham (2010) found a number of work-related factors had an impact on workers' overall subjective well-being. These included characteristics of their work environment (physical, cultural and systemic), interrelationships at work (i.e. with families, colleagues and supervisors) and specific aspects of the job (i.e. factors associated with both workload and type of work).

Mediation

Some theorists identify 'mediation' between upper management and supervisees such as Melissa as one of the functions of supervision (Bourne and Hafford-Letchfield, 2011; Wonnacott, 2012). Here we use the term 'mediation' in terms of a go-between between Melissa and upper management, both in a downward and upward direction. Winston being Melissa's line manager is the human face of the organisation she works for, and Bourne and Hafford-Letchfield (2011: 53) argue that the supervisory relationship has an important mediation function as a channel through which the supervisor conveys organisational culture or, in other words, 'the way we do things around here'. The authors clearly demonstrate the mediation 'piggy in the middle' role supervisors have, such as when they report their 'frequent use of humour, somewhat ironic apologies or other tactics' for defusing conflict and aggravation involved in gaining compliance with the implementation of otherwise unwelcome procedural changes. In theory, the front-line supervisory relationship is also the means for upward communication whereby practitioners can convey information upwards as well as receive information from higher up the hierarchy. Through his mediation role Winston can potentially influence Melissa's work environment so as to support and promote her subjective well-being, and enable her to effectively support the Nowak family, as when adjustments resulted from Winston raising with upper management Melissa's concerns that new procedures were not working.

Outcomes of supervision

The outcomes of supervision can be potentially beneficial to families, employing organisations and workers. When considering the outcomes of supervision, it is common to divide these up into three categories: worker outcomes (including their well-being), organisational outcomes (including staff turnover) and service user outcomes (including worker effectiveness). Researchers and theorists commonly conceptualise the relationship between supervision and its outcomes in terms of those brought about by direct effects and those brought about by indirect effects. Supervision has direct effects on workers, whether for the better or worse, and indirect effects (via the worker) on the organisation they work for and the families they work with. The effects on the organisation include staff retention and turnover, as workers who are unhappy with their supervision, or the lack of it, are more likely to change jobs or their profession (Webb and Carpenter, 2012). Effects on families include workers receiving effective supervision are more likely to work effectively with families (Mor Barak et al., 2009: 28).

Mor Barak et al. (2009: 6) developed a conceptual model featuring supervision outcomes divided into five beneficial outcomes and five potential detrimental outcomes. The beneficial outcomes were job satisfaction, organisational commitment, worker effectiveness, retention and psychological well-being. The detrimental outcomes were job stress, burnout, worker anxiety, staff turnover and worker depression. The idea is that Winston and Melissa should participate in supervision in such a way that fosters beneficial outcomes and limits detrimental outcomes. Through effective supervision, Winston can positively enhance Melissa's overall work experience and, as a result, improve the outcomes for the families she works with, while reducing staff turnover by her remaining in her job.

Mor Barak et al. (2009) carried out a meta-analysis of 27 research articles and found links between effective supervision and positive worker outcomes. The researchers constructed effective supervision as encompassing three distinct dimensions, involving the supervisor's ability to (1) offer guidance and education on work-related issues in a knowledgeable and skilful manner, (2) provide emotional and social support to staff and (3) interact effectively with and influence supervisees. The authors found that all three dimensions significantly relate to increasing beneficial worker outcomes and mitigating against detrimental worker outcomes. The authors use exchange theory to explain the link between effective supervision and beneficial worker outcomes. The theory suggests that workers who experience good supervision through task assistance, emotional support and effective relationships with their supervisors reciprocate with positive feelings and behaviours towards their jobs and their organisation. Importantly, workers who feel confident and positive about their job and the organisation they work for are more likely to effectively support families.

Chapter Key Points

1. This chapter has stressed the potentially important role supervision can play in supporting families.

2. The quality of supervision determines whether its outcomes are beneficial or detrimental to practitioners, the organisations they work for and the families they work with.

3. Whether the potential of supervision to produce good outcomes can be realised depends on the nature of the supervisory relationship and the organisational context in which supervision takes place.

4. In one-to-one supervision, the nature of the supervisory relationship influences whether practitioners feel safe enough to engage in critical reflection on their work with families and the emotions this work evokes within them.

5. Reflective supervision provides a safe space, promotes critical thinking, provides emotional support, contains anxiety, encourages reflective learning and is supportive to carrying out of responsibilities and accountabilities.

6. The micropolitics of supervision and mirroring processes can explain some of the relationship dynamics that can get in the way of reflective supervision.

7. When one-to-one supervision does not provide supportive reflective supervision, 'peer supervision' can provide a safe space in which deeper thinking and reflection can take place.

Reflective Exercises

1. How would you describe the supervisory relationship you have with your supervisor? What adjectives would you use?

2. What is the supervisory 'style' of your supervisor – active intrusive, active reflective or passive? What actions and behaviour does your supervisor engage in that makes you think they have that supervisory style?

3. Think about and make notes of how the supervision you receive or don't receive affects your work with families.

Putting into Practice

Do you feel confident and safe enough to openly discuss in supervision the emotions a particular family evoke within you? If you answer 'yes', can you pinpoint what enables you to feel safe enough? If you answer 'no', what can you do to get the emotional support you need?

Does your supervisor ask you questions that make you think more deeply about your work with a particular family? If you answer 'yes', describe the types of questions she/he asks you. If you answer 'no' what questions could she/he ask you to encourage you to think more deeply about your work with the family?

If you participate in one form or other of peer supervision, what are the potential benefits and drawbacks of your participation? If you do not currently participate in peer supervision, do you think you would benefit from such supervision, and if so, can you think of ways in which you could participate in peer supervision?

Further Resources

Chapter Two 'Understanding the Foundations', in J. Wonnacott (2012) *Mastering Social Work Supervision*, London: Jessica Kingsley, 36–67. If time is scarce, read pages 36–50, 'Developing the Relationship', which is on developing a good quality supervisory relationship.

This chapter argues that relationships are fundamental to social work and to supervision and that a negotiated agreement provides a strong foundation for achieving effective supervision.

Carpenter, J., Webb, C., Bostock, L. and Coomber, C. (2012) *Effective Supervision in Social Work and Social Care: SCIE Research Briefing* 43 [online] www.scie.org/publications/briefing43 [Accessed 15/04/2016].

This SCIE Research Briefing gives an overview of the evidence on the value of supervision in supporting practice, different models of supervision and outcomes for workers, employers and service users and carers.

Turner-Daly, B. and Jack, G. (2014) 'Rhetoric vs. reality in social work supervision: the experiences of a group of child care social workers in England', *Child and Family Social Work*, Advance Publication.

This article reports on a small-scale study that examines the supervisory experiences of a group of child care workers in England.

REFERENCES

Abramson, J. S. and Mizrahi, T. (1996) 'When social workers and physicians collaborate: positive and negative interdisciplinary experiences', *Social Work*, 41(3), 270–281.

Adams, M. and Coltrane, S. (2005) 'Boys and men in families: The domestic production of gender, power, and privilege', in M. S. Kimmell, J. Hearn and R. W. Connell (eds) *Handbook of Studies on Man and Masculinities*, Thousand Oaks, CA: Sage, 230–248.

Aggett, P., Swainson, M. and Tapsell, D, (2015) '"Seeking permission": an interviewing stance for finding connection with hard to reach families', *Journal of Family Therapy*, 37(2), 190–209.

Al, C. M. W., Stams, G. J. J. M., Asscher, J. J. and van der Laan, P. H. (2014) 'A programme evaluation of the Family Crisis Intervention Program (FCIP): Relating programme characteristics to change', *Child and Family Social Work*, 19(2), 225–236.

Al, C. M. W., Stams, G. J. J. M., van der Laan, P. H. and Asscher, J. J. (2011) 'The role of crisis in crisis intervention: Do crisis experience and crisis change matter?', *Children and Youth Services Review*, 33(6), 991–998.

Aldgate, J. and Bradley, M. (1999) *Supporting Families through Short-term Fostering*, London: The Stationary Office.

Aspland, H., Llewelyn, S., Hardy, G. E., Barkham, M. and Stiles, W. (2008) 'Alliance ruptures and rupture resolution in cognitive-behavioural therapy: A preliminary analysis', *Psychotherapy Research*, 18(6), 699–710.

Ball, W. (2014) 'Providing multi-agency children's services in an austere climate: professional narratives on parenting support in Wales', *Family, Relationships and Societies*, 3(3), 321–337.

Barker, J. D. (2012) 'Social capital, homeless young people and the family', *Journal of Youth Studies*, 15(6), 730–743.

Barn, R. (2006): *Parenting in Multi-Racial Britain: Findings Informing Change*, York: Joseph Rowntree Foundation.

Barnard, M. and Barlow, J. (2003) 'Discovering parental drug dependence: Silence and Disclosure', *Children and Society*, 17(1), 45–56.

Barnard, M. and Bain, C. (2015) 'Resisting your good intentions: substance-misusing parents and early intervention to support and monitor children in need', *Child and Family Social Work*, 20(2), 171–180.

Barnardo's (2011) *Reaching Families in Need: Learning from Practice in Barnardo's Children Centres*, Barnardo's Policy, Research and Media Unit [online] http://www.barnardos.org.uk/reaching_families_in_need.pdf [Accessed 07/11/2014].

Beck, U. and Beck-Gernsheim, E. (2002) *Individualization*, Sage: London.

Beddoe, L. (2010) 'Surveillance or reflection: professional supervision in "the risk society"', *British Journal of Social Work*, 40(4), 1279–1296.

Beddoe, L., Davys, A. M. and Adamson, C. (2014) 'Never trust anybody who says "I don't need supervision": practitioners' beliefs about social worker resilience', *Practice Social Work in Action*, 26(2), 113–130.

Belsky, J. (1984) 'The determinants of parenting: A process model', *Child Development*, 55(1), 83–96.

Belsky, J. (1997) 'Determinants and Consequences of Parenting: Illustrative Findings and Basic Principles', in W. Hellinckx, M. J. Colton and M. Williams (eds) *International Perspectives in Family Support*, Aldershot: Arena, 1–21.

Bengtson, V., Giarrusso, R., Mabry, B. and Silverstein, M. (2002) 'Solidarity, conflict and ambivalence: Complementary or competing perspectives on intergeneration relationships', *Journal of Marriage and Family*, 64(3), 568–576.

Berzin, S. C., Cohen, E, Thomas, K. and Dawson, W. C. (2008) 'Does Family Group Decision Making Affect Child Welfare Outcomes? Findings from a Randomized Control Study', *Child Welfare*, 87(4), 35–54.

Biehal, N. (2005) *Working with Adolescents: Supporting Families, Preventing Breakdown*, London: British Association for Adoption and Fostering.

Biehal, N. (2008) 'Preventive Services for Adolescents: exploring the process of change', *British Journal of Social Work*, 38(3) 444–461.

Biestek, F. P. (1961) *The Casework Relationship*, London: Unwin University Books.

Billings, J. A. and Block, S. D. (2011) 'Part III: A guide for structured discussions', *Journal of Palliative Medicine*, 14(9), 1058–1064.

Bion, W. (1962) *Learning from Experience*, London: Heinemann.

Blaug, R. (1995) 'Distortion of the face to face; communicative reason and social work practice', *British Journal of Social Work*, 25(4), 423–439.

Bloor, M. and McIntosh, J. (1990) 'Surveillance and concealment: a comparison of techniques of client resistance in therapeutic communities and health visiting', in S. Cunningham-Burley and N. P. McKeganey, (eds) *Readings in Medical Sociology*, London: Routledge, 159–181.

Bolin, A. (2015) 'Children's agency in interprofessional collaborative meetings in child welfare work', *Child and Family Social Work*, Advance Publication, 1–10.

Booth, T., Booth, W. and McConnell, D. (2005) 'Care proceedings and parents with learning difficulties, comparative prevalence and outcomes in an English and Australian count sample', *Child and Family Social Work*, 10(4), 353–360.

Borenstein, J. and McNamara, P. (2015) 'Strengthening kinship families: scoping provision of respite care in Australia', *Child and Family Social Work*, 15(1), 50–61.

Bourdieu, P. (1986) 'The forms of capital', in J. G. Richardson (ed) *Handbook of Theory and Research for the Sociology of Education*, New York: Greenwood Press, 241–258.

Bourne, D. F. and Hafford-Letchfield P. (2011) 'The role of social work professional supervision in conditions or uncertainty', *International Journal of Knowledge, Culture and Change Management*, 10(9), 41–56.

Bracha, A. and Brown, P. J. (2010) 'Affective decision making: A theory of optimism bias', *Research Review*, 14 (Jul–Dec Issue), 33–34.

Bradley, N., Whisenhunt, J., Adamson, N. and Kress, V. E. (2013) 'Creative approaches for promoting counselor self-care', *Journal of Creativity in Mental Health*, 8(4), 456–469.

Brandon, M., Belderson, P., Warren, C., Gardner, R., Howe D. and Dodsworth, J. and Black, J. (2008a) *Analysing child deaths and serious injury through abuse and neglect: what can we learn? A biennial analysis of serious case reviews 2003–2005, Research Report DCSF-RR023*, Department for Children, Schools and Families: The Stationery Office.

Brandon, M., Belderson, P., Warren, C., Gardner, R., Howe D. and Dodsworth, J. (2008b) 'The preoccupation with thresholds in cases of child death or serious injury through abuse and neglect', *Child Abuse Review*, 17(5), 313–330.

Brayne, H. and Carr, H. (2010) *Law for Social Workers*, Oxford: Oxford University Press.

Brimicombe, A. J., Ralphs, M. P., Sampson, A. and Yuen Tsui, H. (2001) 'An analysis of the role of neighbourhood ethnic composition in the geographical distribution of racially motivated incidents', *British Journal of Criminology*, 41(2), 293–308.

Broadhurst, K. (2003) 'Engaging parents and carers with family support services: What can be learned from research on help-seeking?' *Child and Family Social Work*, 8(4), 341–350.

Bronfenbrenner, U. (1979) *The Ecology of Human Development: Experiments by Nature and Design*, Cambridge, MA: Harvard University Press.

Bronfenbrenner, U. (1986) 'Ecology of the family as a context for human development: research perspectives', *Developmental Psychology*, 22(6), 723–742.

Brown, J., Lewis, L., Ellis, K., Stewart, M., Freeman, T. R. and Kasperski, M. J. (2011) 'Conflict on interprofessional primary health care teams: can it be resolved?' *Journal of Interprofessional Care*, 25(1), 4–10.

Bunting, L. and McAuley, C. (2004) 'Research Review: Teenage Pregnancy and Motherhood: The Contribution of Support', *Child and Family Social Work*, 9(2), 207–215.

Burgess, R. (1984) *In the Field: An Introduction to Field Research*, London: Allen and Unwin.

Burke, P. (2010) 'Brothers and sisters of disabled children: The experience of disability by association', *British Journal of Social Work*, 40(6), 1681–1699.

Butler, J., Bor, I. and Gibbons, J, (1978) 'Task-centred casework with marital problems', *British Journal of Social Work*, 8(4), 393–409.

Butler, S., Baruch, G., Hickley, N. and Fonagy, P. (2011) 'A randomized controlled trial of multisystemic therapy and a statutory therapeutic intervention for young offenders', *Journal of the American Academy of Child and Adolescent Psychiatry*, 50(12), 1220–1235.

Butrym, Z. T. (1976) *The Nature of Social Work*, London and Basingstoke: Macmillan.

Cabinet Office (2008) *Think Family: Improving the life chances of families at risk*, London: Social Exclusion Task Force.

Callan, T., Nolan, N., Whelan, B. J., Whelan, C. T. and Williams, J. (1996) *Poverty in the 1990s: Evidence from the 1994 Living in Ireland Survey*, Dublin: Oak Tree Press.

Cameron, G., Coady. N. and Hoy, S. (2014) 'Perspectives on being a father from men involved with child welfare services', *Child and Family Social Work*, 19(1), 14–23.

Caplan, G. (1964) *Principles of Preventive Psychiatry*, London: Tavistock Publications.

Carpenter, J., Webb, C., Bostock, L. and Coomber, C. (2012) *Effective Supervision in Social Work and Social Care: SCIE Research Briefing* 43 [online] www.scie.org/publications/briefing43 [Accessed 15/04/2016].

Carr, A. (2000) *Family Therapy, Concepts, Process and Practice*, Chichester: Wiley.

Carr, A. (2014) 'The evidence base for family therapy and systemic interventions for child-focused problems', *Journal of Family Therapy*, 36(2), 107–157.

Carter, B. and McGoldrick, M. (1989) 'Overview: The changing family life cycle: A framework for family therapy', in B. Carter and M. McGoldrick (eds) *The Changing Family Life Cycle: A Framework for Family Therapy*, Needham Heights, MA: Allyn and Bacon, 3–28.

Chahal, K. and Julienne, K. (1999) *Findings: The Experience of Racist Victimisation*, York: Joseph Rowntree Trust.

Chow, A. Y. M., Lam, D. O. B., Leung, G. S. M., Wong, D. F. K. and Chan, B. F. P. (2011) 'Promoting reflexivity among social work students: the development and evaluation of a programme', *Social Work Education*, 30(2), 141–156.

Clarke, H. and Hughes, N. (2010) 'Introduction: Family minded policy and whole family practice – developing a critical research framework', *Social Policy and Society*, 9(4), 527–531.

Cleaver, H., Unell, I. and Aldgate, J. (2010) *Children's Needs and Parenting Capacity: The Impact of Parental Mental Illness, Learning Disability, Problem Alcohol and Drug Use and Domestic Violence on Children's Development: Second Edition*, London: The Stationery Office.

Cohen, O. (2012) 'Agreement reached through court mediation conducted by social workers: impact on the co-parenting relationship', *British Journal of Social Work*, 42(2), 227–244.

Collins, S. (2008) 'Statutory Social Workers: Stress, Job Satisfaction, Coping, Social Support and Individual Differences', *British Journal of Social Work*, 38(6), 1173–1192.

Connolly, M. (2006) 'Up Front and personal: confronting dynamics in family group conferences', *Family Process*, 45(3), 345–357.

Cooper, A. (2005) 'Surface and depth in the Victoria Climbié inquiry report', *Child and Family Social Work*, 10(1), 1–9.

Copello, A. G., Velleman, R. D. B. and Templeton, L. J. (2005) 'Family intervention in the treatment of alcohol and drug problems', *Drug and Alcohol Review*, 24(4), 369–385.

Copperman, J. and Newton, P. D. (2007) 'Linking social work agency perspectives on interprofessional education into a school of nursing and midwifery', *Journal of Interprofessional Care*, 21(2), 141–154.

Corcoran, J. (2006) 'A comparison group study of solution-focused therapy versus "treatment as usual" for behavior problems in children', *Journal of Social Service Research*, 33(1), 69–81.

Corcoran, J. and Pillai, V. (2009) 'A review of the research on solution-focused therapy', *British Journal of Social Work*, 39(2), 234–242.

COSW/BASW (2012) *Professional Capability Framework: Qualifying Social Worker Capabilities*, Birmingham: The British Association of Social Workers.

Cree, V. E., Macrae, R., Smith, M., Knowles N., O'Halloran, S., Sharp, D. and Wallace, E. (2014) 'Critical reflection workshops and knowledge exchange: findings of a Scottish project', *Child and Family Social Work*, Advance Publication, 1–9.

Crompton, R. (2006) 'Class and family' *The Sociological Review*, 54(4), 658–677.

Cropanzano, R. and Mitchell, M. S. (2005) 'Social exchange theory: an interdisciplinary review', *Journal of Management*, 31(6), 874–900.

Cross, B. (2011) 'Becoming, being, and having been: practitioner perspectives on temporal stances and participation across children's service's', *Children and Society*, 25(1), 26–36.

Curtis Committee (1946) *Report of Care of Children Committee*, Cmnd 6922, London: HMSO.

Cutrona, C. E. (2000) 'Social Support Principles for Strengthening Families: Messages from America', in J. Canavan, P. Dolan and J. Pinkerton (eds) *Family Support: Direction from Diversity*, London: Jessica Kingsley, 103–122.

D'Amour, D., Ferrada-Videla, M., San Martin Rosriguez, L. and Beaulieu, M. D. (2005) 'The conceptual basis of interprofessional collaboration: Core concepts and theoretical frameworks', *Journal of Interprofessional Care*, Supplement 1, 116–131.

Darcy, C. and McCarthy, A. (2007) 'Work-family conflict: an exploration of the differential effects of a dependent child's age on working parents', *Journal of European Industrial Training*, 31(7), 530–549.

Darlington, Y., Feeney, J. A. and Rixon, K. (2004) 'Complexity, conflict and uncertainly: issues in collaboration between child protection and mental health services', *Child and Youth Services Review*, 26(12), 1175–1192.

Darlington, Y., Feeney, J. A. and Rixon, K. (2005) 'Practice challenges at the intersection of child protection and mental health', *Child and Family Social Work*, 10(3), 239–247.

Davis, A. and Wainwright, S. (2005) 'Combating Poverty and Social Exclusion: Implication for Social Work Education', *Social Work Education*, 24(3), 259–273.

Davis, L. (2009) *The Social Worker's Guide to Children and Families Law*, London: Jessica Kingsley.

de Boer, C. and Coady, N. (2007) 'Good helping relationship in child welfare: learning from stories of success', *Child and Family Social Work*, 12(1), 32–42.

De Haan, L., Hawley, D. R. and Deal, J. E. (2002) 'Operationalizing family resilience: A methodological strategy,' *The American Journal of Family Therapy*, 30(4), 275–291.

De Mol, J., Buysse, A. and Cook, W. L. (2010) 'A Family Assessment Based on the Social Relations Model', *Journal of Family Therapy*, 32(3), 259–279.

De Shazer, S. (1995) *Keys to Solutions in Brief Therapy*, New York: W. W. Norton.

Dempsey, M., Halton, C. and Murphy, M. (2001) 'Reflective learning in social work education: scaffolding the process', *Social Work Education*, 20(6), 631–641.

Department of Health (1995) *Child Protection: Messages from Research*, London: HMSO.

Department of Work and Pensions (2012) *Social Justice: Transforming Lives*, Cm8314, London: Department of Work and Pensions.

Devaney, J. (2008) 'Inter-professional working in child protection with families with long-term and complex needs', *Child Abuse Review*, 17(4), 242–261.

Dewey, J. (1933) *How We Think*, Boston: Heath and Co.

Dixon, A. L. (2007) 'Mattering in the later years: older adults' experiences of mattering to others, purpose in life, depression, and wellness', *Adultspan Journal*, 6(2), 83–95.

Department of Health (2000) *Framework for the Assessment of Children in Need and their Families*, London: Stationery Office.

Dolan, P., Pinkerton, J. and Canavan J. (2006) 'Family support: from description to reflection', in P. Dolan, J. Canavan and J. Pinkerton (eds) *Family Support as Reflective Practice*, London: Jessica Kingsley, 11–23.

Dowling, M. and Dolan, L. (2001) 'Families with children with disabilities: Inequalities and the social model', *Disability and Society*, 16(1), 21–35.

Drakeford, M. and Gregory, L. (2008) Anti-poverty practice and the changing world of credit unions: new tools for social workers', *Practice: Social Work in Action*, 20(3), 141–150.

Drijber, B. C., Reijinders, U. J. L. and Ceelen, M. (2013). 'Male Victims of Domestic Violence', *Journal of Family Violence*, 28(2), 173–178.

Duncan, S. (2007) 'What's the problem with teenage parents? And what's the problem with policy?, *Critical Social Policy*, 27(3), 307–334.

ECCE (2015) *Organisation of Children's Centres in England (ECCE, Strand 3)*, London: Department of Education [online] https://www.gov.uk/government/uploads/system/uploads/attachment_data/file/433853/RR433A_-_Organisation_Services_and_Reach_of_Childrens_Centres_.pdf [Accessed 16/09/2015].

Edwards, R. and Gillies, V. (2012) 'Farewell to family? Notes on an argument for retaining the concept', *Families, Relationships, Societies*, 1(1), 63–69.

Edwards, R. and Weller, S. (2014) 'Sibling relationships and the construction of young people's gendered identities over time and in different spaces', *Families, Relationships and Societies*, 3(2), 185–199.

Elder, L. and Paul, R. (2002) 'Critical thinking: distinguishing between inferences and assumptions', *Journal of Developmental Education*, 25(3), 34–35.

Elliott, G. C. (2009) *Family Matters: The Importance of Mattering to Family in Adolescence*, Chichester: Wiley-Blackwell.

Elliott, G. C., Cunningham S. M., Colangelo, M. and Gelles, R. J. (2011) 'Perceived mattering to the family and physical violence within the family by adolescents', *Journal of Family Issues*, 32(8), 1007–1029.

Elliott, G. C., Kao, S. and Grant, A. (2004) 'Mattering: Empirical Validation of a Social-Psychological Concept', *Self and Identity,* 3(4), 339–354.

Elliott, R. and Leonard, C. (2004) 'Peer pressure and poverty: exploring fashion brands and consumption symbolism among children of the British poor', *Journal of Consumer Behaviour*, 3(4), 347–359.

Ensink, T. and Saucer, C. (2003) 'Social–functional and cognitive approaches to discourse interpretation', in T. Ensink and C. Saucer (eds) *Framing and Perspectivising in Discourse,* Amsterdam/Philadelphia: John Benjamin's Publishing Company, 1–20.

Evans, S., Huxley, P., Gately, C., Webber, M., Mears, A., Pajak, S., Medina, J., Kendall, T. and Katona, C. (2006: 75) 'Mental health, burnout and job satisfaction among mental health social workers in England and Wales', *British Journal of Psychiatry*, 188(1), 75–80.

Ewart-Boyle, S., Manktelow, R. and McColgan, M. (2015) 'Social work and the shadow father: lessons for engaging fathers in Northern Ireland', *Child and Family Social Work*, 20(4), 470–479.

Falloon, I. R. H., Laporta, M., Fadden, V. and Graham-Hole, V. (1993) *Managing Stress in Families: Cognitive and Behavioural Strategies for Enhancing Coping Skills*, London: Routledge.

Family Rights Group (undated) *Family Group Conferences*, London: Family Rights Group [online] www.frg.org.uk [Accessed 23/09/2014].

Farmakopoulou, N. (2002) 'Using an integrated framework for understanding inter-agency collaboration in the special educational needs field', *European Journal of Special Needs Education*, 17(1), 49–59.

Featherstone, B. (1999) 'Taking mothering seriously: the implications for child protection', *Child and Family Social Work*, 3(1), 43–53.

Featherstone, B. (2004) *Family Life and Family Support*, Basingstoke: Palgrave Macmillan.

Featherstone, B., Morris, K. and White, S. (2014) 'A marriage made in hell: early intervention meets child protection' *British Journal of Social Work,* 44(7), 1737–1749.

Ferguson, H. (2009) 'Performing child protection: home visiting, movement and the struggle to reach the abused child', *Child and Family Social Work*, 14(4), 471–480.

Finch J. and Mason, J. (1993) *Negotiating Family Responsibilities*, London: Routledge.

Fonagy, P., Butler, S., Goodyer, I., Cottrell. D., Scott, S., Pilling, S., Eisler, I., Fuggle, P., Kraam, A., Byford, S., Wason, J. and Haley, R. (2013) 'Evaluation of multisystemic therapy pilot services in the Systemic Therapy for At Risk Teens (START) trial; study protocol of a randomised controlled trial', *Trials*, 14(265) [online] http://www.trialsjournal.com/content/14/1/265 [Accessed 20/11/2014].

Forrester, D., Holland, S., Williams, A. and Copello, A. (2014) 'Helping families where parents misuse drugs or alcohol? A mixed methods comparative evaluation of an intensive family preservation service', *Child and Family Social Work*, Advance Publication, 1–11.

Forrester, D., Kershaw, S., Moss, H. and Hughes, L. (2008a) 'Communication skill in child protection: How do social workers talk to parents?' *Child and Family Social Work*, 13(1), 41–51.

Forrester, D., McCambridge, J., Waissbein, C. and Rollnick, S. (2008b) 'How do family social workers talk to parents about child welfare concerns?', *Child Abuse Review*, 17(1), 23–35.

Forrester, D., Westlake, D. and Glynn, G, (2012) 'Parental resistance and social work: Towards a theory of motivational social work', *Child and Family Social Work*, 17(2), 118–129.

Fox, R. A. and Holtz, C. A. (2009) 'Treatment outcomes for toddlers with behavioural problems from families in poverty', *Child and Adolescent Mental Health*, 14(4), 183–189.

Fox, S. and Ashmore, Z. (2014) 'Multisystemic Therapy as an intervention for young people on the edge of care', *British Journal of Social Work*, Advance Publication, 1–17.

Friedlander, M. L., Escudero, V., Horvath, A. O., Heatherton, L., Cabero, A. and Martens, M. P. (2006) 'System for observing Family Therapy Alliances: a tool for research and practice', *Journal of Counseling Practice*, 53(2), 214–224.

Frost, N., Abram, F. and Burgess, H. (2014) 'Family group conferences: evidence, outcomes and future research', *Child and Family Social Work*, 19(4), 501–507.

Garrett, P. M. (2007) 'The relevance of Bourdieu for social work: A reflection on obstacles and omissions', *Journal of Social Work*, 7(3), 355–379.

George, E., Iveson, C. and Ratner, H. (2000) *Solution Focused Brief Therapy Course Notes*, London: Brief Therapy Practice.

Ghate, D. and Hazel, N. (2002) *Parenting in Poor Environments: Stress, Support and Coping*, London: Jessica Kingsley.

Gilbert, M. (2001) 'Collective preferences, obligations, and rational choice', *Economics and Philosophy*, 17(1) 109–119.

Gingerich, W. J. and Peterson, L. T. (2013) 'Effectiveness of solution–focused brief therapy: a systematic review of controlled outcome studies', *Research on Social Work Practice*, 23(3), 266–283.

Glisson, C. and James, L. R. (2002) 'The cross-level effects of culture and climate in human service teams', *Journal of Organizational Behavior*, 23(6), 767–794.

Goffman, E. (1986) [1974] *Frame Analysis: An Essay on the Organisation of Experience*, Boston: Northeastern University Press.

Golan, N. (1987) 'Crisis intervention', in A. Minahan (ed) *Encyclopaedia of Social Work*, 18th edn, vol. 1, Washington, D.C.: National Association of Social Workers, 360–372.

Golia, G. M. and McGovern, A. R. (2015) 'If you save me, I'll save you: the power of peer supervision in clinical training and professional development', *British Journal of Social Work*, 45(2), 634–650.

Golombok, S. (2000) *Parenting: What Really Counts?* London: Routledge.

Golombok, S. and Badger, S. (2010) 'Children raised in mother-headed families from infancy: a follow-up of children of lesbian and single heterosexual mothers at early adulthood', *Human Reproduction*, 25(1), 150–157.

Goodman, S. and Trowler, I. (2012) *Social Work Reclaimed: Innovative Frameworks for Child and Family Social Work Practice*, London: Jessica Kingsley.

Grant, L. and Kinman, G. (eds) (2014) *Developing Resilience for Social Work Practice*, Basingstoke: Palgrave Macmillan.

Grant, L., Kinman, G. and Baker, S. (2014) '"Put on your own oxygen mask before assisting others": social work educators' perspectives on an "emotional curriculum"', *British Journal of Social Work*, Advance Publication, 1–17.

Green, S. E. (2007) '"We're tired, not sad": Benefits and burdens of mothering a child with a disability', *Social Science and Medicine*, 64(1), 150–163.

Griffiths, H. (2013). 'Mediation Approaches' in T. Lindsay (ed) *Social Work Intervention: Second Edition*, London: Sage Learning Matters, 167–184.

Griggs, J., Tan, J.-P., Buchanan, A., Attar-Schwartz, S. and Flouri, E. (2010) '"They've always been there for me": grandparental involvement and child well-being', *Children and Society*, 24(3), 200–214.

Grotberg, E. H. (1995) *A Guide to Promoting Resilience in Children: Strengthening the Human Spirit*, The Hague: Bernard Van Leer Foundation.

Gunn, S. (2005) 'Translating Bourdieu: Cultural capital and the English middle class in historical perspective', *British Journal of Sociology*, 56(1), 50–65.

Hall, C. and Slembrouch, S. (2001) 'Parent participation in social work meetings; the case of child protection conferences', *European Journal of Social Work*, 4(2), 143–160.

Hallett, C., Murray, C. and Punch, S. (2003) 'Young people and welfare: negotiating pathways', in C. Hallett and A. Prout (eds) *Hearing the Voices of Children: Social Policy for a New Century*, London: Routledge, 123–138.

Hardiker, P. (2002) 'A Framework for Conceptualising Need and its Application to Planning and Providing Services', in H. Ward and W. Rose (eds) *Approaches to Needs Assessment in Children's Services*, London: Jessica Kingsley, 49–69.

Harlow, E. and Shardlow, S. M. (2006) 'Safeguarding children: challenges to the effective operation of core groups', *Child and Family Social Work*, 11(1), 65–72.

Hawley, D. R. (2000) 'Clinical implications of family resilience', *The American Journal of Family Therapy*, 28(2), 101–116.

Hayden, C. and Jenkins, C. (2013) 'Children taken into care and custody and the 'trouble families' agenda in England', *Child and Family Social Work*, Advance Publication, 1–11.

Hayes, D. and Houston, S. (2007) '"Lifeworld", "system" and family group conferences: Harbermas's contribution to discourse in child protection', *British Journal of Social Work*, 37(6), 987–1006.

Healy, K., Darlington, Y. and Yellowlees, J. (2012) 'Family participation in child protection practice: an observational study of family group meetings', *Child and Family Social Work*, 17(1), 1–12.

Henricson, C. (2012) *A Revolution in Family Policy*, Bristol: The Policy Press.

Herlofson, K. (2013) 'How gender and generation matter: Examples from research on divorced parents and adult children', *Families, Relationships and Societies*, 2(1), 43–60.

Herring, J. (2011) *Family Law*, 5th edn, Harlow: Pearson Education Ltd.

Hicks, S. (2000) '"Good lesbian, bad lesbian ...": Regulating heterosexuality in fostering and adoption assessments', *Child and Family Social Work*, 5(2), 157–168.

Hill, M., Stafford, A., Seaman, P., Ross, N. and Daniel, B. (2007) *Parenting and Resilience*, York: Joseph Rowntree Foundation.

Holland, S. and Rivett, M. (2008) '"Everyone started shouting": Making Connections between the process of family group conferences and family therapy practice', *British Journal of Social Work*, 38(1), 21–38.

Holt, S., Buckley, H. and Whelan, S. (2008) 'The impact of exposure to domestic violence on children and young people: A review of the literature', *Child Abuse and Neglect*, 32(8), 797–810.

Hordern, J. (2013) 'What's wrong with "compassion"? Towards a political, philosophical and theological context', *Clinical Ethics*, 8(4), 91–97.

Horwath, J. and Morrison, T. (2007) 'Collaboration, integration and change in children's services: critical issues and key ingredients', *Child Abuse and Neglect*, 31(1), 55–69.

Houston, S. (2010a) 'Prising open the black box: Critical realism, action research and social work', *Qualitative Social Work*, 9(1), 73–91.

Houston. S. (2010b) 'Building resilience in a children's home: Results from an action research project' *Child and Family Social Work*, 15(3), 357–368.

Howe, D (1996) 'Surface and depth in social work practice', in N. Parton (ed) *Social Theory, Social Change and Social Work*, London: Routledge, 77–97.

Hoyle, C. (2013). 'A critique of the life cycle model used within family therapy: A social work perspective' *Cumbria Partnership Journal of Research Practice and Learning*, 3(1), 5–9.

Hughes, L. and Pengelly, P. (1997) *Staff Supervision in a Turbulent Environment: Managing Process and Task in Front-line Services*, London: Jessica Kingsley.

Hughes, N. (2010) 'Models and Approaches in Family-Focused Policy and Practice', *Social Policy and Society*, 9(4), 545–555.

Humphreys, C., Thiara, R. K. and Skamballis, A. (2011). 'Readiness to change: mother-child relationship and domestic violence intervention', *British Journal of Social Work*, 41(1), 166–184.

Hutchings, J., Bywater, T., Eames, C. and Martin, P. (2008) 'Implementing child mental health intervention in service settings: lessons from three pragmatic randomised controlled trials in Wales', *Journal of Children's Services*, 3(2), 17–27.

Ingram, R. (2013) 'Emotions, social work practice and supervision: an uneasy alliance', *Journal of Social Work Practice*, 27(1), 5–19.

Ingram, R. (2015) 'Exploring emotions within formal and informal forums: messages from social work practitioners', *British Journal of Social Work*, 45(3), 896–913.

Jack, G, (2000) 'Ecological influences on parenting and child development', *British Journal of Social Work*, 30(6), 703–720.

Jack, G. and Gill, O. (2003) *The Missing Side of the Triangle: Assessing the Importance of Family and Environmental Factors in the Lives of Children*, Ilford: Barnardo's.

Jackson, D. (2003) 'Broadening constructions of family violence: Mothers' perspectives of aggression from their sons', *Child and Family Social Work*, 8(4), 321–329.

Jackson, S. (2008) 'Families, Domesticity and Intimacy: Changing Relationships in Changing Times', in D. Richardson and V. Robinson (eds) *Introducing Gender and Women's Studies*, 3rd edn, Basingstoke: Palgrave Macmillan, 125–143.

James, A. N. (1998) 'Supporting families of origin: an exploration of the influence of the Children Act 1948', *Child and Family Social Work*, 3(3), 173–181.

Jamieson, L., Morgan, D., Crow, G. and Allan G. (2006) 'Friends, Neighbours and Distant Partners: Extending or Decentring Family Relationships?', *Sociological Research Online*, 11(3), 1–9 [online] http://www.socresonline.org.uk/11/3/jamieson.html [Accessed 28/05/2015].

Jo, Y. N. (2013) 'Psycho-social dimensions of poverty: when poverty becomes shameful', *Critical Social Policy*, 13(3), 514–520.

Jones, A. and Jones, D. (2011) 'Improving teamwork, trust and safety: an ethnographic study of an interprofessional initiative', *Journal of Interprofessional Care*, 25(3), 175–181.

Kahn, R. L. and Antonucci, T. C. (1980) 'Convoys over the Life Course: Attachment, Roles, and Social Support', in P. B. Baltes and O. G. Brim Jr. (eds) *Life-Span Development and Behaviour*, New York: Academic Press, 253–286.

Kearns, S. and McArdle, K. (2012) '"Doing it right"? – accessing the narratives of identity of newly qualified social workers through the lens of resilience: "I am, I have, I can"', *Child and Family Social Work*, 17(4), 385–394.

Keeping, C. (2014) 'The Processes Required for Effective Interprofessional Working' in J. Thomas, K. C. Pollard and D. Sellman (eds) *Interprofessional Working in Health and Social Care: Professional Perspectives*, 2nd edn, Basingstoke: Palgrave Macmillan, 22–34.

Khatib, Y., Bhui, K. and Stansfeld, S, A. (2013) 'Does social support protect against depression and psychological distress? Findings from the RELACHS study of East London adolescents', *Journal of Adolescence* 36(2) 393–402.

Kinman, G. and Grant, L. (2011) 'Exploring stress resilience in trainee social workers: the role of emotional and social competences', *British Journal of Social Work*, 41(2), 261–275.

Kinney, J., Haapala, D. and Booth, C. (1991) *Keeping Families Together: The Homebuilders Model*, New York: Aldine de Gruyter.

Knoll, B. (2004) 'Living with an elephant: growing up with parental substance misuse', *Child and Family Social Work*, 9(2), 129–140.

Koeske, G. F. and Kelly, T. (1995) 'The impact of overinvolvement on burnout and job satisfaction', *American Journal of Orthopsychiatry*, 65(2), 282–292.

Koritsas, S., Coles, J. and Boyle, M. (2010) 'Workplace violence towards social workers: the Australian experience', *British Journal of Social Work*, 40(1), 257–271.

Kosonen, M. (1996) 'Siblings as providers of support and care during middle childhood: children's perceptions', *Children and Society*, 10(4), 267–279.

Krane, J. and Davies, J. (2000) 'Mothering and child protection: rethinking risk assessment', *Child and Family Social Work*, 5(1), 35–45.

Krumer-Nevo, M., Monnickendam, M. and Weiss-Gal, I. (2009) 'Poverty-aware social work practice: a conceptual framework for social work education', *Journal of Social Work Education*, 45(2), 225–242.

Lavee, Y., McCubbin, H. I. and Olsen, D. H. (1987) 'The effects of stressful life events and transitions on family functioning and well-being', *Journal of Marriage and Family*, 49(4), 857–873.

Layder, D. (2006) *Understanding Social Theory*, 2nd edn, London: Sage.

Lazarus, R. S. (1991) *Emotion and Adaptation*, New York: Oxford University Press.

Lee, N. (2001) *Childhood and Society: Growing Up in an Age of Uncertainty*, Buckingham: Open University Press.

Leeson, C. (2010) 'The emotional labour of caring about looked after children', *Child and Family Social Work*, 15(1), 483–491.

Leever, A. M., Hulst, M. V. D., Berendsen, P. M., Boendemaker, P. M., Roodenburg, J. L. N. and Pols, J. (2010) 'Conflicts and conflict management in the collaboration between nurses and physicians: qualitative study', *Journal of Interprofessional Care*, 25(6), 612–624.

Leftwich, A. (2004) (ed) *What is Politics? The Activity and its Study*, Cambridge: Polity Press.

Lethem, J. (2002) 'Brief solution focused therapy', *Child and Adolescent Mental Health*, 7(4), 189–192.

Leung, K. K. P. (2012) 'An exploration of the use of power in social work supervisory relationships in Hong Kong', *Journal of Social Work Practice*, 26(2), 151–162.

Levitas, R. (2012) *There May Be 'Trouble' Ahead: What We Know About Those 120,000 Families*, London: Poverty and Social Exclusion UK.

Levitt, M. J. (2005) 'Social relations in childhood and adolescence: The convoy model perspective', *Human Development*, 48(1/2), 28–47.

Liebmann, M. (ed) (2000) *Mediation in Context*, London: Jessica Kingsley.

Lietz, C. A. (2008) 'Implementation of group supervision in child welfare: findings from Arizona's supervision circle project', *Child Welfare*, 87(6), 31–48.

Lietz, C. A, (2010) 'Critical Thinking in Child Welfare Supervision', *Administration in Social Work*, 34(21), 68–78.

Lindemann, E. (1944) 'Symptomatology and management of acute grief', *American Journal of Psychiatry*, 101, 141–148.

Lishman J. (2009) *Communication in Social Work,* Basingstoke: Palgrave Macmillan.

Lister, R, (2004) *Poverty*, Cambridge: Polity Press.

Littell, J. H., Popa, M. and Forsythe, B, (2005) *Multisystemic Therapy for Social, Emotional and Behavioural Problems in Youth Aged 10–17*, Cochrane

Database of Systematic Reviews [online] http://onlinelibrary.wiley.com/doi/10.1002/14651858.CD004797.pub4/pdf [Accessed 21/02/2015].

Littlechild, B. (2005) 'The stresses arising from violence, threats and aggression against child protection social workers', *Journal of Social Work,* 5(1), 61–81.

Lord Laming (2003) *The Victoria Climbié Inquiry: Report of an Inquiry by Lord Laming,* London: The Stationery Office.

Luthar, S. S., Cicchetti, D. and Becker, B. (2000) 'The Construct of resilience: A critical evaluation and guidelines of future work', *Child Development,* 71(3), 543–562.

Luthar, S. S., Sawyer, J. A. and Brown, P. J. (2006) 'Conceptual issues in studies of resilience: Past, present and future research', *Annals of New York Academy of Sciences,* 1094, 105–115.

Mandell, D., Stalker, C, Wright, M., Frensch, K. and Harvey, C. (2013) 'Sinking, swimming and sailing: experiences of job satisfaction and emotional exhaustion in child welfare employees', *Child and Family Social Work,* 18(4), 383–393.

Mann, S. (2004) '"People-work": emotion management, stress and coping', *British Journal of Guidance and Counselling,* 32(2), 206–221.

Manning, V., Best, D., Faulkner, D. and Titherington, E. (2009) 'New estimates of the number of children living with substance misusing parents: results from UK national household surveys', *BMC Public Health,* 9(327), 1–12.

Maslach, C. and Jackson, S. E. (1986) *The Maslach Burnout Inventory,* Palo Alto, CA: Consulting Psychologists Press.

Mason, C. (2012) 'Social work the 'art of relationship': parents' perspectives on an intensive family support project', *Child and Family Social Work,* 17(3), 368–377.

Masten, A. S., Best, K. M. and Garmezy, N. (1990) 'Resilience and development: contributions from the study of children who overcome adversity', *Development and Psychopathology,* 2(4), 425–444.

Mattinson, J. (1975) *The Reflection Process in Casework Supervision,* London: Tavistock Institute of Marital Studies.

Maxwell, N., Scourfield, J., Featherstone, B., Holland, S. and Tolman, R. (2012) 'Engaging fathers in child welfare: a narrative review of recent research evidence', *Child and Family Social Work,* 17(2), 160–169.

Maybery, D., Reupert, A. and Goodyear, M. (2015) 'Goal setting in recovery: families where a parent has a mental illness or dual diagnosis', *Child and Family Social Work,* 20(3), 354–363.

McConnell, D. and Llewellyn, G. (2002) 'Stereotypes, parents with intellectual disability and child protection', *Journal of Social Welfare and Family Law,* 24(3), 297–317.

McConnell, D., Savage, A. and Breitkreuz, R. (2014) 'Resilience in families raising children with disabilities and behavior problems', *Research in Developmental Disabilities,* 35(4), 833–848.

McLaughlin, H. (2013) 'Motherhood, apple pie and interprofessional working', *Social Work Education,* 32(7), 956–963.

McLean, S. (2012) 'Barriers to collaboration on behalf of children with challenging behaviours: a large qualitative study of five constituent groups', *Child and Family Social Work*, 17(4), 478–486.

McLeod, A. (2012) 'What research findings tell social workers about family support' in D. Davies (ed) *Social Work with Children and Families*, Basingstoke: Palgrave Macmillan, 53–73.

Meltzer, H., Doos, L., Vostais, P., Folrd, T. and Goodman, R. (2009) 'The mental health of children who witness domestic violence', *Child and Family Social Work*, 14(4), 491–501.

Menzies, I. E. P. (1960) *A Case Study in the Functioning of Social Systems as a Defence Against Anxiety: A Report on a Study of the Nursing Service of a General Hospital*, London: The Tavistock Institute.

Merkel-Holguin, L. and Bross, D. C. (2015) 'Commentary: taking a deep breath before reflecting on differential response', *Child Abuse and Neglect*, 39, 1–6.

Millar, J. and Ridge, T. (2013) 'Lone mother and paid work: the "family-work" project', *International Review of Sociology*, 23(3), 564–577.

Miller, E., Buys, L. and Woodbridge, S. (2012) 'Impact of disability on families: Grandparents' perspectives', *Journal of Intellectual Disability Research*, 56(1), 102–110.

Montgomery, S. A. and Steward, A. J. (2012) 'Privileged allies in lesbian and gay rights activism: Gender, generation and resistance', *Journal of Social Issues*, 68(1), 162–177.

Moore, C. (1986) *The Mediation Process: Practical Strategies for Resolving Conflict*, San Francisco: Jossey-Boss.

Mor Barak, M.E., Travis, D.J., Pyun, H. and Xie, B. (2009) 'The impact of supervision on worker outcomes: a meta-analysis', *Social Service Review*, 82(1), 3–32.

Moran, P. and Ghate, D. (2005) 'The effectiveness of parenting support', *Children and Society*, 19(4), 329–336.

Morgan, D. H. J. (1996) *Family Connections: An Introduction to Family Studies*, Cambridge: Polity Press.

Morgan, D. H. J. (1999) 'Risk and Family Practices: Accounting for Change and Fluidity in Family Life', in E. B. Silva and C. Smart (eds) *The New Family?* London: Sage, 13–30.

Morris, K. (2012) 'Family Support: Policies for Practice', in M. Davies (ed) *Social work with Children and Families*, Basingstoke: Palgrave Macmillan, 12–25.

Morris, K. (2013) 'Troubled families: vulnerable families' experiences of multiple service use', *Child and Family Social Work*, 18(2), 198–206.

Morris, K. and Connolly, M. (2012) 'Family Decision Making in Child Welfare: Challenges in Developing a Knowledge Base for Practice', *Child Abuse Review*, 21(1), 41–52.

Morris, K., Hughes, N., Clarke, H. Tew, J., Mason, P., Galvani, S., Lewis, A. and Loveless, L. (2008) *Think Family: A Literature Review of Whole Family Approaches*, London: Cabinet Office.

Morris, K., White, S., Doherty, P. and Warwick, L. (2015) 'Out of time: theorizing family in social work practice', *Child and Family Social Work*, Advance Publication, 1–10.

Morrow, G., Malin, N. and Jennings, T. (2005) 'Interprofessional team working for child and family referral in a Sure Start local programme', *Journal of Interprofessional Care*, 9(2), 93–101.

MST-UK (undated) *Multisystemic Therapy* [online] http://mstuk.org/ [Accessed 09/06/2015].

Muir, K. and Strnadová, I. (2014) 'Whose responsibility? Resilience in families of children with developmental disabilities', *Disability and Society*, 29(6), 922–937.

Munro, E. R. and Ward, H. (2008) 'Balancing parents' and very young children's rights in care proceedings: decision-making in the context of the Human Rights Act 1989', *Child and Family Social Work*, 13(2), 227–234.

Munro, E. (1996) 'Avoidable and unavoidable mistakes in child protection work', *British Journal of Social Work*, 26(6), 793–808.

Munro, E. (2008) 'Improving reasoning in supervision', *Social Work Now*, August 3–10.

Munro, E. (2008) *Effective Child Protection, Second Edition*, London: Sage.

Munro, E. (2011) *The Munro Review of Child Protection: Final Report*, London: Department of Education.

Neale, B. (2000) *Theorising, Family, Kinship and Social Change*, CAVA Workshop Paper 6 [online] http://www.leeds.ac.uk/cava/papers/wsp6.pdf [Accessed 17/07/2014].

Ney, T., Stoltz, J. and Maloney, M. (2011) 'Voice, power and discourse: Experiences of participants in family conferences in the context of child protection', *Journal of Social Work*, 13(2), 184–202.

Nickerson, R. S. (1998) 'Confirmation bias: A ubiquitous phenomenon in many guises', *Review of General Psychology*, 2(2), 175–220.

Noble, C. and Irwin, J. (2009) 'Social work supervision; an exploration of the current challenges in a rapidly changing social, economic and political environment', *Journal of Social Work*, 9(3), 245–358.

O'Dell, L., Crafter, S., de Abreu, G. and Cline, T. (2010) 'Constructing 'normal childhoods': young people talk about young carers', *Disability and Society*, 25(6), 643–655.

O'Donoghue, J. B. (2014) 'Towards an interaction map of the supervision session: an exploration of supervisees and supervisors experiences', *Practice: Social Work in Action*, 26(1), 53–70.

O'Donovan, O. (2006) *The Problem of Self-love in St Augustine*, Eugene, OR: Wipf and Stock.

O'Reilly, M. and Parker, N. (2013) 'You can take a horse to water but you can't make it drink: exploring children's engagement and resistance in family therapy', *Cotemporary Family Therapy*, 35(3), 491–507.

Oakeshott, M. (1989) *The Voice of Liberal Learning*, New Haven: Yale University Press.

Ochieng, B. M. N. (2011) 'The effect of kin, social network and neighbourhood support on individual well-being', *Health and Social Care in the Community*, 19(4), 429–437.

Oliver, M. (2013) 'The social model of disability: Thirty years on', *Disability and Society*, 28(7), 1024–1026.

Orr, L. C., Barbour, R. S. and Elliott, L. (2014) 'Involving families and carers in drug services: are families "part of the problem"?', *Families, Relationships and Societies*, 3(3), 405–424

Osmo, R. (2001) 'A conceptual tool: making social workers' assumptions explicit', *Social Work Education*, 20(2), 209–217.

Parker, R. (1995) *Torn in Two: The Experience of Maternal Ambivalence*, London: Virago.

Parr, S. (2009) 'Family intervention projects: A site of social work practice', *British Journal of Social Work*, 38(7), 1256–1273.

Parton, N. (2009) 'From Seebohm to '*Think Family*': reflections on 40 years of policy change of statutory children's social work in England', *Child and Family Social Work*. 14(1) 68–78.

Parton, N. (2011) 'Child protection and safeguarding in England: changing and competing conceptions of risk and their implications for social work', *British Journal of Social Work*, 41(5), 854–875.

Patterson, J. M. (2002) 'Integrating family resilience and family stress theory', *Journal of Marriage and Family*, 64(2), 349–360.

Payne, M. (2000) *Teamwork in Multiprofessional Care*, Basingstoke: Palgrave Macmillan.

Pilgram, D. (2002) 'The biopsychosocial model in Anglo-American Psychiatry: Past, Present and Future', *Journal of Mental Health*, 11(6), 585–594.

Pearson, R. (2009) 'Working with unco-operative or hostile families', in L. Hughes and H. Owen (eds) *Good Practice in Safeguarding Children: Working Effectively in Child Protection*, London: Jessica Kingsley, 85–101.

Pitcher, D. and Arnill, M. (2010) '"Allowed to be there": the wider family and child protection', *Practice: Social Work in Action*, 22(1), 17–31.

Platt, D. (2001) 'Refocusing children's services: evaluation of an initial assessment process', *Child and Family Social Work*, 6(2), 139–148.

Platt, D. (2007) 'Congruence and cooperation in social workers' assessments of children in need', *Child and Family Social Work*, 12(4), 326–335.

Potrac, P. and Jones, R. (2009) 'Power, Conflict, and Cooperation: toward a micropolitics of coaching', *Quest*, 16(2), 223–336.

Reder, P. and Duncan S. (2003) 'Understanding communication in child protection networks', *Child Abuse Review*, 12(2), 82–100.

Reid, W. J. and Epstein, L. (1972) *Task-Centred Casework*, New York: Columbia University Press.

Reid, W. J. (1985) *Family Problem Solving*, New York: Columbia University Press.

Reupert, A. and Maybery, D. (2010) '"Knowledge is power": educating children about their parent's mental illness', *Social Work in Health Care*, 49(7), 630–646.

Reupert, A. E., Green, K. T. and Maybery, D. J. (2008) 'Care plans for families affected by parental mental illness', *Families in Society: The Journal of Contemporary Social Services*, 89(1), 39–43.

Ridge, T. (2011) 'The everyday costs of poverty in childhood: a review of qualitative research exploring the lives and experiences of low-income children in the UK', *Children and Society*, 25(1), 73–84.

Riessman, C. K. (2008) *Narratives Methods for the Human Sciences'*, Thousand Oaks, CA: Sage.

Roberts, L. (2015a) 'Time to change? Exploring the impact of time-limited service provision in a family support service', *Child and Family Social Work*, Advance Publication, 1–10.

Roberts, L. (2015b) 'Using part-time fostering as a family support service: advantages, challenges and contradictions', *British Journal of Social Work*, Advance Publication, 1–17.

Röndahl, G., Bruhner, B. and Lindle, J. (2009) 'Heteronormative communication with lesbian families in antenatal care, childbirth and postnatal care', *Journal of Advanced Nursing*, 65(11), 2337–2344.

Rose, J, (2011) 'Dilemmas of inter-professional collaboration: can they be resolved?', *Children and Society*, 25(2), 151–163.

Rouf, K., Larkin, M. and Lowe, G. (2011) 'Making decisions about parental mental health: An exploratory study of community mental health team staff', *Child Abuse Review*, 21(3), 173–189.

Ruch, G. (2007a) 'Reflective practice in contemporary child-care social work: the role of containment', *British Journal of Social Work*, 37(4), 659–680.

Ruch, G. (2007b) '"Thoughtful" practice: child care social work and the role of case discussion', *Child and Family Social Work*, 12(4), 370–379.

Ruch, G., Turney, D. and Ward, A. (eds) (2010) *Relationship-Based Social Work: Getting to the Heart of Practice*, London: Jessica Kingsley.

Rudoe, N. (2014) 'Becoming a young mother: Teenage pregnancy and parenting policy', *Critical Social Policy*, 34(3), 293–311.

Russell, A. and Saebel, J. (1997) 'Mother-son, mother-daughter, father-son and father-daughter: are they distinct relationships?', *Development Review*, 17(2), 111–147.

Rustin, M. (2005) 'Conceptual analysis of critical moments in Victoria Climbié's life', *Child and Family Social Work*, 10(1), 11–19.

Rutter, M. (1987) 'Psychosocial resilience and protective mechanisms', *Journal of American Orthopsychiatry*, 57(3), 316– 331.

Rutter, M. (2006) 'Implications of resilience concepts for scientific understanding', *Annals of New York Academy of Sciences*, 1094, 1–12.

Saltiel, D. (2013) 'Understanding complexity in families' lives: the usefulness of "family practices" as an aid to decision-making', *Child and Family Social Work*, 18(1), 15–24.

Salway, S., Chowbey, P. and Clarke, L. (2009) *Understanding the Experiences of Asian Fathers in Britain: Findings Informing Change*, York: Joseph Rowntree Foundation.

Sanders, J., Munford, R., Liebenberg, L. and Unger, M. (2014) 'Peer paradox: the tensions that peer relationships raise for vulnerable youth', *Child and Family Social Work*, Advance Publication, 1–12.

Sanders, M. R., Markie-Dadds, C., Tully, L. A. and Bor, W. (2000) 'The triple P Positive parenting program: a comparison of enhanced, standard, and self-directed behavioural family intervention for parents of children with early onset conduct problems', *Journal of Consulting and Clinical Psychology*, 68(4), 624–640.

Santos, J. D. and Levitt, M. J. (2007) 'Intergenerational Relations with In-Laws in the Context of the Social Convoy: Theoretical and Practical Implications', *Journal of Social Issues*, 63(4), 827–843.

Savage, M., Devine, F., Cunningham, N., Taylor, M., Li, Y., Hjellbrekke, J., Le Roux, B., Friedman, S. and Miles, A. (2013) 'A new model of social class? Findings from the BBC's Great British Class Survey Experiment', *Sociology*, 47(2), 219–250.

Savage, M., Warde, A. and Devine, F. (2005) 'Capitals, assets and resources: some critical issues', *The British Journal of Sociology*, 56(1), 31–46.

Seebohm Committee (1968) *Report of the Committee on Local Authority and Allied Personal Services*, Cmnd 3703, London: HMSO.

Seymour, J. and McNamee, S. (2012) 'Being parented? Children and young people's engagement with parenting activities', in J. Waldren and I.-M. Kaminski (eds) *Learning from Children: Childhood, Culture and Identity in a Changing World*, Oxford: Berghahn Books, 92–107.

Sheppard, M. (2004) 'An evaluation of social support intervention with depressed mothers in child and family care', *British Journal of Social Work*, 34(7), 939–960.

Sheppard, M. (2012) 'Preventive orientations in children's centres: a study of centre managers', *British Journal of Social Work*, 42(2), 265–282.

Shepperd, J. A., Klein, W. M. P., Waters, E. A. and Weinstein N. D. (2013) 'Taking stock of unrealistic optimism', *Perspectives on Psychological Science*, 8(4), 395–411.

Shier, M. L. and Graham, J. R. (2010) 'Work-related factors that impact social work practitioners' subjective well-being: well-being in the workplace', *Journal of Social Work*, 11(4), 402–421.

Silva, E. B. and Smart, C. (1999) 'The "New" Practices and Politics of Family Life', in E. B. Silva and C. Smart (eds) *The New Family?*, London: Sage, 1–12.

Simmonds, J. (2010) 'Relating and relationship in supervision: supportive and companionable or dominant and submissive', in G. Ruch, D. Turney and A. Ward (eds) *Relationship Based Social Work: Getting to the Heart of Practice*, London: Jessica Kingsley, 214–228.

Sloper, P. (2004) 'Facilitators and barriers for co-ordinated multi-agency services', *Child: Care, Health, Development*, 30(6), 571–580.

Smart, C. (2006) 'Children's narratives of post-divorce family life: from individual experience to an ethical disposition', *The Sociological Review*, 54(1), 155–170.

Smith, M. (2004) 'Parental mental health: disruption to parenting and outcomes for children', *Child and Family Social Work*, 9(1), 3–11.

Smith, M., McMahon, L. and Nursten, J. (2003) 'Social workers' experiences of fear', *British Journal of Social Work*, 33(5), 659–671.

Smith, R. (2008) *Social Work and Power*, Basingstoke: Palgrave Macmillan.

Smith, R. and Anderson, L. (2008) 'Interprofessional Learning: aspiration or achievement?', *Social Work Education*, 27(7), 759–776.

Social Work Reform Board (2010) *Building a Safe, Confident Future: One Year On*, London: Department of Education [online] https://www.gov.uk/government/uploads/system/uploads/attachment_data/file/180787/DFE-00602-2010-1.pdf [Accessed 26/02/2015].

Somerset County Council (2007) *Pod Working: Initial Review*, Taunton: Somerset County Council [online] www.six.somerset.gov.uk/eis/do_download.asp?did=26909 [Accessed 11/12/2013].

Stalker, C. A., Mandell, D., Frensch, K. M., Harvey, C. and Wright, M. (2007) 'Child welfare workers who are exhausted yet satisfied with their jobs: how do they do it? *Child and Family Social Work*, 12(2), 182–191.

Stanley, N., Penhale, B., Riordan, D., Barbour, R. S. and Holden, S. (2003) 'Working on the interface: identifying professional responses to families with mental health and child-care needs', *Health and Social Care in the Community*, 11(3), 208–218.

Staudt, M. and Drake, B. (2002) 'Intensive family preservation services: Where's the crisis?', *Children and Youth Services Review*, 24(9/10), 777–795.

Stockdale, S. E., Wells, K. B., Tang, L., Belin, T. R., Zhang, L. and Sherborne C. D. (2007) 'The importance of social context: Neighbourhood stressors, stress-buffering mechanisms, and alcohol, and mental health disorders', *Social Science and Medicine*, 65(9), 1867–1881.

Stratton, P. (2011) *The Evidence Base of Systemic Family and Couples Therapies*, Warrington: The Association for Family Therapy and Systemic Practice.

Strier, R. (2009) 'Community anti-poverty strategies: a conceptual framework for a critical discussion', *British Journal of Social Work*, 39(6), 1063–1081.

Sturrock, F., Gray, D., Fergusson, D., Horwood, J. and Smits, C. (2014) *'Incredible Years' Follow-up Study: Long-term Follow-up of the New Zealand 'Incredible Years' Pilot Study*, Wellington: Ministry of Social Development [online] https://www.msd.govt.nz/documents/about-msd-and-our-work/publications-resources/evaluation/incredible-years-follow-up-study/indredible-years-follow-up-study.pdf [Accessed 05/04/2015].

Sullivan, K. (2015) 'An application of family stress theory to clinical work with military families and other vulnerable populations', *Clinical Social Work Journal*, 43(1), 89–97.

Sundell, K. and Vinnerljung, B. (2004) 'Outcomes of family group conferencing in Sweden: A 3-year follow up', *Child Abuse and Neglect*, 28(3), 267–287.

Suter, E., Arndt, J., Arthur, N., Parboosingh, J., Taylor, E. and Deutschlander, S. (2009) 'Role understanding and effective communication as core competencies for collaborative practice', *Journal of Interprofessional Care*, 23(1), 41–51.

Tarleton, B. and Porter, S. (2012) 'Crossing no man's land: A specialist support service for parents with learning disabilities', *Child and Family Social Work*, 17(2), 233–243.

Taylor, C. and White, S. (2000) *Practicing Reflexivity in Health and Welfare: Making Knowledge*, Buckingham: Open University Press.

Templeton, L. (2014) 'Supporting families living with parental substance misuse M-PACT (Moving Parents and Children Together) programme', *Child and Family Social Work*, 19(1), 76–88.

Tew, J. (2006) 'Understanding power and powerlessness: towards a framework for emancipatory practice in social work', *Journal of Social Work*, 6(1), 33–51.

Tew, J. and Nixon, J. (2010) 'Parent abuse: Opening up a discussion on a complex instance of family power relations', *Social Policy and Society*, 9(4), 579–589.

Thoburn, J., Copper, N., Brandon, M. and Connolly, S. (2013) 'The place of "think family" approaches in child and family social work: Messages from a process evaluation of an English pathfinder service', *Children and Youth Services Review*, 35(2), 228–236.

Thomas, C. (2004) 'How is disability understood? An examination of sociological approaches', *Disability and Society*, 19(6), 569–583.

Thylefors, I., Persson, O. and Hellström, D. (2005) 'Team types, perceived efficiency and team climate in Swedish cross-professional teamwork', *Journal of Interprofessional Care*, 19(2), 102–114.

Townsend, P. (1997) *Poverty in the United Kingdom: A survey of Household Resources and Standards of Living*, Harmondsworth: Penguin.

Tunstill, J., Aldgate, J. and Thoburn, J. (2010) 'Promoting and safeguarding the welfare of children: A bridge too far?', *Journal of Children's Services*, 5(3), 14–24.

Turner-Daly, B. and Jack, G. (2014) 'Rhetoric vs. reality in social work supervision: the experiences of a group of child care social workers in England', *Child and Family Social Work*, Advance Publication, 1–11.

Turney, D. (2012) 'A relationship-based approach to engaging involuntary clients: the contribution of recognition theory', *Child and Family Social Work*, 17(2), 149–159.

Ulvik, O. S. (2015) 'Talking with children: professional conversations in a participation perspective', *Qualitative Social Work*, 14(2), 193–208.

Ungar, M. (2011) 'The social ecology of resilience: Addressing contextual and cultural ambiguity of a nascent construct', *American Journal of Orthopsychiatry*, 81(1), 1–17.

Uprichard, E. (2008) 'Children as "being and becomings": children, childhood and temporality', *Children and Society*, 22(4), 303–313.

Van Puyenbroeck, H., Loots, G., Grietens, H., Jacquet, W., Vanderfaeillie, J. and Escudero, V. (2009) 'Intensive family preservation services in Flanders: an outcome study', *Child and Family Social Work*, 14(2), 222–232.

Van Volkom, M., Machiz, C and Reich, A. E. (2011) 'Sibling relationships in the college years: do gender, birth order, and age spacing matter?', *North American Journal of Psychology*, 13(1), 35–50.

Waisbrod, N., Buchbinder, E. and Possick, C. (2012) 'In-home intervention with families in distress: changing places to promote change', *Social Work*, 57(2), 121–132.

Walsh, F. (2003) 'Family resilience for clinical practice', *Family Process*, 42(1), 1–18.

Walter, U. M. and Petr, C. G. (2000) 'A template for family-centered interagency collaboration', *Families in Society*, 81(5), 494–503.

Warren-Adamson, C. (2006) 'Research review: family centres: a review of the literature', *Child and Family Social Work*, 11(2), 171–182.

Waterhouse, L. and McGhee, J. (2009) 'Anxiety and child protection: implications for practitioner-parent relations', *British Journal of Social Work*, 14, 481–490.

Wattis, L., Standing, K. and Yerkes, M. A. (2013) 'Mother and work-life balance: exploring the contradictions and complexities involved in work-family negotiations', *Community: Work and Family*, 16(1), 1–19.

Webb, C. M. and Carpenter, J. (2012) 'What can be done to promote the retention of social workers? A systemic review of interventions', *British Journal of Social Work*, 42(7), 1235–1255.

Webber, M., McCree, C. and Angeli, P. (2013) 'Inter-agency joint protocols for safeguarding children in social care and adult mental health agencies: a cross-sectional survey of practitioner experiences', *Child and Family Social Work*, 18(2), 149–158.

Webster-Stratton, C. (1989) *The Incredible Years: The Parents and Children Series*, Seattle, WA: University of Washington.

Weeks, J., Heaphy, B. and Donovan, C. (2001) *Same Sex Intimacies: Families of Choice and Other Life Experiments*, London: Routledge.

Welbourne, P. (2012) *Social Work with Children and Families: Developing Advanced Practice*, Abingdon: Routledge.

Welshman, J. (2012) '"Troubled Families": the lessons of history', 1880–2012, [online] http://www.historyandpolicy.org/papers/policy-paper-136.html [Accessed 11/04/2014].

West, C. and Zimmerman, D. H. (1987) 'Doing Gender', *Gender and Society*, 1(2), 125–151.

White, C., Warrener, M., Reeves, A. and La Valle, I. (2008) *Family intervention projects: An evaluation of their design, set-up and early outcomes*, London: National Centre for Social Research.

White, S. and Featherstone, B. (2005) 'Communicating misunderstandings: multi-agency work as social practice', *Child and Family Social Work*, 10(3), 207–216.

Whittaker, K. A. and Cowley, S. (2012) 'An effective programme is not enough: A review of factors associated with poor attendance and engagement with parenting support programmes', *Children and Society*, 24(2), 138–149.

Whittaker, K. A., Cox, P., Thomas, N. and Cocker, K. (2014) 'A qualitative study of parents' experiences using family support services: applying the concept of surface and depth', *Health and Social Care in the Community*, 22(5), 479–487.

Wilińska, M. (2014) 'Shame on me … emotions in the fieldwork on old age in Japan', *Qualitative Social Work*, 13(5), 602–618.

Wilkinson, E. and Bell, D. (2012) 'Ties that blind: on not seeing (or looking) beyond the family', *Families, Relationships and Societies*, 1(3), 423–429.

Williams J. (2001) '1998 Human Rights Act: Social Work's New Benchmark', *British Journal of Social Work*, 31(6), 831–844.

Wilson, K., Rush, G., Lymbery, M. and Cooper, A. (2008) *Social Work: An Introduction to Contemporary Practice*, Harlow: Pearson Education.

Winter, K. and Connolly, P. (2005) 'A small-scale study of the relationship between measures of deprivation and child-care referrals', *British Journal of Social Work*, 35(6), 937–952.

Wonnacott, J. (2012) *Mastering Social Work Supervision*, London: Jessica Kingsley.

Woodcock, J. and Sheppard, M. (2002) 'Double trouble: Maternal Depression and alcohol dependence as combined factors in child and family social work', *Children and Society*, 16(4), 232–245.

Yahav, R. and Sharlin, A. (2002) 'Blame and family conflict: symptomatic children as scapegoats', *Child and Family Social Work*, 7(2), 91–98.

York Consulting (2011) *Turning around the lives of family with multiple problems– an evaluation of the Family and Young Carer Pathfinders Programme* [online] https://www.gov.uk/government/uploads/system/uploads/attachment_data/file/182428/DFE-RR154.pdf [Accessed 07/04/2016].

Zimmerman, S. L. (2013) 'Conceptualizing family well-being', in A. Morerno Mínguez (ed) *Family Well-Being: European Perspectives*, Dordrecht: Springer, 9–25.

Zwarenstein, M., Reeves, S. and Perrier, L. (2005) 'Effectiveness of pre-licensure interprofessional education and post-licensure collaborative interventions', *Journal of Interprofessional Care*, Supplement 1, 148–165.

AUTHOR INDEX

SUBJECT INDEX